D0428493

THE

BAMBOO

NETWORK

How Expatriate Chinese Entrepreneurs Are
Creating a New Economic Superpower
in Asia

MURRAY WEIDENBAUM
SAMUEL HUGHES

MARTIN KESSLER BOOKS
THE FREE PRESS
New York   London   Toronto   Sydney   Tokyo   Singapore

To

PHYLLIS AND SUSAN

for their constant encouragement, support, and patience

THE FREE PRESS
A Division of Simon & Schuster Inc.
1230 Avenue of the Americas
New York, NY 10020

Designed by Carla Bolte

Manufactured in the United States of America

10 9 8 7 6 5 4 3 2 1

Library of Congress Cataloging-in-Publication Data

Weidenbaum, Murray L.
    The bamboo network: how expatriate Chinese entrepreneurs are creating a new
economic superpower in Asia / Murray Weidenbaum, Samuel Hughes.
      p. cm.
    Includes bibliographical references and index.
    ISBN 0–684–82289–X (cloth)
     1. Investments, Foreign—China.   2. Entrepreneurship—East Asia.
3. Chinese—East Asia.   4. China—Economic conditions—1976–
I. Hughes, Samuel. II. Title.
HG5782.W44   1996
332.6' 73' 095—dc20   95–42655
                                   CIP

ISBN 0–684–82289–X

CONTENTS

PREFACE

I never expected to write a book on the Orient, much less one dealing with Chinese entrepreneurs. But, at least in this regard, one seemingly unrelated event surely led to another.

In the fall of 1992, I was invited to visit Hong Kong as the Wei Lun lecturer at Chinese University. My major lecture focused on the global marketplace, with only a minor reference to the growth of Southeast Asia. To some degree, I felt obliged out of sheer courtesy to include my host's region in my discussion of key economic centers such as Europe, North America, and Japan. More importantly, however, the remarkable and pervasive cross-border movement of people and goods in Southeast Asia (which I dubbed the "bamboo network") was a fine example of my broader point that economic pressures are making political borders less important. Goods, services, money, and people are increasingly flowing across this region, despite the substantial differences voiced so noisily by leaders in Beijing, Taipei, and Hong Kong.

To my surprise, most of the questions and comments I received following my lecture were related to the part dealing with the area I called Greater China (Hong Kong, Taiwan, and the mainland of China). When I tried to find out why, I received some compliments about my grasp of the special developments occurring in this region, especially the rise of the bamboo network. I was also urged to convey this understanding to my fellow Americans.

On returning to the United States, I spun off the "Chinese" part of the Wei Lun lecture and amplified it with the knowledge I had gained during my recent visit. The result was a pamphlet published in 1993 by the Center for the Study of American Business at Washington University. Once again, I was surprised by the intensity of the reaction to this research. Several newspapers converted the piece into a major article, while others utilized my comments as part of more general articles on Greater China. In response to this favorable reaction, as well as to my own budding interest in the subject, I began what has been a continuing series of interviews, speaking with Chinese officials as well as Americans who live or do business in Southeast Asia. Much of the analysis in this book is based on the insights provided by these special, albeit informal, sources of information.

My follow-on research focused increasingly on the bamboo network of Chinese entrepreneurs in Southeast Asia. It became clear to me that an important new force had arrived on the world scene, a factor not adequately appreciated in the West. The bamboo network of overseas Chinese family-oriented businesses was indeed a subject worthy of further analysis, as it helped to explain the rapid movement of mainland China toward private enterprise. In 1994, an extended trip to Southeast Asia (a combination of sightseeing, lectures, and interviews) provided additional insight and further increased my interest in this special phenomenon.

During this period, I joined forces with Samuel Hughes, the John M. Olin Fellow at the Center for the Study of American Business. After immersing himself in the subject, he came to share my enthusiasm for communicating the fascinating developments of the bamboo network. In writing this book, which has truly been a joint effort and mutual learning experience, we have also drawn on the work of a wide variety of specialists on China and the surrounding area. We have tried to fully acknowledge that contribution—without blaming them for our results, with many of which they may disagree.

Thus, the analysis and conclusions are our own. We believe that we have brought to this enterprise a certain detachment and perhaps even new insights that will be valuable to the reader. Indeed, we hope that our enthusiasm for learning about a truly fascinating and increasingly important part of the world will be contagious.

We are grateful to a great many people for meeting with Samuel Hughes and/or with me, and for the frank and helpful interactions that resulted. Much of the information in this book was obtained from informal interviews with these overseas Chinese business executives, Western businesspeople, and Asian studies specialists: Nik Mohd Ariffin Jaafar, Assistant Director, Enforcement Division, Ministry of Domestic Trade and Consumer Affairs, Malaysia; James K. Berthold, President and Chairman of the Board, Sunnen Products Company, USA; Charles D. Booth, Faculty of Law, University of Hong Kong; Ray Bowen, Professor, University of Missouri, St. Louis; Robert Brooks, Chairman and CEO, Brooks Telecommunications, USA; Chen Chun Feng, Secretary General, Hebei Province, PRC; Chi Liqun, Vice Mayor, Jinxi Municipal Government, Liaoning Province, PRC; Fu Ying, Division Chief, Asian Department, Ministry of Foreign Affairs, PRC; Ge Songxue, First Secretary, Science and Technology Office, Embassy of the PRC; Charles Ingene, Distinguished International Professor, Chinese University of Hong Kong; Susan Inslee, Director, World Trade Center, St. Louis; Diane Jacobsen, CEO, DeMell Group, USA; Jack Moran, Vice President, British-American Forfaiting Co., USA; Michael Morgan, Partner, Bryan Cave, Hong Kong; Robert Ogrodnik, Vice President–International, Emerson Motor Company, USA; Ong Beng Seng, Managing Director of Hotel Properties, Ltd., Singapore; Jopie H.K. Ong, Group Managing Director, Metro Holdings Limited, Singapore; Carole Petersen, Faculty of Law, University of Hong Kong; Betty Chan Po-king, Director, Yew Chung Education Foundation, Hong Kong; William Purvis, Chairman, HSBC Holdings (holding company of Hong Kong Shanghai Bank); Qin Chaozhen, Director, Hebei Economic and Trade Committee, PRC; Kyle St. Peter,

Senior Associate, Hellmuth, Obata, & Kassabaum, Inc., USA; Sally Stewart, Head, Department of Management Studies, University of Hong Kong; Jack H. Su, Esq., White & Case, Hong Kong; Sun Ming, Vice Mayor, Yingkou Municipal Government, Liaoning Province, PRC; Wang Hui, Deputy Secretary General, State Economic Trade Council, PRC; Wang Jun, Deputy Division Chief, Department of International Organizations & Conferences, Ministry of Foreign Affairs, PRC; Wang Junyi, Professor, University of Beijing, PRC; Greg Wong, International Trade Specialist, World Trade Center, St. Louis; Richard Yue-chim Wong, Director, Center for Economic Research, University of Hong Kong; Remi Wrona, International Trade Consultant, USA; William Shoutian Wu, Washington University Medical School, USA; Ye Liansong, Governor, Hebei Province, PRC; James Yeh, President, Lay International Consulting Services, USA; Eric T. M. Yeung, Vice President, Perfekta Enterprises, Ltd., Hong Kong; Paul Yip, Chairman, Informtech Industrial, Ltd., Hong Kong; Eden Siu-hung Yu, Professor of Operations and Systems Management, Chinese University of Hong Kong; Chia Siow Yue, Professor of Economics and Statistics, National University of Singapore; Zhang Mujin, Consulate General of PRC, Chicago.

—*Murray Weidenbaum*

St. Louis

August 1995

PART I

INTRODUCTION

CHAPTER 1

The Strategic Role of the Bamboo Network

Bamboo bends; it does not break.
—a Southeast Asian aphorism

OVERVIEW

The most significant global development since the end of the Cold War is occurring without fanfare and in the most unexpected place: Southeast Asia. An emerging Greater China—comprising mainland China, Hong Kong, and Taiwan—is moving rapidly from entrenched communism to a market economy. This unprecedented transformation is being financed and managed in large measure not by wealthy Western investors but by a "bamboo network" of overseas Chinese. Ironically, most of these ethnic Chinese investors were forced out of their homeland by the communist takeover in the 1940s, or they are the descendants of those refugees.

To say that many of these overseas Chinese are now revisiting the mainland in style is to miss the main point. The members of what we call the bamboo network are essential players in all of

Southeast Asia, financing both China's transition from totalitarian to marketplace decisionmaking and the rapid expansion of
the other regional economies. The People's Republic of China
(PRC) could not have achieved the sweeping changes that have
occurred over the last two decades without the very substantial
help of these resourceful entrepreneurs who now live outside of
their ancestral homeland. Nor is it likely that Thailand, Malaysia,
and Indonesia would have attained such rapid growth without
the bamboo network's active participation.

In a powerful demonstration of the benefits of free markets,
the resilient overseas Chinese have progressed through three very
different, and difficult, stages in order to achieve their current position of prominence within the economy of Greater China. The
first and essential stage was to go literally from rags to riches.
Most overseas Chinese left the mainland with little wealth and
could not rely on the governments of other Southeast Asian
countries for assistance. Often battling prejudice and discrimination, these families created their own businesses, and in the
process developed much of the modern private business sector
throughout Southeast Asia—in Taiwan, Hong Kong, Singapore,
Malaysia, Thailand, Indonesia, the Philippines, and, to a more
limited extent, Vietnam. These Horatio Alger-style success stories
were not flukes. As we will show in the next chapter, they were
repeated again and again, drawing upon traditional Chinese cultural traits of frugality, entrepreneurship, and perseverance.

The second stage of development was the duplication of the
House of Rothschild phenomenon—the internationalization of
the family business—on an unprecedented scale. Again, this was
achieved on a uniquely Chinese basis. Always wary of their new
local governments, the overseas Chinese discovered that a common background provided a basis for mutual trust and, therefore, presented an opportunity for business and trade throughout
the region. Language, culture, and ethnicity could serve as such
common ground, but family ties provided the most reliable and
secure assurances in an area where formal business agreements
were difficult to enforce. Thus, to facilitate the cross-border
movement of their goods, many overseas Chinese firms estab-

lished outposts of their firms elsewhere in Southeast Asia. Control of the business and of its regional offshoots was almost always kept within the family, with sons (and, less frequently, daughters) of the founder rising up through the organization to position themselves for future senior leadership. Even today, it is common for the father-CEO stationed in Hong Kong or Bangkok or Singapore to send one son to Shanghai, another to Taipei, a son-in-law to Manila, and a nephew to Kuala Lumpur.

The third and most surprising stage is the current turnaround: massive investments are being made by overseas Chinese capitalists to establish new businesses in their original home, or that of their parents and grandparents. These extensions into China have largely overshadowed the efforts of even the most successful Western firms. Indeed, to date, most Western companies that have attempted to expand their operations into the mainland have faced a treacherous business environment. Few have significant profits to show for their efforts.

The very positive experiences of the Chinese who migrated from the mainland have had a vital but unintended effect. Hong Kong, Singapore, and Taipei—the jewels of the overseas Chinese—provide vivid and nearby examples to the mainland government authorities that successful capitalism is not exclusively a Western institution, nor does it require a Japanese-style adaptation. It is becoming increasingly clear that the ancient Chinese trading tradition can adjust very well to the high-tech world economy that is currently dominated by the United States, Japan, and Germany, and that this Chinese approach to economic development can generate unprecedented wealth. Singapore in particular has demonstrated the compatibility of successful private enterprise with a powerful public sector.

In China, the members of the bamboo network are currently providing three essential ingredients lacking in a communist society—entrepreneurship, risk-taking capital investment, and business management capability. Not only have the overseas Chinese provided the largest share of "foreign" investment to the mainland, they are also developing and training the future managers of China's businesses. Their efforts have propelled Greater China onto the fastest growth track seen anywhere on the face of the globe. This is a story worth telling. The purpose of this book is to do so.

CROSSING NATIONAL BOUNDARIES

The numerous cross-border enterprises of the overseas Chinese are not unique. Throughout the world, arbitrary national boundaries mark political units that fragment ethnically, culturally, and economically linked groups. In today's global marketplace, a combination of economic incentives and technological advances work to overcome these political barriers. The major actors in this new drama being played out on the world stage are a breed generally overlooked by students of politics and international relations—individual entrepreneurs and their private business firms.

Despite efforts by governments to restrain or redirect trade and investment, many businesses are able to circumvent the laws and regulations that serve as obstacles to private decisionmaking. The mobility of enterprises—of their people, capital, and information—is effectively reducing the power of government. Technological advances have provided business firms with an expanding international reach by way of computers, satellite telecommunications, and fax machines that allows information to flow quickly and cheaply throughout the world. Nowhere is this internationalization more evident than in emerging Third World economies where American, European, and Asian firms are fighting over new and potentially lucrative markets.

Increasingly, governments are discovering the simple fact that private enterprises inexorably seek out profitable opportunities, regardless of geographic location. In response to this, many countries have opened up their borders to trade and investment, hoping to attract the capital, technology, and resources that would otherwise seek locations in more hospitable business climates. Within the last several years, the world has witnessed monumental free trade agreements in North America and Europe. The United States, Canada, and Mexico are linked by

NAFTA, the North American Free Trade Agreement. Most of the Western European nations have joined together to form a European Union (note the progressive changes in name to match the growth in membership: from the Common Market to the European Community and now to the European Union). On a broader scale, GATT (the General Agreement on Tariffs and Trade) has been transformed into a more ambitious World Trade Organization.

Clearly, the formal powers of government are not to be discounted outright. Throughout history, the destructive potential of political units has been vividly demonstrated in ways that range from military action to punitive regulation. Nevertheless, the continuing ability of business entrepreneurs to exploit economic opportunities despite the presence of formidable governmental barriers is impressive. The power of the state has not completely withered away, but much of it has shifted towards private, profit-driven enterprises in a global economy that does not always adhere to arbitrary lines drawn on a map.

Compelling examples of this new competition among economic and political units are seen in the rise of what scholars have termed natural economic territories. These are regions whose economic linkages straddle portions of two or more countries. In many ways, these territories are similar to large metropolitan areas that stretch beyond state or provincial boundaries. In the United States, for example, the southern portion of Illinois is economically oriented to St. Louis, Missouri. Greater New York City (the metropolitan area measured by statisticians) straddles three different states, but does not contain the prime governmental authority of any of them.

By far, the most striking case of natural economic territories is provided by the area comprising the South China coast, Hong Kong, Macao, and Taiwan. In this region, wars and revolutions have created national boundaries that artificially separate ethnic Chinese cultural and trading groups. Whatever their political status, Hong Kong, Macao, and Taipei are all effectively Chinese cities: in each case, most of the population is ethnically Chinese, speaks Chinese, and adheres to Chinese heritage and culture.

Despite the heated rhetoric on both sides, Taiwan and China are also inextricably linked by geography, culture, and language—as well as by massive financial investments.

Beyond that close linkage, companies owned by ethnic Chinese families in Singapore, Malaysia, Thailand, Indonesia, and the Philippines make up about 70 percent of the private business sector in those countries—and are rising influences in Vietnam and Australia.

THE NATURE OF THE NETWORK

The massive cross-investments among these nations are evidence of a new but poorly understood economic power in the region. This force is both a potential ally and a formidable competitor of Western business. It possesses tremendous financial wealth, and has repeatedly demonstrated the ability to capture large profits from emerging markets, in spite of political fragmentation and economic uncertainty. This power that we refer to is the bamboo network of ethnic Chinese entrepreneurs who have relocated to the Southeast Asia diaspora. The individuals who make up this network are responsible in large part for the entire region's unparalleled economic success. The bamboo network has been fueling vibrant business activity in Hong Kong, Taipei, Singapore, Bangkok, Kuala Lumpur, Jakarta, Manila, Saigon, and the other Southeast Asian metropolises. However, while continuing to be extremely active in each of these economies, ethnic Chinese businesses are increasingly focusing on profit opportunities in their homeland.

Although ethnic Chinese trading circles have existed on a cross-border basis for many centuries, the exodus of millions of Chinese citizens during and after the Communist Revolution of 1949 was responsible for the rapid expansion of this entrepreneurial network. Most of these refugees fled the mainland to nearby safe havens in Southeast Asia. Some, through foresight and providence, managed to escape with much of their accumulated family savings. Others left with little more than the proverbial shirts on their backs. For example, Hong Kong real estate tycoon Li Ka-shing started work at the age of 12 at a Hong Kong plastics factory in order to support his family, which had fled from the communist forces. In 1949, he started his own plastics business with $7,000 in savings. Today, Li's fortune is estimated at nearly $6 billion.

As in the case of Li Ka-shing, a unique combination of circumstance and opportunity led many other overseas Chinese to start their own businesses. These refugees often had little choice, as they were barred from owning farmland or holding government jobs in their new home countries. Many of these newly created businesses conducted transactions that crossed over national borders, with overseas Chinese in one country trading with other ethnic Chinese throughout the region. As a result of such trade, tightly knit family-owned and family-run business groups arose, creating great economic power and financial wealth not only for their owners but also for the nations in which they reside. Local politicians have welcomed these hardworking and thrifty newcomers, encouraging their contribution to local development (as well as to the politicians' personal well-being) and not fearing any competition from them in the political arena.

Today, family-run ethnic Chinese business empires are increasingly directed by a new generation of leaders. Despite holdings that often total billions of dollars, these companies have maintained strong family control and have shown a near fanatical reluctance to admit professional outsiders into the management of their firms. A fascinating example of this phenomenon is offered by the fracturing of Y.K. Pao's Hong Kong-based shipping and property empire before his death in 1992. Because he had only daughters, Pao divided management of his businesses among his four sons-in-law, despite their unusually diverse backgrounds: a Chinese doctor, a Japanese architect, a Shanghai banker, and an Austrian lawyer.[1] Apparently, Pao had no thought of turning over the business to professional management.

As we will show, this is not an unrepresentative example. In one recent case, the retiring head of a Hong Kong Chinese family enterprise summoned his oldest son to take over the business. Dutifully, the son—a UCLA M.D.—closed down his medical practice in Los Angeles and complied with the parental request to return to Hong Kong. Similarly, a neurosurgeon in St. Louis took a one-year leave of absence to "straighten up" outstanding business affairs resulting from the death of his father in Taiwan. In that case, Shi Hui Huang found the management of the 30 enterprises so challenging that he, too, changed careers. Today, he is chairman of Taipei-based Ching Fong Global Corporation, a group of 35 industrial and investment companies in Taiwan, Vietnam, Brazil, the United Kingdom, and the United States.[2]

Historically, family-dominated, geographically diversified business groups have not been unique to Southeast Asia. The earlier European experience of the House of Rothschild comes to mind. Of the founding father's five sons, one managed the main office in Frankfurt and the others established branches in London, Paris, Vienna, and Naples, the main European commercial centers of the time. Today, in a similar fashion, the Grande International Group—a Macao-based conglomerate of industrial companies—has its headquarters in Hong Kong, its research and development center in Taiwan, and its production facilities in the mainland province of Guangdong.

The family-oriented style of management that is characteristic of many overseas Chinese firms is both a strength and a weakness. On the positive side, family control allows for a less bureaucratic management structure that permits rapid decisionmaking. Family loyalty also serves to minimize dissension and destructive in-fighting. On the negative side, however, family members may not possess the managerial talent necessary for a firm to remain competitive in the world economy. Furthermore, the anticipation of a large inheritance may decrease the ambition and drive of relatives admitted into the family business. This helps to explain the old saying among overseas Chinese that the first generation makes the family fortune, the second generation enjoys it and builds on it, but the third generation squanders it. In private conversation, more colorful terms are used by family leaders when describing the shortcomings of their offspring.

The typical overseas Chinese conglomerate is privately held and is involved in such a wide variety of business transactions that it is virtually impossible to discern its true structure. The reluctance of family members to disclose much information about the business to outsiders further complicates any systematic analysis of the bamboo network. Some reasons for this secrecy are obvious. It makes good sense to minimize the jealousy of less successful participants in the local economy when such people have at times, as in Indonesia, launched violent physical assaults against ethnic Chinese. Even financially hard-pressed governments have been known to put the squeeze on the possessors of great wealth. A by-product of this reticence is that only limited amounts of data are available on the detailed operations of these financial empires.

Nevertheless, there is enough information available about the more well-known overseas Chinese business families to provide a good understanding of this important sector of the Southeast Asian economy. While researching this book, the authors met with many Chinese entrepreneurs and government personnel, as well as with Western business officials who deal with them. Considerable insight can be gleaned from these mini-case studies which, in turn, provide information about the current state of the Greater Chinese economy and the workings of the bamboo network. In most cases, we have been able to cross-check the information obtained from these interviews with published sources.

When we step away from examining individual entrepreneurial families, some intriguing overall patterns emerge. In particular, there has been a recent turnaround in the relationship between the overseas Chinese and their homeland. Ironically, overseas Chinese who once fled the mainland under difficult circumstances are now by far the largest *investors* in mainland China. It is fascinating to contemplate the unfolding of this uneasy relationship between the politically powerful yet capital-hungry mainland and the economically powerful but politically vulnerable members of the bamboo network. So far, a tentative symbiotic relationship has developed. The living standard of mainland China is rising rapidly with the influx of foreign investment; that investment, in turn, appears to be earning substantial profits for overseas Chinese investors.

However, serious tensions between these two groups are already visible. From the viewpoint of Beijing and the senior leadership of the Communist Party, it is becoming increasingly difficult to manage a polarized, two-economy nation. Extraordinarily rapid growth has occurred in the coastal zones that began opening up to private enterprise in 1978. However, this economic development has not yet carried over to the remainder of China to any substantial degree. Outside the coastal area, business expansion has been fitful and, as we will see, much less successful. China's wealthy, capitalist zones have aroused the envy of the far larger yet poorer state sector, which is still dominated by agriculture and nationalized, government-run industry. The simultaneous existence of capitalism and socialism has bred corruption throughout the governmental bureaucracy. And, as economic power becomes increasingly decentralized, Beijing is losing its power to maintain full political control.

For the overseas Chinese, large-scale investments in the mainland present threats as well as opportunities. Uncertainty surrounds China's future political climate as fears of extortion and expropriation grow. Most of the overseas Chinese entrepreneurs have already lived through revolution and war. These experiences surely affect their evaluation of future investment risks. As we will show in later chapters, should mainland China squeeze too hard when it incorporates Hong Kong in 1997, the result is likely to be a shift of wealth and capital to Singapore and other areas of Southeast Asia. The bamboo network is strong enough to operate quite independently of the mainland if drastic change becomes necessary once again.

Under these delicate circumstances, the role of Western entrepreneurs in the Chinese economy is extremely chancy. The task to be performed by European and North American businesses and governments is far more challenging than the currently fashionable activity of simply forecasting the expanding market potential of Greater China or even signing highly publicized contracts for future sales. Rather, there is a compelling need to understand the powerful and conflicting forces that are determining the economic future of the region and that will influence the lives of those business contracts, particularly their profitability. Given the limited knowledge that most Westerners have of this region, a variety of background considerations need to be introduced and carefully examined.

PROGRESS AND PROBLEMS

We begin by noting that, unlike cultural ties, the present close economic relationships between overseas Chinese commercial interests and the mainland are not long-standing. For roughly 30 years after the 1949 revolution, mainland China was economically isolated, closed to virtually all commercial trade except for limited black market activity with nearby Hong Kong and Taiwan. But in 1978, with the beginning of Deng Xiaoping's "open door" policy instituted after the death of Mao Tse Tung, the most populous nation in the world emerged from isolation, eager to engage in commerce, trade, and finance with the international economic community. Overseas Chinese entrepreneurs, with their language, family, and cultural ties to the mainland, were in the best position to aggressively pursue investment opportunities in this new market.

Since that time, mainland China has enjoyed economic progress on an unprecedented scale. Twenty years ago, an observer standing on the edge of the New Territories of Hong Kong and looking inland would have seen only rice paddies. Today, that land is filled with skyscrapers, factories, and a busy transportation network. Indeed, it is difficult to see where the New Territories end and where the mainland's rapidly expanding Shenzhen Special Economic Zone begins. The provinces of Guangdong and Fujian, home to many of China's new private enterprises, are booming with industrial activity. (Not coincidentally, these provinces are also the original homelands of most of the overseas Chinese.) Simultaneously, Shanghai is regaining its historical position as the mainland's premier commercial and financial center. Throughout China, quiet villages have been transformed into bustling cities. Their streets are crammed not only with bicycles and motor scooters, but also with the automobiles that symbolize this region's newfound wealth.

These rapid economic changes have resulted from a series of reforms that laid the foundations for a market economy: prices set by supply and demand, wages linked to employee performance, and private enterprises free to compete in world markets. Today, over half of China's industrial output is produced outside of the state sector. An even larger fraction of the entire economy now responds to market incentives rather than government planning. During the period 1978 to 1994, over $90 billion in foreign direct investment entered the mainland. Investment projects on the drawing board involve several hundreds of billions more.

Significant political change also has occurred. Although China's Communist Party continues to monopolize political power and suppress any opposition, it has loosened its grip on the society. Individuals are allowed, to a degree unheard of during the Maoist era, to make career, travel, and lifestyle choices. Living standards for the average Chinese are much higher than they were in 1978. Millions are escaping from poverty and filling the ranks of a new middle class.

U.S. companies and other Western entrepreneurs have followed these developments with growing interest, albeit with an undercurrent of concern over developments they do not fully comprehend. Many private interests are eager to harness the productive energy that has been unleashed along China's coastline. For producers of labor-intensive goods, the mainland seems to offer virtually unlimited supplies of low-wage workers. At the same time, companies that make consumer goods view China as an enormous, increasingly accessible market for everything from soft drinks to luxury automobiles. Other firms seek to extract the oil, natural gas, and mineral resources of China's vast western regions, which remain unexplored or at least undeveloped due to a lack of technology or supporting infrastructure.

Yet, despite its massive potential, the Chinese marketplace has not yet generated significant returns for most Western businesses. Indeed, many firms have yet to earn any profit at all from their Chinese operations. One major U.S. law firm catering to Western companies trying to do business in China reports that it may begin to break even in its sixth year of operation. Far more companies are reluctant to provide any data on their profits (or losses) in individual overseas markets.

The problems encountered by U.S. businesses in China seem endless. Rules and regulations are often not publicized by Beijing, and those that are may be changed without notification. Currency is not freely convertible, so many firms have difficulty bringing their money home. Signed contracts are not legally binding, and judicial recourse is very limited. Copyright infringement and other forms of intellectual piracy are widespread. With a few sporadic and well-publicized exceptions, this form of economic theft is rarely punished by government officials who look the other way—and on occasion profit from the piracy.

In addition to these formidable problems, Western business-people also find themselves facing a completely foreign business environment. The lack of a common cultural ground between Westerners and Chinese can complicate even routine transactions. Mystical practices such as *feng shui*, somewhat akin to Western astrology, govern certain types of business decisionmaking. *Guanxi*, the use of personal influence on a massive scale, is accepted as a matter of course in China. Gifts lubricate the deal-making process to an extent bordering on bribery, which is explicitly outlawed in the United States.

Securing necessary business permits frequently requires the development of close relationships with the local Communist Party hierarchy. At times, these officials become *de facto* business partners. A son or daughter of a Beijing leader may request a 10 percent share of a business. Only the most intrepid (or perhaps foolhardy) businessperson would turn down such a request from the powerful, even though no payment for the valuable equity is ever likely to be received.

For all these reasons, Western companies have been reluctant to commit heavily to an expensive, risky presence in the Chinese market. Overseas Chinese investors, with a far greater understanding of the mainland, have not been as cautious. A flood of overseas investment is pouring into China, mainly through Hong Kong (which handles financial transactions for overseas Chinese throughout the region). Taipei-based businesses, despite Taiwan's severed trade links with the mainland, are also leading investors.

What accounts for this discrepancy between Western and ethnic Chinese investors? Not only do overseas Chinese speak the same language as their mainland counterparts, they also share similar religious, cultural, and historical backgrounds. As a result, the overseas Chinese have a far better understanding of *guo qing*, or the unique characteristics of Chinese society that must be taken into consideration if a product or business practice is to enjoy widespread acceptance. Many have family members or friends with the necessary *guanxi* to grease the wheels of the still powerful government bureaucracy. They have established networks to aid them with the movement of financial capital and the securing of informal contracts in a region where the rule of law is weak and its administration often chaotic.

THE BAMBOO NETWORK AND SOUTHEAST ASIA

The net result of these cross-border investment flows by the overseas Chinese community has been the rapid emergence of a new Chinese-based economy that is the epicenter for industry, commerce, and finance in Southeast Asia. The region has substantial technological and manufacturing capability, entrepreneurial and marketing skills, and very large endowments of land, resources, and labor. Moreover, it possesses its own huge pool of financial capital.

Yet the power of the bamboo network should not be overemphasized or misconstrued. One of the most common beliefs of overseas Chinese entrepreneurs is reflected in an ominous admonition based on a great deal of experience: Keep your bags packed at all times. Even the most aggressive overseas Chinese investors concede that business on the mainland is a risky proposition (as it has also been elsewhere in Southeast Asia). China is still an authoritarian nation, ruled by leaders with a great deal of arbitrary power. Its banking system is severely underdeveloped. High and persistent inflation continues to plague the economy. And, most importantly, China does not possess the necessary political institutions—such as an established legal system and an effective judiciary—that Westerners take for granted as essential prerequisites to long-term economic growth. Indeed, some overseas Chinese business owners report grievous personal harm inflicted by mainland authorities with whom they ran afoul.

Furthermore, China's senior political leadership is unstable. It is possible that the rising wealth produced by the economic transformation may encourage the continuation of recent progress. On the other hand, the ruling regime could crack, or even collapse, following the death of Deng Xiaoping. Alternatively, it may be superseded by a new form of authoritarian government that will reverse the recent economic reforms and accelerate the current buildup of military forces. Some fear that ethnic and political tensions in China will tear the country apart. The dismal experience of Yugoslavia is taken seriously by the Chinese, be they at home or abroad.

Even if the current political hierarchy is able to overcome these problems, other, longer-term concerns may threaten the political and economic relationship between China and the West, and thus dampen the currently bright prospects for all of Southeast Asia. China's military forces have been growing rapidly in recent years, and may move to fill the strategic vacuum created by the breakup of the Soviet Union. Historical territorial disputes between China and its neighbors (e.g., Vietnam, Taiwan, the Philippines) may turn into military flashpoints. The South China Sea, the locale of one such dispute, may not sound important to most Americans, but one-fourth of the world's shipping moves through the area.

China's rapid economic growth has also created severe environmental problems, many of which are being ignored by investors who myopically focus on short-term profits. Furthermore, the mainland's primitive infrastructure has already been pushed beyond its limits. Congestion and delays are encountered by virtually all travelers. Sustained, long-term development will require a more balanced investment approach than has been typical of the last decade.

Despite these fundamental concerns, money continues to flow

into the mainland on a large scale. High risk can equate with high returns for those who are able to navigate their way through the government bureaucracy, consistently supply their factories with raw materials and skilled labor, *and* efficiently withdraw their profits from the country. Investment figures suggest that the overseas Chinese community possesses the skills necessary to meet these challenges. Many Western companies, including the largest and traditionally most successful firms, are finding out that they do not possess the requisite capabilities for success in China, at least not yet. Some high-technology firms, however, constitute a special case. They possess something the Chinese authorities very much want: the capability to design, develop, and manufacture products that either are needed by China or are attractive to its growing export markets. Often, the result is especially cooperative treatment by governmental authorities.

The Western entrepreneurs who operate most successfully in China typically have enjoyed strong relationships with one or more of the leading overseas Chinese firms. At least in the early stages, this combination of forces—often formalized in the terms of a joint venture—has been essential. Even the most successful American companies, such as Wal-Mart, feel obliged to establish a joint venture with an overseas Chinese partner before trying to penetrate this exotic market.

U.S. analysts and investors alike are observing the economic transformation of Greater China with awe. Despite the tenor of most discussions on the subject in the United States, neither prison labor nor totalitarian government is the key to this phenomenal economic growth. A far more positive force is at work: China is throwing off the shackles of communism while moving aggressively, albeit irregularly, to a market economy. Since 1978, Beijing has instituted increasingly liberal economic reforms that have opened up Southeast China to foreign entrepreneurs at a faster pace than almost anyone expected. What began as only a few foreign trade zones designed to attract some outside investment has become an explosion of economic activity along the coast and, increasingly, into the inland provinces. In the words of author Paul Theroux, the Long March has taken a sharp right turn, down the capitalist road.[3]

The implications of this change are unprecedented. Never before in recorded history have so many—literally hundreds of millions of people—risen from poverty so quickly. At the same time, however, large numbers of uneducated, unskilled workers currently employed in the unproductive state sector face a threatening future in the form of large-scale unemployment. Change is often painful, and the rapidity of change in mainland China has placed great strain on that country's social and cultural foundations.

There is unambiguous evidence, however, that the average Chinese has benefited greatly from the reforms. Diets have improved, consumption of luxury items has increased, and real incomes are rising rapidly. As a result, a new middle class is emerging that is hungry for Western consumer goods. Given a total population of 1.2 billion, this potential market is too large for most firms to ignore.

Indeed, as the world's most rapidly expanding marketplace, Greater China has become a magnet for foreign investment. China's sustained double-digit annual economic growth contrasts dramatically with the paltry 2 to 4 percent yearly increases experienced in the United States, Europe, and Japan. The resulting consumer market in China is developing faster than any other in the world.

However, these economic attractions are offset—at least in part—by political volatility, a primitive legal system, and an unstable outlook, all of which pose significant risks to investors. The worst-case scenario is the political collapse of China following the demise of Deng, which would severely disrupt the global order with potentially tens of millions of refugees swarming across the seas to Japan, Indonesia, Malaysia, and elsewhere. But even a stable China will add substantially to the world's resource and environmental problems. As noted by Lee Kuan Yew of Singapore, "The size of China's displacement of the world balance is such that the world must find a new balance in thirty to forty years . . . This is the biggest player in the history of man."[4]

Greater China is the most exciting if not also the most scary business opportunity in the global economy, both today and into the foreseeable future. No other region contains its potent combination of physical, financial, and human resources. The historical record bolsters that perspective. You do not have to accept controversial multicultural approaches to education in order to acknowledge that, for most of recorded history, China has been more developed, prosperous, sophisticated, and civilized than the West. In the broad sweep of world history, China has not been the backward nation that most Americans typically visualize, but rather the innovator that Western nations have later imitated. China invented gunpowder, the magnetic compass, the clock, the wheelbarrow, movable type, and nautical innovations such as the rear rudder. Chinese technicians were casting molten iron 17 centuries before Europeans discovered the process. Unlike the great civilizations of ancient Egypt, Greece, and Rome, the Chinese civilization that was their contemporary remains intact today.[5]

Today, China is on a road that could potentially restore its earlier greatness. It is vital for the political and economic interests of the West to better understand the developments taking place in that hitherto exotic part of the world. That is not an easy task. Fortunately, the operations of the bamboo network provide an important, albeit neglected, key to that understanding.

PART II

THE NETWORK AND CHINA

CHAPTER 2

Understanding the Bamboo Network

They are your most formidable competitors in both China and Southeast Asia;
they are also your most likely allies . . .[1]

The preceding quotation refers not to well-prepared Japanese business executives or to energetic German sales representatives. Rather, it is a reference to the Chinese entrepreneurs who live outside of their home country: the "overseas Chinese." Louis Kraar, the distinguished journalist who has lived in the Orient for several decades, goes on to note: "This is not some quaint ethnic sideshow; the overseas Chinese are increasingly the main event in Asian business today."[2] Many other observers of the region share the belief that ethnic Chinese businesses operating off the mainland are the driving force in the new wave of Asian trade, manufacturing, and investment.

Since the 1500s, southern China has served as a springboard for emigrants to Vietnam, Thailand, Indonesia, and elsewhere in Southeast Asia. These overseas Chinese have developed a bamboo network that transcends national boundaries. This informal array of complementary business relationships extends throughout the region, where entrepreneurs, business executives, traders, and financiers of Chinese background are major players in local economies. The heart of the Chinese network is Hong Kong, Taiwan, and the China coast. Singapore, with a predominantly Chinese population, is also an important factor in cross-border Chinese business relationships.

Companies owned by overseas Chinese dominate the private business sectors of every Southeast Asian country. Typically, the founders of these overseas Chinese businesses possessed little wealth and built their firms from scratch, contributing substantially to the development of the local economy in the process. A former student of one of the authors tells of his grandfather, who migrated from the mainland of China to the United States. He got a job in a traditional Chinese hand laundry and, over the course of many years ironing garments, managed to save a very large sum from his modest earnings. He then moved to Hong Kong, where he was able to invest 50,000 Hong Kong dollars in the rice business. This gutsy move was the basis of the current family fortune, which is now diversified across Southeast Asia and into Australia.

Today, many of these small family firms have grown into enormous conglomerates, each of which maintains interests in dozens of highly diversified companies. In 1994, the total assets of the 500 largest public companies in Asia controlled by overseas Chinese exceeded $500 billion (see table below).[3] These numbers exclude the many privately owned enterprises controlled by the same families.

As S. Gordon Redding notes in his landmark study, *The Spirit of Chinese Capitalism*, it is difficult to recognize the true significance of the overseas Chinese in Southeast Asia because their impact is spread across so many boundaries. Thus, they cannot as a total be represented in any national statistics. "Even adding together Taiwan, Hong Kong, and Singapore is grossly inadequate, as it leaves out much going on in Malaysia, Indonesia, Thailand, and the Philippines, to say nothing of China or of Vancouver, Toronto, New York, San Francisco, London, Sydney, etc."[4] The World Bank estimates that the combined economic output of the

Location	Number of Companies	Market Capital-ization (in billions)	Total Assets (in billions)
Hong Kong	123	$155	$173
Taiwan	159	111	89
Malaysia	83	55	49
Singapore	52	42	92
Thailand	39	35	95
Indonesia	36	20	33
Philippines	8	6	8
Total	500	424	539

overseas Chinese was nearly $400 billion in 1991, an impressive sum for 40 million people. Today, considering the explosive economic growth of Southeast Asia, the figure is probably closer to $600 billion.[5]

In Indonesia, overseas Chinese make up only 3 to 4 percent of the population, yet they own about 70 percent of private domestic capital and run more than 160 of the 200 largest businesses. Liem Sioe Liong's Salim Group alone is estimated to account for 5 percent of the country's gross domestic product. In 1995, every reported Indonesian billionaire was ethnic Chinese.[6]

In Thailand, overseas Chinese account for about 10 percent of the population and control the four largest private banks. One of these, the Bangkok Bank, is the largest and most profitable in the region, and a key lender to the bamboo network. In Malaysia, ethnic Chinese control roughly half of that nation's corporate assets. In the Philippines, they make up less than 2 percent of the population, but control over one-third of the 1,000 largest corporations.[7]

The economic dominance of the bamboo network within these countries is a source of great tension. The overseas Chinese are often seen as profiteers, stealing the wealth of a country from its indigenous people. This misguided view often results in discrimination, both formal and informal, as well as outright violence. From the late 1930s to the mid-1950s, the Thai government took over large numbers of private Chinese firms. During the 1960s and 1970s, Indonesia and the Philippines formally blocked Chinese businesses from operating in certain sectors of the economy, a type of affirmative action for the majority. In Indonesia, tens of thousands of ethnic Chinese were killed in 1965 during an attempted communist coup. In Malaysia, ethnic tension in May 1969 fueled riots that resulted in massive property damage and nearly 200 deaths.[8]

As recently as April 1994, anti-Chinese riots erupted in Medan, Indonesia, effectively paralyzing the city. During the riots, over 100 ethnic Chinese-owned shops and businesses were looted and vandalized by indigenous protesters demanding higher wages. One Chinese-owned shopping mall was overrun by thousands of Indonesians, many wielding machetes. An ethnic Chinese factory owner was beaten to death while attempting to drive to his factory and protect it from rioters. Leaflets distributed among the crowd detailed the wealth of ethnic Chinese families and their alleged exploitation of Indonesian workers.[9]

Events such as these provide further incentive for overseas Chinese to deal primarily with other members of the bamboo network, and foster an "us against them" mentality that is not completely unjustified. Parallels with Jewish business leaders, historical targets of discrimination, are hard to avoid. Indeed, sensationalistic Japanese newspapers have reported off-the-wall conspiracy theories that blame overseas Chinese and Jewish businesspeople for engineering declines in Tokyo's stock market during the early 1990s. These stories are indicative of the widespread hostility faced by overseas Chinese throughout Asia.[10]

Partly in response to such discrimination, the overseas Chinese have attempted to blend in with their local cultures. Many change their names to avoid persecution. Corazon Aquino's maiden name—Cojuangco—appears to be Spanish but in reality is derived from her immigrant grandfather's name—Ko Hwan Ko. In Thailand, ethnic Chinese were required to take Thai names from a government list.[11]

As further protection against discrimination and violence, the overseas Chinese have diversified their wealth outside of their home countries. In the process, they have become the largest cross-border investors in Thailand, Malaysia, Indonesia, Hong Kong, the Philippines, and Vietnam. In recent years, much of this investment capital has been flowing into the Chinese mainland, especially the southern coastal region. Since Deng Xiaoping launched his economic open door policy in 1978, overseas Chinese have invested more than $50 billion in their motherland, representing about 80 percent of all foreign investment.

To date, the members of what we call the bamboo network have formed more than 100,000 joint ventures in China. In the process, they have generated export industries, brought in management skills and technology, and provided international connections to the mainland. William Overholt, a senior official in the Hong Kong office of Bankers Trust, describes the ongoing phenomenon of overseas Chinese executives training mainland Chinese in capitalist methods as "the biggest business school for managers ever created in the world."[12]

THE RISE OF CHINESE BUSINESSES

One of the most striking characteristics of the typical overseas Chinese business is its international diversification. A good example of such geographic diversification is furnished by Hong Kong entrepreneur Lee Shau Kee, who owns a controlling interest in the Henderson Land Development Company (with an estimated market value in 1995 of $9.1 billion). That wealthy firm invests in Beijing, Shanghai, Guangdong, and Hong Kong. It also has interests in a Singapore convention center, as well as in residential developments in the United States and Canada. In 1995, Lee's personal net worth was estimated at $6.5 billion.[13]

Many of these cross-border enterprises have a fundamentally different organizational structure than their Western counterparts. In large measure, the bamboo network consists of cross-holdings of privately owned family-run, trade-oriented firms, rather than the huge publicly owned manufacturing corporations that are typical in the United States, Japan, and Western Europe. Of the world's 500 largest corporations in 1994, only six were located in Greater China: one in Hong Kong, two in Taiwan, and three on the mainland. In comparison, 149 Japanese enterprises made the list, as did 151 U.S. companies.[14]

The tendency of Chinese merchants to establish themselves at locations away from their home country is a long-standing practice, going back at least several centuries. As Americans traditionally migrated to the West, the Chinese moved south into Malaysia, Thailand, and Indonesia. However, despite this migratory tradition, these individuals remain Chinese in some deep and significant sense. According to Redding, "the majority of them have not psychologically left China, or at least . . . some ideal and perhaps romanticized notion of Chinese civilization."[15]

Ever since the fifth century B.C., every generation of students in China has learned the sayings of Confucius (K'ung fu-tzu) by rote. The Confucian tradition is remarkably persistent. Most Chinese who have immigrated to other nations have carried these principles with them and preserved them as they adapt to the values of their new countries. Traditional Chinese thought continues to be marked by acceptance of the course of events and pragmatism with regard to order. The common core of Confucian teaching includes such values as loyalty to a hierarchical structure of authority, a code of defined conduct between children and adults, and trust among friends.[16]

Other characteristics of the Confucian tradition are beneficial to a market economy. A sense of collective responsibility, pride in the work ethic, and a disdain for conspicuous consumption make for high saving rates, an especially valuable trait in fostering rapid industrialization. As we will see, the resultant state of mind is expressed in business dealings, networks, and family management of companies.

More than half of today's overseas Chinese population can be traced to only two southeastern coastal provinces: Guangdong (located next to Hong Kong) and Fujian (across the strait from Taiwan). Another large portion fled from Shanghai to Hong Kong in the late 1940s to avoid being swept up in the Communist Revolution. Many of these refugees were owners of textile factories who helped provide the British colony with the technical know-how that fueled its first industrial boom.

As Robert Elegant wrote in 1959, "The Chinese came seeking economic opportunity or political asylum. . . . They are now fishermen and pawnbrokers, rubber tappers and tin miners, capitalists and servants. But everywhere the largest single group is engaged in some form of commerce, from the corner grocery store to the international trading firm."[17]

Wary of government, the expatriate Chinese found that kinship, dialect, or a common origin (in a clan, a village, or even a county) provided a basis for mutual trust in business transactions, even ones conducted at great distances. Hakka tended to deal with Hakka, Chiu Chownese with Chiu Chownese. These relationships provided both certainty and informality, facilitating transactions that at times may have skirted the letter of the law.[18]

Traditionally, overseas Chinese businesses have tried to develop close ties with the leaders of the government of their host country. Unlike the expatriate managers of Japanese and Western firms, Chinese family members frequently become citizens of the countries in which they do business. This gives them a critical advantage in assimilating, understanding, and adopting the local culture, as well as the nuances of local politics and economics. It also helps them to circumvent discriminatory legislation or to seek the protection needed by a productive but unpopular minority. In Malaysia, the phenomenon known as the "Ali Baba" business arose in response to the official discrimination against foreign businesses. "Ali" refers to the native partner whose main contribution is to help the firm qualify for the special government subsidy available only to native Malays. "Baba" is the Chinese entrepreneur with the capital and skill to really run the enterprise.[19]

The overseas Chinese network is often "maddeningly impenetrable" to outsiders, according to *Institutional Investor* magazine. Ross H. Munro of the Foreign Policy Research Institute, who worked in Beijing and Hong Kong for many years, concludes that Chinese businesses in Southeast Asia are extremely secretive about their business activities at home and abroad. He notes especially that, in China, empathetic local officials cater to their secretiveness.[20]

Capital moves throughout the network in circuitous ways, providing safety against unforeseen political and economic events. Bankers speak of transactions that involve six or seven countries, with the funds flowing back to their original source at the end of it all.[21] Even when Taiwan had strict exchange controls, it was possible for an individual in the network to deposit a large sum with a gold shop in Taipei and for a relative to withdraw the equivalent on the next day from an affiliated gold dealer in Hong Kong. Such "underground" transactions still take place.

THE FAMILY BUSINESS IN OPERATION

Sociologist Peter L. Berger, who has studied in depth the relation between Chinese culture and economics, concludes that the "absolutely central institution" for understanding Chinese business is the overseas Chinese family. Berger notes that Chinese firms are almost always family firms because, within traditional Chinese culture, "you can only trust close relatives." After interviewing the people in many Chinese businesses, Berger concluded that managers who were not family members were the most unhappy people he encountered. The reasons were all interrelated: nobody trusted them, they knew they were not going to get anywhere, and their constant thought was to leave the business as soon as possible and start their own.[22]

Because so much of the typical overseas Chinese business is privately held, very little information is released about the firm's operations—in contrast to the vast amounts of public information available regarding the standard U.S. corporation. Nevertheless, some of the holdings of the larger overseas Chinese firms are publicly held and listed on stock exchanges, providing some idea of their size and structure.

Charoen Pokphand Group of Thailand

The Charoen Pokphand (CP) Group, a Thai agribusiness conglomerate, is a typical example of the overseas Chinese family business. The CP Group had its beginnings in a small seed company named Chia Tai, founded in 1921 by two Chinese brothers—Chia Ekchor and Chia Seow Nooy. Although originally headquartered in Shantou, a seaport in China's southeastern Guangdong province, Chia Tai developed a network of seed outlets with locations in Bangkok, Hong Kong, Taipei, Kuala Lumpur, and Singapore. After the 1949 Communist Revolution, Chia Ek Chor moved his company headquarters to Bangkok and, as is the custom in Thailand, took a Thai name—Chearavanont (which means "long established wealth" in Thai).

In the early 1950s, the Charoen Pokphand Company was born out of a venture to expand the market for Chia Tai seed (Charoen Pokphand means "commodity development" in Thai). CP was a struggling business until the 1970s, when Bangkok Bank (described later in this chapter) asked it to assume control of a bankrupt chicken farm. Following this experience, CP began lending money to farmers, providing technical expertise, and selling poultry feed. The firm also purchased grown chickens for distribution to grocers and restaurants. This business strategy worked phenomenally well: CP expanded its operations into Indonesia, Taiwan, China, Turkey, Portugal, and the Philippines.[23]

Today, although its primary specialty continues to be agribusiness, CP has expanded into nine other divisions, including such disparate enterprises as petrochemicals and property development. One of CP's largest ventures outside of its agribusiness core is its stake in TelecomAsia, a joint venture with the U.S. telecommunications giant NYNEX. In 1990, TelecomAsia was granted a 25-year license to build and operate two million telephone lines in Bangkok. More recently, it has acquired interests in satellite launch, cable television, and mobile telephone services.[24]

In all, CP controls more than 200 affiliated companies, of which only 14 are listed on stock exchanges. The fact that so much of the group is privately held by the family (all of the founders' sons sit on the board of directors) makes it difficult to ascertain its true wealth or structure. Figure 1 shows some of its complex cross-holdings.

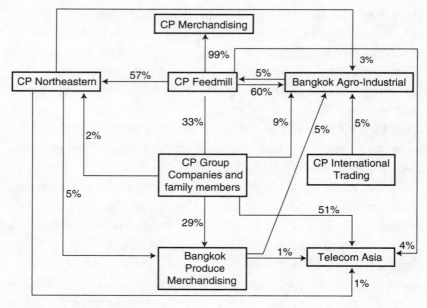

FIGURE 1
Important Cross-Holdings of the Charoen Pokphand Group

Officially, CP reports that its 1993 revenues exceeded $5 billion (only half of which came from operations in Thailand). Chia Ek Chor's son, Dhanin Chearavanont, controls the family empire. Contrary to custom, Dhanin took over at the age of only 25 despite being the youngest of Chia's four sons. Dhanin's older brother, Sumet Jiaravanon, is vice chairman and operates out of Hong Kong. In 1995, the family wealth was estimated at $5.5 billion.

It is not surprising that most Westerners are unfamiliar with conglomerates such as CP, because these business groups have specialized almost exclusively in Southeast Asian operations, particularly the rapidly growing Chinese market. CP is reportedly the single largest investor in the mainland, where each one of its divisions has established a joint venture. Its agribusiness division operates in 26 of China's 30 provinces. CP currently commands 5 percent of China's enormous (and growing) feed meal market, and derives over one-fifth of its total revenue from the mainland.[25] According to Prasert Poongkumain, group president in charge of agroindustry, "We have an advantage because we are of Chinese origin. We speak the language and look the same."[26]

There seems to be more to it than common culture, however. The equity of most of CP's dozens of joint ventures in China is divided rather evenly with partners on the mainland. These diverse business partners range from the provincial grain bureau to provincial and municipal governments to NORINCO—a state-owned industrial conglomerate controlled by the army. The exact contribution of these PRC partners is difficult to assess. We must wonder whether the local party receives its ownership share by virtue of the influence it brings to bear at crucial points in the business relationship—rather than in exchange for any contribution of funds or physical assets. In return for their stake in the partnership, local officials are often hired as employees of the joint venture. These types of arrangements replace the commissions that are often paid under such circumstances, and thus may obviate the need for outright bribery.

CP's joint venture with Continental Grain, Conti Chia Tai International, is reported to pay 15 percent of its earnings to Shenzhen Development. That government-owned firm controls the site on which the joint venture has built its feed mill. Given the secrecy with which these companies operate (Continental Grain is a privately held U.S. enterprise), it is difficult to determine the extent to which their practices depart from traditional arms-length relationships that result from competition in Western markets.

The diversification of CP provides a flexibility that allows it to seize profitable opportunities unrelated to its core businesses. In 1985, CP established the Ek Chor motorcycle company (using the Chinese name of the founder). Lacking any experience in motor manufacturing, the firm licensed the necessary technology from leading manufacturers such as Honda and then relied on CP's managerial experience and mainland connections to set up the business. Today, Ek Chor produces 300,000 motorcycles a year at its two plants on the mainland and has gained a 15 percent share of the Chinese motorcycle market (a distant second behind NORINCO). It plans to dramatically expand production in 1996, when it completes a more modern plant in Shanghai's Pudong area.[27]

Li Ka-shing Group of Hong Kong

The personal net worth of Hong Kong real estate tycoon Li Ka-shing was estimated in 1995 at nearly $6 billion, placing him among the world's ten richest people. Li grew up in Guangdong province, but moved with his family to Hong Kong in 1940 as a refugee from China's civil war. His father died two years later and, to help support his family, Li began to work for a company that produced plastic flowers and watchbands. By the age of 20,

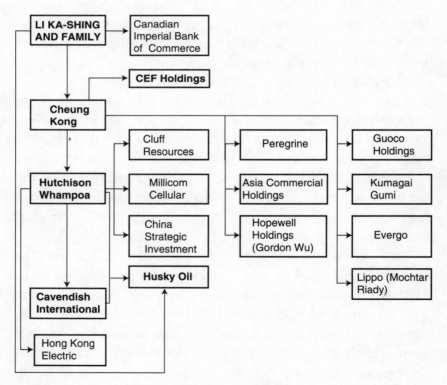

Boldface = controlling interest; others are minority interests

FIGURE 2
Li Ka-shing's Business Network

Li was general manager of that enterprise, and two years later he started his own plastics company—Cheung Kong. Soon after that, Li purchased his own factory, a move that began his legendary real estate trading business. His two young sons, Richard and Victor, were given pieces of the business to run when they were in their twenties.[28]

In recent years, Li has diversified beyond real estate into telecommunications, infrastructure, and energy industries. Figure 2 illustrates a portion of the complicated financial arrangements of Li's empire. At the top of the structure is Cheung Kong (with a 1995 market value of $10.8 billion); Li Ka-shing and his family hold a controlling interest.

Cheung Kong holds a large interest (44 percent) in Hutchison Whampoa, which in 1995 had a market capitalization of $18.3 billion, making it one of the biggest ex-British "hongs" that traditionally dominated Hong Kong. Cheung Kong also controls the Husky Oil Company of Canada. Li holds smaller interests in a variety of enterprises controlled by other ethnic Chinese, notably Gordon Wu's Hopewell Holdings and Mochtar Riady's Lippo Group. Hutchison Whampoa also holds interests in a variety of businesses—including Husky Oil, Cavendish International, and Cluff Resources. Some of these companies are publicly owned, being listed on the stock exchanges of Great Britain, Canada, and Hong Kong. Others are unlisted and privately owned.[29]

Clearly, Li Ka-shing is a powerful business and financial force. Some insight into his fabulous business success can be gleaned from his personal conduct. This billionaire lives in an unassuming house on the unfashionable south side of Hong Kong Island and sports a well-worn inexpensive electronic watch. In the late 1970s, he earned the trust of the territory's business elite when he turned down an extremely lucrative offer for a property he had already agreed to sell—at a much lower price. But this sense of honor cuts two ways. In 1987, when investment bankers who had agreed to underwrite a stock issue wanted to pull out of the deal after the stock market crash, he insisted that they meet their commitments.[30]

The close relationships between Li Ka-shing and government

leaders is legendary. The PRC has appointed him to its advisory council for the takeover of Hong Kong. Cheung Kong has a strategic stake in a Hong Kong-listed company, Shougang Concord Grand, in which Deng Xiaoping's second son, Zhifang, is executive director. On occasion, however, Li's good connections can turn sour. He enjoyed a good relationship with Zhou Beifang, head of the Hong Kong division of Shougang, one of China's most powerful state enterprises whose chairman was Beifang's father Zhou Guanwu. In February 1995, when Deng Xiaoping (an old comrade of Zhou senior) was reported to be in failing health, the elder Zhou was replaced and his son arrested.

Seeing an asset perhaps about to turn into a liability, Li Ka-shing quickly rushed to Beijing, where he was photographed with Prime Minister Li Peng. In return for this favor, Li agreed to reduce by one-half his investment in the development of the Wangfujing area of Beijing to make way for investors from the mainland.[31]

Richard Li, the youngest son of Li Ka-shing, continues the family's entrepreneurial tradition. Unlike his father, Richard was born into great wealth. He attended prep school in the United States and studied economics and computer engineering at Stanford. At 23, he returned home to Hong Kong to work with his father. Eager to make his own fortune, Richard raised over $100 million from the family's Hutchison Whampoa conglomerate to start up Star TV, a satellite broadcasting system that transmitted throughout Asia. The company's performance surpassed all expectations: less than three years later, he sold two-thirds of the company to Great Britain's Rupert Murdoch for over $500 million. Since then, Richard Li has paid off his debts to his family and personally financed his next venture—Pacific Century Group—to adapt telecommunications and health care technologies for use in Southeast Asia. Meanwhile, he remains vice-chairman of his father's Hutchison Whampoa.[32]

Ong Beng Seng of Singapore

Most successful overseas Chinese business groups set up an intricate network of subsidiaries and associated companies, some public and some private. A good example is the group led by Ong Beng Seng of Singapore. The group's umbrella public corporation is Hotel Properties Limited (HPL), of which Ong is managing director. HPL controls a variety of construction, hotel and restaurant management, and entertainment subsidiaries.

HPL owns hotels and properties in Singapore, Hong Kong, Malaysia, and Australia. Its wholly owned subsidiaries include food distributors and retailers in Hong Kong, Singapore, and Malaysia, a travel and tour service in Hong Kong, and a variety of investment holding companies. The group is perhaps best known for its high-profile restaurant franchises, including Planet Hollywood, a movie-theme restaurant chain co-owned by Sylvester Stallone and Arnold Schwarzenegger. HRC Holdings, of which 50 percent is controlled by HPL, has established Hard Rock Cafes in Beijing, Taipei, Singapore, Kuala Lumpur, Bangkok, Jakarta, and Bali.

In addition, HPL holds controlling interests in a variety of businesses, but often they share ownership with other firms (see Figure 3). Aside from direct subsidiaries, it also owns at least 20 percent of the equity and exercises "significant influence" in the financial and operating policy decisions of several "associated companies."[33] For example, HPL owns 60 percent of Cleaton Investments, which holds a controlling interest in the Four Seasons Resort in Bali. HPL also holds a "substantial" interest in the Ramada Renaissance Hotel in Colombo, Sri Lanka, and a 50 percent interest in Poussain, a joint venture that is developing a major condominium project in Singapore.

The range of HPL's holdings is extensive. The company controls 95 percent of the equity of Luang Sing Restaurant and Recreation Company of Beijing, as well as 80 percent of Waterfront Cruises and 38 percent of Trans Asia Hotel (a hotelier in Sri Lanka). Its many other investments include investment holding companies headquartered in Singapore and other Southeast Asian centers. In February 1995, Ong's private investment arm, Kuo International, was given the go-ahead to set up an automotive assembly plant in Vietnam, jointly with Toyota and a Vietnamese state firm under the Ministry of Heavy Industry.[34]

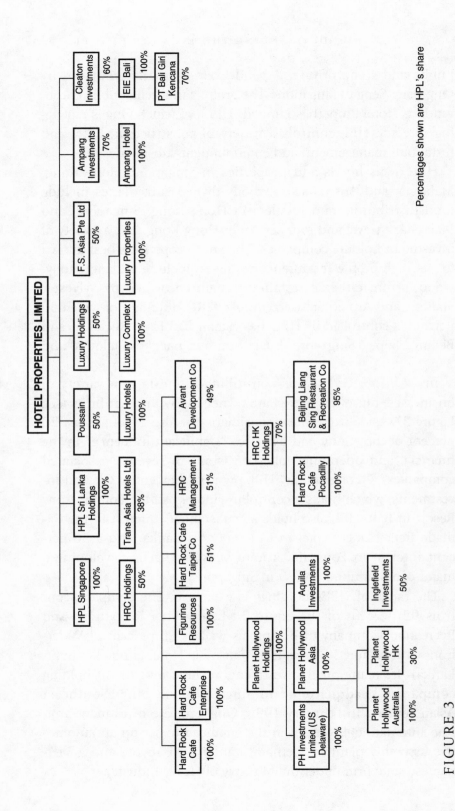

Percentages shown are HPL's share

FIGURE 3

Ong Beng Seng Group—Major Public Holdings

Like some other members of the bamboo network, Ong has diversified heavily into Australia and beyond in recent years. In addition to its Brash Holdings and Planet Hollywood investments, the Ong group owns a luxury hotel in Melbourne and the local franchise for the Hyundai and Chrysler/Jeep automobile companies. In 1994, Ong purchased for $19.2 million an ailing U.S. fashion chain that belonged to Italian designer Giorgio Armani. Ong's wife, Christine, is active in the world of high fashion.

Reef Holdings is a private investment company controlled by Ong. In 1994, HPL and Reef Holdings joined forces in providing the funds necessary to keep cash-starved Brash Holdings (Australia's largest music and electronics dealer) in operation. Ong is married to a daughter of Fu Yun Siak, the head of Kuo International, which has diverse interests ranging from oil to property.[35] Fu is chairman of HPL. He is also president of Oakville N.V., a Netherlands Antilles corporation which, in turn, is a wholly owned subsidiary of Kuo Investment Limited, a Cayman Islands corporation. Ong is vice-president of Oakville.

Ong Beng Seng has been described by *Asiaweek* as a "secretive oil trader turned property tycoon."[36] However, in an interview with one of the authors in the fall of 1994, Ong was not reluctant to talk about his various business interests. He was particularly proud of arranging Michael Jackson's tours of Southeast Asia and bringing Hard Rock Cafes to the area. By his friends and acquaintances, this impressive entrepreneur prefers to be called "B.S."

Y. C. Wang of Taiwan

Another example of the family-controlled overseas Chinese conglomerate is provided by the Formosa Plastics Group (FPG) business empire of Yung-ching Wang. Wang has accumulated personal holdings with an estimated value of over $2 billion, centered on the Taiwan-based Formosa Plastics Corporation—the world's number one producer of PVC, a widely used plastic polymer. When combined with the other components of FPG—Nan Ya Plastics and Formosa Chemical and Fibre Company—the entire Wang business empire enjoyed a market capitalization estimated at over $11 billion in late 1994.

In recent years, the Wang family has encountered resistance in developing its petrochemical empire outside of Taiwan. In 1991, Formosa Plastics was fined $4 million for improper handling of hazardous waste in Texas. More recently, the firm canceled high-profile plans to construct a $700 million rayon plant in Louisiana, as well as a $7 billion industrial zone on the mainland. Because of these problems, the Wangs have been diversifying into electronics and computer manufacturing.[37]

Several of these new enterprises are headed by Wang's children. Wang (often called "Y. C.") has displayed a strong commitment to keeping control of his empire within the family. Each of his ten children is an executive in the family business. His brother, Y. T. Wang, is president of Formosa Chemicals and Fibre, and runs that business with Y. C. Wang's son, William. Y. C.'s daughter, Cher Wang, is president of Everex Systems, a personal computer manufacturer based in California. Another son, Winston Wang, is senior vice president of Nan Ya Plastics, which produces circuit boards, notebook computer screens, and other electronic components.

The formal percentage of Wang family ownership of each of the enterprises in which it is involved varies substantially. Daughter Charlene Wang and her husband Ming Chien are respectively president and chairman of First International Computer, the world's largest manufacturer of motherboards, the circuit boards used to make personal computers. Charlene started this business on her own but secured the necessary initial financing with her father's guarantee.

Sophonpanich Group of Thailand

In Thailand, the Sophonpanich family—with an estimated net worth of $2.4 billion—is synonymous with banking. The family controls at least one-third of the Bangkok Bank, the largest commercial financial institution in Southeast Asia, with $35 billion in assets and offices in Hong Kong, Vietnam, Laos, and China. At home, the bank's 400 branches account for 24 percent of the bank deposits in Thailand.

Chin Sophonpanich, the founder of the Sophonpanich family empire, was born in Thailand to a Chinese father and Thai mother. Chin received his primary education in southern China before returning to Bangkok at age 17. He worked as a laborer until a Chinese insurance company gave him his first real break, letting him manage a construction company. He also established a hardware and canned goods store that traded with businesses in Hong Kong and Singapore.

In 1944, Chin helped found the Bangkok Bank, of which he was named director. Several years later, he established the Asia Trust group, which invested in finance and insurance firms. In 1952, Chin was named president of both Bangkok Bank and a Thai commercial banking association, allowing him to develop close connections with the ruling Thai government.

After a political upheaval in 1957, Chin fled the country to Hong Kong, leaving his son Chatri to run the family business. Chin made the most of his exile by establishing the first overseas branch of Bangkok Bank in Hong Kong. Upon his return to Thailand in 1963, Chin began to aggressively acquire shares in Bangkok Bank, controlling roughly a third by the early 1980s.

Also during this time, Chin increased the responsibilities of his sons in managing the family's diversified holdings. By the time of Chin's death in 1988, his oldest son, Rabin, was running the Hong Kong branch of Bangkok Bank, while Chote Sophonpanich had the London branch. Another son, Chai, was director of Bangkok First Investment and Trust. Choedchu Sophonpanich was director for Asia Insurance and a top manager at Bangkok First Investment and Trust. The number two son, Chatri, had the key positions of chairman and president of Bangkok Bank. When Chatri retired in late 1994, *his* eldest son Chartsiri (Tony) took over control of the family business.[38] By then, the many enterprises controlled by the family conformed to the bamboo network's typical pattern of intricate cross-holdings (see Figure 4).

The Sophonpanich family has been instrumental in helping other overseas Chinese entrepreneurs to get started, notably In-

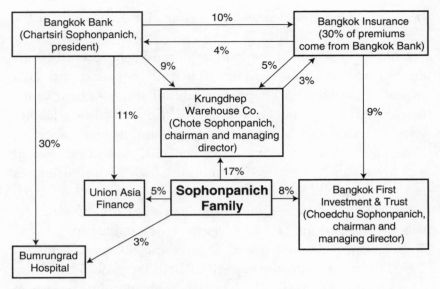

FIGURE 4
The Sophonpanich Family's Network of Cross-Holdings

donesia's Liem Sioe Liong and Malaysia's Robert Kuok—both now fabulously successful billionaires. The Sophonpanich family's financing capabilities also assisted the late Chua Kin Bun, founder of the Pacific Trading Company. Sensing the imminent political upheaval in China during the 1940s, Pacific Trading shifted its base of operations to Hong Kong and invested in textiles, real estate, and construction in Indonesia, Singapore, Malaysia, and Thailand. With the strong support of the Sophonpanich family, Chua ventured into other businesses, ranging from fiberglass to monosodium glutamate (MSG). In 1971, Chua established Pacific Finance and Securities Company (PACFIN) in Thailand. In 1992, PACFIN acquired several other leading Thai companies, including Citi Capital Ltd., an affiliate of Citibank.[39]

The outlook for the Sophonpanich Group is a mixture of the old and the new. The Bangkok Bank has opened a branch in Shantou to process remittances from ethnic Chinese in Southeast Asia who are helping their relatives on the mainland. Clearly, the family remains fully in control of the Bangkok Bank and its related interests. The future effectiveness of the group will depend in good measure on the relatively untested ability of its third generation of leadership. Chartsiri Sophonpanich served only a one-year internship with Citibank in New York before being catapulted into the top management of the Bangkok Bank. Chartsiri's education—two masters degrees from the Massachusetts Institute of Technology, one in business and one in science—typifies the Western reorientation of the new overseas Chinese business leadership.

Salim Group of Indonesia

The Salim Group, founded by Liem Sioe Liong (also known by his Indonesian name, Sudono Salim), exemplifies the transnational nature of the bamboo network. Witness the group's major holdings in Hong Kong and Singapore, in addition to its home base in Indonesia. The Salim Group controls and owns more than 60 enterprises, including the majority of Indonesia's blue chip companies: Indocement, Indosteel, Indomilk, Unggul Indah Chemical, and Bogasari Flour. In 1995, Indocement alone reported a market value of $4.4 billion.

A penniless Liem left Fuqing, China, in 1938 for Kudus, a county in Java. The very next year, he and a friend started a company dealing in local products. During the 1947–1949 Indonesian war of independence, Liem supplied the rebels with clothing, food, and arms, forging links with the native forces that would rise to power after the Dutch left. In free Indonesia, he founded companies trading in everything from nails to bicycle parts. In 1957, he acquired Bank Central Asia, now the country's largest private-sector bank. Subsequently, he befriended army general Suharto, whose relatives joined him in many ventures. After Suharto took power in 1965, Liem acquired state licenses to control much of the logging, clove, flour milling, and cement industries.

Salim's flagship enterprise in Hong Kong is the First Pacific Group, which, in turn, has two listed companies on the local stock exchange—First Pacific Company Ltd. and FPB Bank Holding Company. With a market capitalization of $1.2 billion, First

Pacific operates in 25 countries in Asia, North America, and Europe and maintains business interests in marketing and distribution, property, and financial services. Salim's interests in Hong Kong include cellular telephone, paging, and telepoint services.

In Singapore, the Salim Group's chief investment vehicle is the United Industrial Corporation, whose activities range from property development to trade to manufacturing. Its Singapore Land subsidiary is one of the largest property firms in the country, holding a sizable portfolio in the central business district. The group also controls property interests and business development activities in China, Britain, Canada, Thailand, and Turkey.[40]

In 1995, Salim founder Liem Sioe Liong and family had a reported net worth of $4.6 billion, making him one of the richest members of the bamboo network.[41] Nevertheless, Liem usually maintains a low profile. In 1994, however, he was widely criticized in Indonesia for hosting a lavish party in Singapore to celebrate his fiftieth wedding anniversary.

Although the Salim Group remains securely under the control of Liem Sioe Liong, the founder has put his youngest son Anthony in charge of operations. Anthony, 42, leapfrogged past two older brothers who supposedly are less adroit in business matters. With a different approach to business than his father, Anthony has surrounded himself with a group of professional managers who rely more on business skills than on personal relationships and political connections.[42] Two distant relatives of Liem also maintain a strong interest in the Salim Group. Djuhar Sutanto (his Chinese name is Liem Oen Kian) and his son control nearly 20 percent of First Pacific and over $1 billion in other Salim Group holdings.[43]

The scope of Liem's business activities continues to expand. In 1994, he joined forces with Malaysia's Robert Kuok to form a new holding company in the Sumatran sugar business. Kuok is one of the largest sugar producers in Malaysia and the Indonesian undertaking is estimated, in the aggregate, to cover an area twice the size of Singapore.

Most new overseas investments by the Liem family are not undertaken directly by the Salim Group in Jakarta. Rather, foreign-based associates are used to offset accusations of capital flight. For example, a three-times-removed Salim unit went into a joint venture with CWT, a listed Singapore government-linked company, to manage two ports in Fuqing. The Salim Group operated through a company owned by the Netherlands-listed Hagemeyer Group which, in turn, is owned by its Hong Kong-listed company, First Pacific Company (see Figure 5 for a display of the major holdings of First Pacific). In 1994, First Pacific reported profits of over $120 million on sales of approximately $3.5 billion.[44]

Lippo Group of Indonesia

A good example of the interactions among the overseas Chinese business leaders—as well as the family orientation of the bamboo network—is furnished by Indonesia's Lippo Group. Lippo,

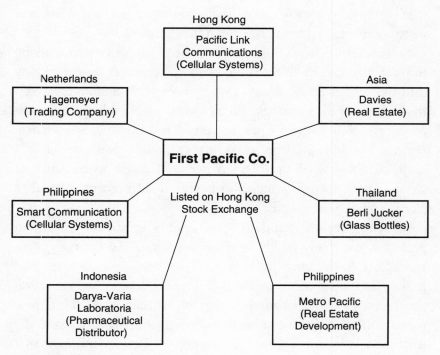

FIGURE 5
A Salim Group Public Company

which means "energy" in Chinese, is controlled by the Riady family through a series of private trusts. This heavily diversified financial and property conglomerate controls dozens of both private and public companies with about $6 billion in assets. In Indonesia, the Riady family controls seven listed companies. In Hong Kong, it controls six listed corporations through its flagship Lippo Limited, which concentrates on merchant banking. The others include the Hong Kong Chinese Bank and Asia Securities for strategic investment and Hong Kong China for property investment.

Chairman Mochtar Riady built his global business by leveraging the contacts he has developed throughout his life. A native of Indonesia, Riady studied banking in China and added many mainland friends to his network of acquaintances. He later teamed up with Liem Sioe Liong, the wealthy Indonesian Chinese entrepreneur, to manage Bank Central Asia, which he subsequently joined with other overseas Chinese banks to form Indonesia's largest private bank. When Riady was ready to go out on his own, Liem was instrumental in arranging the initial financing.

Subsequently, Riady sold 9.4 percent of Lippo Ltd. to Cheung Kong, controlled by Li Ka-shing, who, in turn, has brought Riady into many real estate deals. To penetrate the mainland market, Riady entered into strategic alliances with two leading PRC companies in Hong Kong, China Resources and China Travel Service. It turns out that a former classmate of Riady's is a partner in a bank that Riady set up in Shenzhen and a senior executive of China Travel Service, which has acquired 50 percent of Riady's Hong Kong Chinese Bank.

Most of Lippo's mainland investments have been in Fujian province, the Riady family's former homeland. So far, these ventures have been primarily in real estate, land development, and tourism. Lippo has secured a franchise to develop an island off the coast of Fujian that is already popular with Taiwanese tourists. It appears that the Riady family is looking forward to the further development of direct mainland–Taiwan trade, which would increase the flow of businessmen and tourists across the straits.

Riady has delegated considerable authority to his two sons. His older son, James, runs the day-to-day business in Indonesia. Stephen Riady, the younger son, acts as his father's deputy in Hong Kong, with the title of chairman. Stephen, a graduate of the University of Southern California, has a reputation for being a high flyer. He has been criticized by the Hong Kong Securities and Futures Commission for his role in battling for control of Asia Securities, but will not respond to inquiries.[45]

Stephen Riady sees the future of Asia as revolving around three "golden triangles." The northernmost comprises Japan, Korea, and Northeast China. The central triangle consists of Hong Kong, Taiwan, and southern China. The southernmost covers Indonesia, Malaysia, and Singapore. The Lippo Group is well entrenched in the third triangle, its home base. The northern triangle is already well developed—and dominated by Japan. Thus, the central area is Lippo's major target of opportunity and Chinese entrepreneurs are the major business and financial force.

Kuok Group of Malaysia

The Kuok Group of Malaysia is another good example of cross-border business relationships in Southeast Asia (see Figure 6). Group leader (Robert) Kuok Hock Nien (often called Robert Kuok in Western circles) has based himself in Hong Kong for more than a decade. His public appearances are rare and he avoids media contact. The Kuok business empire encompasses a complex web of private and public companies, mostly controlled by relatives or trusts.

In Singapore, Kuok's Shangri-La hotels and Pacific Carriers are listed on the local stock exchange. Pacific Carriers is a diversified maritime company, managing a fleet of 45 vessels and providing technical services, chartering, manning services, and freight trading. Shangri-La Hotels and other properties are located in Singapore, Malaysia, Hong Kong, the Philippines, Myanmar, Indonesia, and Canada.

In Hong Kong, Kuok's extensive activities include a substantial 35 percent ownership of the colony's largest English-language daily

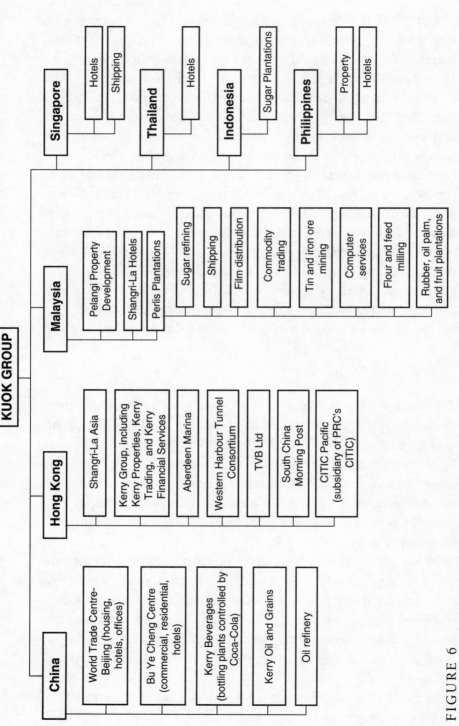

FIGURE 6
International Diversification of Kuok Group

newspaper (the *South China Morning Post*), and Television-Broadcasts, Ltd., as well as 15 development projects in China. Its privately held Kerry Trading Company serves as the flagship holding company of the Kuok Group's main businesses in Hong Kong and China. The company has established numerous ventures on the mainland, including flour and feed mill plants, vegetable oil plants, and an exclusive contract to bottle Coca-Cola in several cities.

Robert Kuok is also a partner in the Beijing World Trade Centre, an office, conference, and hotel complex that is the country's largest commercial property project. In addition, he has invested in a project in his ancestral city of Fuzhou. Although the Kuok Group continues to be a major investor in China, in 1994 it began to shift some of the family investments on the mainland to the publicly held companies that it controls.

Kuok has a good record in entering risky markets with large potential. Back in 1986, Robert Kuok was one of the few foreigners who risked large sums of money in the Philippines, whose economy had been battered by coups and natural disasters. His Manila group now comprises 15 companies, including three luxury Shangri-La hotels.[46]

In 1993, Kuok officially retired from the day-to-day running of the group's vast array of companies, which remains essentially a family-run enterprise. In the traditional Chinese manner, he divided the Hong Kong and Singapore/Malaysian operations between two sons, the elder taking the Hong Kong location. Equally traditionally, Kuok senior has kept a close eye on their activities and remains at the core of the decisionmaking process.[47]

Sy of the Philippines

Henry Sy provides yet another variation on the family-oriented bamboo network. Sy emigrated from Fujian province to the Philippines in 1936. Immediately following World War II, he started his own shoe store in Manila. Throughout the 1950s and '60s, Sy expanded his ShoeMart store chain and diversified his growing retail empire into real estate, tourism, and banking. He also acquired a few manufacturing plants to complement his other investments—cement manufacturing for construction and sandals and slipper production for his stores. By the 1990s, ShoeMart had achieved a nearly 50 percent share of the Filipino department store market. Henry Sy had become as synonymous with retailing in the Philippines as Xerox is with copiers in the United States.[48]

Today, Sy's only publicly owned company is SM Prime Holdings, whose primary activity is the development of retail stores and shopping malls. The Sy family holds 84 percent of the shares of SM Prime, one of the largest companies listed on the Philippines Stock Exchange. All together, the family's estimated net worth approaches $2 billion.[49] Virtually all of Sy's investments are in the Philippines. However, he has begun a large development project in Xiamen, on the China mainland.

As is often the case in the bamboo network, the gap between image and reality is wide. Sy's frequently cited business philosophy is both simple and modest: "Serve the greatest number and make small margins on large volumes." Nevertheless, in 1993, SM Prime Holdings reported a net income of 583 million pesos, which amounted to a very impressive 31 percent of its total revenues of 1.81 billion pesos.

Ironically, the Sy family finds itself protected by the very laws passed in the 1950s to discriminate against ethnic Chinese. The Philippines' Retail Trade Nationalization Act bans foreign ownership of retail businesses, eliminating the threat to the Sy empire from Western retailing giants such as Wal-Mart that are expanding across Southeast Asia.[50]

Sy's eldest daughter Teresita Sy-Coson, president of SM Prime's department stores, is positioned to inherit control of the family empire. All six of Sy's children are managers in the business. Three sons are members of the board of directors. Every Sunday, Sy cooks lunch for his children and grandchildren, which provides a great opportunity for coordinating the family's social and business activities.[51]

Yet all is not serene for Henry Sy or his fellow ethnic Chinese in the Philippines. In 1993, his teenage daughter Charlene was abducted. (Wealthy Chinese have been an especially tempting target for local criminal gangs.) She was killed when police riddled the kidnappers' cars with automatic fire.[52]

Joining Forces

At times, some of the large overseas Chinese business families join forces in the form of joint ventures. Liem Sioe Liong's Salim Group in Indonesia has teamed up with the Kuok family of Malaysia to develop a hotel and golfing resort in Indonesia and a cement factory in Wuhan, China. On occasion, both groups have joined forces with Thailand's CP Group. Stakeholders in the New China Hong Kong Group include Indonesia's Lippo Group, Hong Kong's Li Ka-shing Group, Taiwan International Securities, Singapore's Trade Development Board, and ten mainland Chinese companies and ministries.[53]

Smaller enterprises rely on more formal overseas Chinese mutual aid associations. These organizations are typically based on family, clan, province, or dialect (Cantonese, Hakka, Hokkien, or Chiu Chow). The associations act like banks through which members can borrow money, trade information, recruit workers, and receive business introductions. They help enforce the "handshake" deals on which much of Chinese business is based. If a business owner violates an agreement, he is blacklisted. This is far worse than being sued, because the entire Chinese network will refrain from doing business with the guilty party. Bankruptcy or dishonesty redounds not only on the individual, but on the entire family and clan.[54]

Keeping your word is of vital importance. Overseas Chinese tell of Qiao Tanming, a tanner in Calcutta, who exemplified the ideals of trustworthiness and reliability. Apparently, he traveled through torrential monsoon rains just to pay a rawhide merchant on time. If there is a moral to the tale, it is that Tanming's conscientiousness paid off. This action so impressed the merchant that from then on he always sold Tanming his best hides on very favorable credit terms.[55]

BUSINESS AND CULTURE

Overseas Chinese businesses—particularly those in Hong Kong and Taiwan—are responsible for much of the mainland's recent economic expansion. (The next chapter provides detail on this development.) What explains the overwhelming dominance of these Chinese entrepreneurs? Many believe that the overseas Chinese have an inherent advantage over Western investors. This implies that because of their shared culture, ethics, and language, ethnic Chinese simply prefer to deal with other ethnic Chinese.

However, economists traditionally place little weight on cultural differences when explaining trade patterns and economic development. A conventional economic argument is that preferential treatment of, or discrimination against, a certain group of people is expensive and, in the long run, unsustainable. The logic is this: such treatment creates opportunities for individuals who do not discriminate to acquire resources or sell their products on more favorable terms than those who do.

Although they may be theoretically appealing, such explanations are not very helpful in explaining the sustained success over time of ethnically homogenous trading groups, such as the Jews in medieval Europe, the Lebanese in West Africa, the Indians in East and Central Africa, and the Chinese in Southeast Asia.[56] These important examples cannot be dismissed as either insignificant or the product of a primitive, irrational society.

But if we acknowledge that there *are* costs associated with the preferential treatment of certain trading parties, the long-term existence of these trading groups implies that there must be benefits that outweigh these costs. Specifically, members of the extensive intra-Chinese trading network are able to economize on the high "transaction costs" associated with doing business in China and elsewhere in Southeast Asia.[57]

Throughout Southeast Asia, where many markets are underdeveloped and law is often unpredictable, informal networks have become the preferred vehicle for many complex transactions. The financing for a $100 million property deal can be arranged in a matter of days within the bamboo network. Under such circumstances, personal trust replaces formal—as well as more expensive and time-consuming—"due diligence" reviews. In the process, the cost of doing business is lowered substantially. Without these informal arrangements, many business transactions would be impossible or prohibitively expensive. Seen in this light, the extensive trade among overseas Chinese is a direct response to the high transactions costs inherent in many economies in Southeast Asia—particularly China—that lack sophisticated political and economic institutions.[58]

These transnational trading networks are very much in accord with Chinese tradition. They allow for the flexible and efficient transmission of information, finance, goods, and capital in what are often informal agreements and transactions. Confidence and trust replace contracts as the major guarantees that commitments will be met satisfactorily. In a region where capital markets are rudimentary, financial disclosure is limited, and contract law very weak, interpersonal networks are critical to moving economic resources across political boundaries.

THE POWER OF FAMILY AND PERSONAL RELATIONSHIPS

A traditional—and perhaps the oldest—method to economize on contract enforcement costs is to maintain strong kinship ties that promote repeated interaction among the same people. Although family-controlled business empires are encountered in the United States and Europe, the scale and scope of modern overseas Chinese family businesses are unprecedented. Kinship ties are extremely important and family control over firms is the rule. As we have seen, most Chinese family firms are extremely reluctant to appoint outsiders to key positions.

These examples are not isolated instances. Indeed, the family enterprise tends to be the basic economic unit in Southeast Asia. In an in-depth survey of more than 150 Chinese entrepreneurs conducted by Professor John Kao of the Harvard Business School, 90 percent of the Chinese entrepreneurs he surveyed had experienced war, 40 percent had weathered a political disaster, and 32 percent had lost a home. As we would expect, such experiences have strongly influenced the investment decisions of the bamboo network.

Indeed, Kao's survey identified many common beliefs among ethnic Chinese businesspeople. One is that the only people you can trust are family members. An incompetent relative in the family business is considered to be more reliable than a competent stranger. Also, obedience to patriarchal authority is deemed essential to maintaining the enterprise.

A high level of savings is considered desirable, regardless of immediate need. (The frugality of the overseas Chinese is legendary. In the case of Taiwan billionaire Y. C. Wang, the only way to get him to wear a new suit is for his wife to buy it and secretly put it in his closet.) In turn, investment must be based on kinship or clan affiliations, rather than more general business principles. Hard work is seen as necessary to ward off the hazards present in an unpredictable world. A favorite maxim is the widespread admonition to "keep your bags packed at all times."[59]

In the typical ethnic Chinese family firm, there is little separation between owner and management. The head of a Chinese company typically is an all-powerful "paterfamilias" who entrusts key activities and positions to members of the family. Within the family, confidence in his judgment borders on the absolute. For example, Liem Sioe Liong has been described as a village elder, "poised, consummately wise and of few words, as though he had never left the Sumatran bazaar even for a day."[60]

This extreme centralization of authority avoids many of the "agency" problems that Western businesses must overcome in ensuring that managers promote the interests of the owners rather than themselves. Yet there are also disadvantages associated with the family-run business. Keeping control within the family almost inevitably restricts the size, or at least the complexity, to which it can grow. That is not so much a problem for low-tech firms as it is for high-tech companies that require sophisticated organizational structures.

The track record of second- and third-generation overseas Chinese managers is mixed. Frequently, these sons and daughters must manage the transition of the family firm from an entrepreneurial start-up to a modern corporation. Family ties can be so strong that incompetent relatives are preferred to competent outside professionals. In 1993, William Soeryadjaya, founder of Indonesia's P.T. Astra industrial conglomerate, lost control of his company as a result of his son's mismanagement.

The best and brightest Chinese entrepreneurs are trying to finesse the succession problem by taking their companies public, hiring professional managers, and sending their offspring to Western business schools. Ronnie Chan returned from 16 years in America with an M.B.A. from the University of Southern California to take control of his father's Hang Lung Group. Since 1990, when Chan assumed his position as chairman, the group's market capitalization has more than tripled, to $6 billion.

CONCLUSION

As competitors to Western business, the overseas Chinese bring to the arena a number of specific advantages including intense managerial effort, financial shrewdness, and production efficiency. Most important, however, is the high degree of flexibility made possible within a network of companies allied by ties of mutual obligation. As competitors or partners with this network, Western firms should remember some useful generalizations about its operations.

1. *Most overseas Chinese take a low profile in the commercial world and shy away from publicity.* As a result, rather than produce consumer goods with a Chinese brand name, the members of the bamboo network operate in the interstices of the trading world. They make components, manufacture for others, and perform subassembly work. They are also heavily involved in wholesaling, financing, sourcing, and transporting. Most of these operations are behind the scenes, minimizing the need to market products to end users. The leading businessmen know each other personally and do deals together, with information spreading through an informal network rather than through more conventional channels.

2. Ethnic Chinese family firms rely on strict, centralized control and informal transactions to minimize company bureaucracy and paperwork. Key information is obtained in conversation and retained in the heads of the senior managers, which helps to eliminate the need for formal reporting. Considering the tremendous flow of studies, reports, and memoranda in the typical Western business of any size, the implicit economies of time and effort achieved by the bamboo network are impressive. Money is borrowed from family and friends on trust. Transactions of great size are often dealt with by common understanding and a note jotted in a diary.[61]

For many Chinese entrepreneurs, the enterprise is viewed as a mechanism by which to both exert control and achieve security in a disordered world. As such, the overseas Chinese firm takes on the personality of its founder. Business decisions are made on the basis of experience, intuition, and informal exchanges, rather than statistical reports or the advice of external consultants.[62]

However, the successes of the large overseas Chinese conglomerates are forcing some changes. When a family-owned corporation is listed on a stock exchange, disclosure laws require the firm to fully report its transactions. Compliance with these regulations requires legal documents, and not just a handshake. Nevertheless, most successful ethnic Chinese business families hide their investor identities by retaining a large portion of their wealth in private companies through family trusts and networks of cross-holdings.[63]

3. The successful overseas Chinese business family operates through a network of enterprises rather than the unitary company (e.g., Ford, Wal-Mart) characteristic of U.S. family firms. Most U.S. family business dynasties grew out of a single firm's dominance in a single market or area. For example, the Ford Motor Company, despite its enormous size, has to this day retained its "core competency" as a motor vehicle manufacturer. Its business structure follows a clear hierarchy, with the parent company maintaining full ownership and tight control of its subordinate businesses. Diversification is generally accomplished by internationalization or by obtaining an interest in firms that provide necessary parts for automobile assembly.

In sharp contrast, the typical overseas Chinese business family maintains varying percentage interests in a galaxy of small- to medium-sized firms, many of which have little relationship to the parent company's core competency. For example, although the ascension of Thailand's CP Group from feed mills to poultry farming may have been predictable, the group's tremendous success in motorcycle manufacturing and telecommunications joint ventures is more difficult to explain. The *guanxi* of the overseas Chinese family business provides a perfect complement to high-tech Western firms that lack the necessary economic and political connections to navigate a treacherous foreign business environment.

Overseas Chinese firms have eschewed traditional business structures in order to capitalize on the weak system of contracting and law throughout Southeast Asia, particularly on the mainland. Core business groups develop varying degrees of ownership in dozens, if not hundreds, of small- to medium-sized businesses. In turn, many of these businesses maintain cross-holdings with other family-controlled firms. The resulting web of holdings, when combined with the insertion of family members into key management positions, allows the family to maintain ultimate, albeit circuitous, control. This structure ensures the secrecy and diversification necessary in a region where the threat of governmental expropriation and ethnic discrimination is still pervasive.

A fundamental shortcoming, however, is that the Chinese family business structure makes it extremely difficult to develop the high-tech products and systems that will provide the foundation for future business growth and national economic progress.

4. Overseas Chinese business leaders utilize a management style that is more informal and intuitive than that practiced in a typical Western corporation. The extensive—and expensive—due diligence efforts conducted by U.S. corporations before making major investments are streamlined in the overseas Chinese firm. Senior management performs the analysis itself, rather than delegating the task to technical experts. Decisionmaking is more practical than theoretical, more intuitive than bureaucratic. The resulting rapidity of action allows opportunities to be seized as they arise, creating a fundamentally different organizational structure than is present in most Western firms. The fortunes of the wealthy overseas Chinese are usually based on a variety of activities, such as shipping, hotels, textiles, toys, property management, and trade. There is no Chinese equivalent of such complex, decentralized companies as America's Procter & Gamble, Japan's Sony, or Korea's Daewoo. The exception is in Taiwan, which has cultivated the ability to make long-term investments and to manage complex manufacturing operations.

Some of the younger members of the overseas Chinese community have emigrated to the West, especially to the United States and Canada. Portions of this group, particularly those trained in California's Silicon Valley electronics industry, are now returning with their Western ideas. Those who possess M.B.A.s from American universities are loosening their ties to the ancestral cultural heritage and adopting more modern business techniques. Over time, traditional cultural factors will play a reduced role in Southeast Asian business, especially as the reins of power are passed to a younger generation of business leaders who lack their parents' emotional ties to the mainland.

The ability to rely on personal contacts may also become less significant if—or when—mainland decisionmakers adopt more modern political and legal institutions in order to participate more fully in the global marketplace.[64] In the long run, such adaptation will be essential to maintaining competitiveness in an increasingly high-tech global marketplace. In the short run, family control will continue to be an essential ingredient in dealing effectively with the rudimentary and often chaotic institutional structure that typifies the economies of Southeast Asia.

In examining the fascinating phenomenon that we have labeled the bamboo network, a note of caution is essential. Variations are substantial and stereotyping must be avoided. Not all Chinese entrepreneurs in Southeast Asia are successful. Nor are all Chinese involved in entrepreneurial activity. A wide range of market participation exists in this rapidly growing region, ranging from small traders to heads of large transnational enterprises. Generalizations should be suspect.[65] Yet, as a group, the overseas Chinese family firms have become the pacing element in the economies of Southeast Asia, and they are likely to continue in that role. Western firms will be forced in the years ahead to learn far more about the culture underlying the conduct of the bamboo network enterprises that may eventually become their competitors or partners—or both.

CHAPTER 3

Creating a Greater China

China? There lies a sleeping giant.
Let him sleep! For when he wakes he will move the world.
—attributed to Napoleon

During the 1980s, the world witnessed the emergence of a new Asian economic power. This "dragon" is currently exhibiting an unparalleled dynamism, growing faster than other Pacific Rim dragons such as South Korea and Japan in their early stages of economic development.

This superpower is not a single unified country, nor is it a formalized trading bloc such as the coalescing European Union or the North American Free Trade Area. Instead, this rapidly developing economy is taking shape in the form of a group of workers and businesses that, although separated geographically and politically, nevertheless share common economic strategies and goals. The combined output of this trading community exceeds that of traditional economic powerhouses such as Germany, and is rapidly overtaking that of Japan. In fact, forecasts of the twenty-first century show that—given a reasonable set of assumed conditions, of course—this Asian economic dragon could catch up to the United States by the year 2020. That is right: it is conceivable that in just a few decades the United States may no longer be the world's largest economic superpower.

The label for this emerging world power is Greater China. Most analysts who use this term define it as an aggregation of the people, governments, and economies of mainland China, Taiwan, and Hong Kong (as well as the half million people of neighboring Macao). Such a measurement has the benefit of being cleanly defined, and is justified by the notion that Hong Kong, Taiwan, and Macao are far more closely related to the mainland than to any other territory.

This simple definition is problematic, however. Greater China defies the traditional statistical techniques used to measure fundamental benchmarks such as population, output, and trade. It spills over other national boundaries within Southeast Asia into the ethnic Chinese-dominated business sectors of Thailand, Malaysia, Indonesia, Singapore, and Vietnam. Tenuous political relations among these parties—as well as a highly uncertain outlook—complicate the region's future. Nevertheless, investors within this region have worked to tear down or bypass the mainland's restrictive trade and investment policies. Politically, Greater China is still fragmented. At best, extensive day-to-day relationships between mainland China and its close trading partners represent only a partial integration. As we will see, however, those relationships have become very substantial.

THE TIES ACROSS GREATER CHINA

From a business point of view, Greater China is rapidly emerging as an epicenter for industry, commerce, and finance in the world economy. This strategic area contains substantial amounts of technology and manufacturing capability (Taiwan), outstanding entrepreneurial, marketing, and services acumen (Hong Kong), a fine communications network (Singapore), a tremendous pool of financial capital (all three), and very large endowments of land, resources, and labor (mainland China). A talking doll, to take a modest example, is designed in Hong Kong, contains a computer chip made in Taiwan, and is assembled in China. The common factor in these diverse activities is the presence of ethnic Chinese entrepreneurs.

The thickening webs of international interdependence that link Greater China are creating a unique natural economic territory that consistently defies formal state boundaries. Although most of the business relationships that link the different regions of Greater China are informal (often to overcome political obstacles to cross-country trade), we can still see the closeness of these connections in many ways. We begin by examining the complex economic interdependence among China and its largest trading partners.

HONG KONG AND CHINA

The synergy among the members of Greater China is most apparent in the case of Hong Kong. Despite its extremely small land area (three-quarters that of Rhode Island) and population (just over 6 million people), Hong Kong is the world's eighth largest trading economy. Boasting the best natural harbor on the China coast, Hong Kong possesses the world's busiest container port. Its per capita gross domestic product ($22,000) is second only to Japan in Asia. In earlier times, Hong Kong relied on cheap labor to produce manufactured exports. It has since reshaped itself as a service-oriented economy. Today, Hong Kong is one of Asia's major financial centers. Most of its remaining manufacturing is capital-intensive and high-tech. In 1994, nearly 80 percent of Hong Kong's gross domestic product (GDP) originated in the service sector.[1]

The government of Hong Kong takes pride in its policies minimizing the role of government in business. Government spending is extremely low by Western standards, equal to only 15 to 20 percent of its GDP. These public-sector outlays go mostly toward three ends: infrastructure, education, and security. In contrast, U.S. government spending equals roughly 35 percent of GDP, and is dominated by entitlements and defense. Many countries in Europe report government-to-GDP ratios of 50 percent and more.

Furthermore, the budgets of these Western nations cover a wide range of activities, notably transfer programs to aid the elderly and poor (social insurance, health care, welfare, etc.). Such policies are virtually nonexistent in Hong Kong, which has no comprehensive unemployment benefits, mandatory medical insurance, or transfer-based social security system. By any measure, Hong Kong's economy has flourished in this environment of "positive nonintervention" that minimizes government regulation. With smaller government comes lower tax burdens. The top personal income tax rate in Hong Kong is only 15 percent. Capital gains are not taxed, no income tax is paid at all by the bottom half of wage earners, and the tax code is far less complex than the byzantine U.S. system.[2]

Hong Kong serves as the gateway to China. Its population is overwhelmingly ethnic Chinese and speaks the official languages of English and Cantonese—the latter being one of eight primary dialects of the Chinese language. Although the official language of the mainland is Mandarin, Cantonese is the local dialect of adjacent Guangdong province. Hong Kong executives, who possess technological and management skills scarce in China, help run the burgeoning industrial infrastructure of Guangdong.

The complementary assets of the mainland and Hong Kong are impressive. Hong Kong has money, managerial talent, marketing expertise, worldwide business networks, and advanced technology—but it also suffers from high costs because of the intensive utilization of its very limited space. Mainland China has a great supply of lower-cost land and workers, but it is short of skills, money, and technology. Hong Kong's natural comparative advantages are strengthened by the fact that the nearby coastal province of Guangdong, to its good fortune, is the original homeland of most of Hong Kong's Chinese population (or their ancestors).

The cross-border connections between Hong Kong and the mainland continue to grow. Today's Shenzhen, the Special Economic Zone on the mainland that is closest to Hong Kong, boasts tall buildings, factories, streets full of automobiles, people wearing clothes with designer labels, and a retinue of London and New York investment bankers.[3] It has become, in essence, a mini-

Hong Kong. Indeed, throughout much of southern China, the Hong Kong dollar has become the *de facto* currency.

On a macroeconomic basis, China and Hong Kong are each other's largest investor and trading partner. About 60 percent of China's exports go through Hong Kong, while China is Hong Kong's number one export destination (23 percent, compared to 19 percent for the second-place United States). Hong Kong is more than an entrepôt (or transshipment center) for China. Much investment by overseas Chinese enters the mainland via Hong Kong. Joint projects in China are commonly financed by Indonesian or Thai Chinese investors with the assistance of Hong Kong partners.

Approximately two-thirds of foreign investment in China to date has been made by Hong Kong's Chinese entrepreneurs. (Inevitably, some—perhaps as much as one-fourth—of that "foreign" investment is actually mainland money that is recycled in order to qualify for special import incentives.) These investments extend to over 17,000 businesses and 25,000 factories. Four out of five Hong Kong industrial firms have branches in China. Hong Kong manufacturers own or contract with Chinese enterprises for far more work than is performed in Hong Kong itself. These mainland factories employ 6 million workers, nearly ten times the number of manufacturing jobs in all of Hong Kong. As China experts Nicholas Kristof and Sheryl Wu Dunn write, "China is the factory, and Hong Kong is the storefront."[4]

In the opposite direction, more than 2,000 of China's government agencies and private enterprises have invested about $25 billion in Hong Kong trade, real estate, transport, and financial enterprises, far more than any other country. That portfolio includes airlines, hotels, the second cross-harbor tunnel linking Kowloon and Hong Kong Island, and a multibillion-dollar port expansion. The Bank of China, whose new imposing building is an important part of the Hong Kong financial district, is the second largest bank in Hong Kong (measured by deposits). Some PRC-owned companies already operate major subsidiaries in Hong Kong. The largest, CITIC Pacific, boasted a capitalization of $5.2 billion in 1995.

Financial links are only one dimension of this network, however. The integration of transportation is equally impressive. A network of ferries, hydrofoils, and air routes links Hong Kong and China. In 1994, a 77-mile, $1.1 billion six-lane superhighway built by Hopewell Holdings (controlled by Hong Kong infrastructure tycoon Gordon Wu) directly and symbolically linked Guangzhou and Shenzhen with Hong Kong. About 50,000 managers and professionals commute daily from Hong Kong to Guangdong and over 20 million trips are made by Hong Kong residents to China each year.

Convergence between Hong Kong and the mainland is well under way. Hong Kong newspapers are full of advertisements for townhouses and condominiums across the border, usually costing only a fraction of the price of a comparable Hong Kong apartment. Hong Kong television reaches more than 98 percent of the Chinese households in the crescent around the colony. Between 10 p.m. and midnight, advertisers target special commercials to the mainland by using more Chinese characters and less English. Even gangsters operating on both sides have increasingly close ties.[5]

Yet this convergence is limited primarily to southern China, where ethnic ties have promoted investment and personal interaction. The fate of Hong Kong is thus caught up in the larger struggle within the People's Republic of China between centralization and decentralization and, specifically, between southern China and Beijing.[6]

Under the 1984 Joint Declaration signed by China and the United Kingdom, Hong Kong—which is still officially part of the British empire—will become a special administrative region of mainland China in July 1997. A giant clock in Tiananmen Square counts down the time remaining until China regains control of the British colony. Under the Joint Declaration, Hong Kong is promised a high degree of autonomy, and will be allowed to retain its present social, economic, and legal systems for 50 years. Among the assurances that the Joint Declaration provides to the people of Hong Kong are:

• Continuation of the existing economic and social systems and protection of property rights and foreign investment.

- Free movement of goods and capital and free convertibility of Hong Kong currency.
- Continuation of Hong Kong's monetary and financial policies, with no taxes paid to the mainland.
- Retaining of English common law and protection of all fundamental human rights by law.
- The right of free movement to and from Hong Kong.
- Autonomy in conducting external commercial relations.
- An independent judiciary and a fully elected legislature of local people.

The language of the Sino-British Declaration is sweeping. For example, Article 5 reads: "The current social and economic systems in Hong Kong will remain unchanged and so will the lifestyle . . . Private property, ownership of enterprises, legitimate right of inheritance and foreign investment will be protected by law."

Although the Joint Declaration is an impressive document, the enforcement mechanism for these commitments is not yet apparent—aside from China's self-interest in maintaining the stability of its own economic development. Hong Kong's hypercapitalist culture sets it apart from the mainland and presents difficulties for the 1997 integration. The Chinese catchphrase for the upcoming arrangement is "One country, two systems." With the Chinese leadership's usual fondness for aphorisms, Jiang Zemin (secretary-general of the PRC's Communist Party) says, "The well water should not interfere with the river water." According to this approach, he notes, China can practice socialism while Hong Kong practices capitalism.[7] Nevertheless, there is widespread concern that China will renege, possibly voiding contracts signed prior to 1997 or even nationalizing certain industries. Because of this, the future economic contribution of Hong Kong to Greater China is uncertain.

Increased levels of emigration from Hong Kong attest to the lack of confidence that many have in the mainland's ability to effectively rule the colony. During the first half of the 1980s, emigration averaged 21,000 annually. The yearly exodus steadily increased to an estimated 55,000 in 1990. By 1994, however, the population movement seemed to have stabilized, with a net *inflow* of 86,000. Interestingly, however, much of this inflow is by former Hong Kong citizens who are hedging their bets by temporarily moving overseas to obtain a foreign visa or dual citizenship—mainly in Canada, Australia, or the United States—before returning to the colony. Roughly 500,000 Hong Kong citizens retain a foreign passport. Many others are moving their valuables out of Hong Kong, fearing that China will restrict exports or even expropriate wealth following 1997. Business appears cautious as well: half of the colony's top 200 corporations maintain their registration outside of Hong Kong.[8]

British firms that have long dominated the colony are finding themselves in a particularly awkward position as 1997 approaches, and surely have lost their primary position to ethnic Chinese entrepreneurs. The British "hongs" (which were a controlling influence over the Hong Kong economy) are a thing of the past. As noted in Chapter 2, Li Ka-shing now owns Hutchison Whampoa, a former "hong." HSBC Holdings, the parent company of the Hong Kong Shanghai Bank—the colony's largest financial enterprise and the issuer of most of its currency—is now domiciled in the United Kingdom (the Bank of China is now issuing bank notes used as Hong Kong currency). HSBC is also taking a more politically correct, or at least culturally sensitive, tack on its Hong Kong-based art collection, substituting modern works for paintings of scenes featuring British opium traders and Asians acting as servants for Europeans.[9]

After failing to win approval from the Chinese government for several large investment projects, Jardines (a major Hong Kong-based trading company) has moved its main office to Bermuda. It also has delisted from the Hong Kong stock exchange, following the example of more than half of Hong Kong's listed companies that have shifted their headquarters to other locations. Now listed on the Singapore exchange, Jardine Matheson Holdings had a market capitalization of $5.7 billion in 1995, while Jardine Strategic Holdings was valued at $3.7 billion in the same year. Relations between Beijing and Jardines have always been strained. In 1840, William Jardine was an opium trader who helped to persuade Britain to go to war with China. In the 1950s, Jardines' assets in Shanghai were lost to communist forces. Firms that wish to invest in Hong Kong following 1997 should pay close attention to how long-standing rivalries between Beijing and companies like Jardines are resolved.[10]

Hong Kong's official flower is the bauhinia, a sterile hybrid that produces no seed. A cynic might ask whether the brilliant hybrid of British efficiency and Chinese entrepreneurship that is Hong Kong will wither away in the coming decades. From time to time, the PRC issues reassuring statements. In early 1995, a senior official of the Bank of China reaffirmed the future status of the Hong Kong dollar as the legal tender in Hong Kong after 1997. On the other hand, just a few months later, reports surfaced that China planned to send 15,000 troops into Hong Kong following the 1997 takeover. The reuniting of Hong Kong and the mainland promises to be a complex and difficult task, with significant compromises needing to be made on both sides.

MACAO AND CHINA

Like Hong Kong, the territory of Macao—a small peninsula of the Chinese mainland opposite Hong Kong—is the last vestige of a European empire. Macao was colonized by the Portuguese in 1557 and its foreign government was officially recognized by the Chinese in an 1887 treaty. One hundred years later, Portugal agreed to turn over control of Macao to China at the end of 1999. The problems that have developed during the years prior to the Chinese takeover mirror those in Hong Kong, although the formal relationships between Macao and the mainland are at present much more cordial.

As in Hong Kong, many firms are diversifying their activities as a hedge against governmental expropriation. For example, Macao tycoon Stanley Ho—chairman of Grande International Group, STDM, and Shun Tak Enterprises, all of which do extensive business in Macao, Hong Kong, and Guangdong—has acquired interests in hotels, casinos, and other businesses in the United States, Canada, and Europe.[11]

TAIWAN AND CHINA

Taiwan's relationship with the mainland is much more tenuous than that of Hong Kong or Macao. After the Communist Revolution in 1949, Chiang Kai-shek and the government of the defeated Republic of China (ROC) withdrew to Taiwan. Throughout the 1950s and 1960s, most international organizations recognized the ROC in Taiwan as the legitimate Chinese government. In the 1970s, however, the mainland People's Republic of China (PRC) began to emerge as an official international entity. Taiwan lost its seat in the United Nations to the PRC in 1971, and the United States officially switched diplomatic recognition from Taipei to Beijing in 1979. Taiwan was subsequently expelled from the World Bank and the International Monetary Fund, organizations that provide financial assistance to developing countries.[12]

Taiwan's awkward place on the world stage continues today. At high government levels, Taipei and Beijing frequently hurl insults at each other. The mainland still considers Taiwan to be a rogue province, and routinely expresses its opposition to any recognition by other nations of the island's sovereignty. Technically, a state of war exists between the two.[13] Official visits to Taiwan by even midlevel government officials from the United States or Japan spark cries of protest from Beijing. At best, the political relationship between the two is tenuous and uneasy. At worst, the saber rattling threatens to escalate into military conflict. In 1994, China held large-scale military exercises across the strait from Taiwan. The following year, the PRC conducted ballistic missile training exercises off the Taiwan coast. The day after the tests were announced, the Taipei stock market dropped 4 percent. Having made its point, China ended the military exercise two days ahead of schedule.

Taiwan has a population of 21 million people who generate an annual GDP of over $200 billion, making the island the world's twentieth largest economy. Its military power is also considerable. Despite its substantial achievements, Taiwan is not officially recognized by most countries. In the United States, Taiwanese government diplomatic offices are not allowed to identify the country that they represent. In 1994, when his private jet stopped overnight in Hawaii for refueling, President Lee was not allowed to leave the plane, lest he set foot on American soil. This particular incident sparked a unanimous Senate vote to allow one-day visas to select Taiwanese officials.

Despite such international political isolation, Taiwan has thrived economically. Along with South Korea, Singapore, and Hong Kong, Taiwan is considered to be one of Asia's most successful "Little Dragons." Its extremely high level of "human capital"—Western-trained scientists, engineers, and businesspeople—has fueled its penetration of high-tech markets once dominated by the United States and Japan. In 1994, Taiwan was the world's largest producer of portable computers and the world's fourth largest producer of all computer equipment (after the United States, Japan, and Germany). As an indicator of the high level of education attained by Taiwanese society, consider that more than half of the government's cabinet members have earned doctorates from American universities. President Lee Teng-hui holds a Ph.D. from Cornell and sparked an international controversy when he requested a visa to address his alma mater in Ithaca, New York. The visa was reluctantly granted, over Beijing's vigorous objections. To protest the decision, Beijing canceled high-level official visits and suspended arms control talks with the United States.[14]

Although the ROC continues to maintain that in theory there is only one China (and that Taipei is its legitimate ruling authority), Taiwan has resigned itself in practice to the political, military, and economic realities of its situation. Officially, Taiwan and the PRC refuse to recognize or trade with each other. Unofficially, the two countries have experienced a convergence in recent years, holding tentative political summits, expanding their trade through intermediaries such as Hong Kong, and even embarking on direct cooperation in the environmental area.[15]

Because Taiwan is not recognized by the United Nations, the International Monetary Fund, or most other international agencies, there are few reliable estimates of its economic interactions with other nations. Nevertheless, Taiwan is unquestionably one of the leading traders and investors in Southeast Asia. In the practical world of Chinese business, Taiwan is an integral part of Greater China. Trade between Taiwan and the mainland (mainly through Hong Kong) rose more than fivefold from 1987 to 1993, from $3.5 billion to $20.2 billion. Estimates of Taiwanese direct investments in China exceed $20 billion, in 100,000 factories and business enterprises. Much of this investment has flowed into Fujian province, from which many nationalists fled after the communist takeover in 1949. In the late 1980s, investors from Taiwan accounted for more than half of foreign investment in Fujian's Xiamen Special Economic Zone.[16]

Some Taiwanese businesses have moved entire factories to Fujian in order to take advantage of cheaper labor and natural resources. Virtually all of Taiwan's shoemaking industry has relocated to Guangdong and Fujian provinces, and much of the garment and sportswear industries have moved as well. Cultural links have been taking Taiwanese investors into areas where other foreigners are reluctant to go. The air route between Taipei and Hong Kong is already Asia's busiest. If Taiwan allows direct flights across the strait, it will find itself at one corner of the world's busiest air route, the Asian equivalent of the Boston–New York–Washington corridor.[17]

In early 1995, a major breakthrough in Taiwan–mainland financial relations began to occur. The New York branch of the Bank of China signed an agreement with the New York branch of the Bank of Taipei in which each bank can take deposits and issue letters of credit and export/import guarantees on behalf of the other. Previously, such banking services between China and Taiwan were conducted through foreign banks. The potential magnitude of this change is quite substantial when one considers the volume of cross-border investments between the two nations.[18]

Although there are encouraging signs of a peaceful convergence, the future of the mainland–Taiwan relationship remains potentially ominous. Located less than 200 miles off the coast of mainland Fujian province, Taiwan's population is only one-fiftieth that of the PRC. Although it maintains a modern fighting capability, Taiwan's ability to defend itself against the far greater military power of the People's Liberation Army is questionable. Any move by Taiwan to establish itself as a sovereign nation could force China to declare a quarantine of Taiwan, or even initiate an armed conflict. A shooting war would have severe economic consequences for both sides, as trade and investment within the region would surely plummet.

Today, the limited economic convergence between Taiwan and China has already forced modest political changes. Although Beijing is anxious to obtain control over Taiwan's massive foreign exchange holdings (an estimated $80 billion), it also welcomes the investment and entrepreneurship that has helped the economic development of southern China. Yet by allowing Taiwan to operate as a normal international actor, China may reduce the possibility of future political unification. There is also a potential feedback effect here that worries the PRC: if Taiwan *does* declare independence, it might also encourage greater regionalism on the mainland.

A major breakthrough in this delicate relationship occurred in late 1987, when Taiwan permitted its citizens to visit relatives on the mainland. That year, fewer than 7,000 Taiwanese made the trip. In 1992, that number had swelled to 1.3 million a year. By mid-1994, an estimated cumulative total of 6 million had visited China since the policy change. On any one day, over 50,000 tourists and 100,000 resident managers from Taiwan are estimated to be on the mainland.[19] A measure of rising personal interaction is the fact that, in 1987, people in the Special Economic Zone of Xiamen booked only ten telephone calls a month to Taiwan. By 1993, the rate averaged 60,000 a month.[20] Invariably, some people relocate, strengthening the cultural and social linkages between the two countries. As in Hong Kong, cross-border marriages are becoming more common.

Increasingly, the barriers that prevent Taiwanese businesspeople from conducting business on the mainland are also coming down. Taiwanese investors have been allowed to acquire mainland passports for travel in the province of Fujian. As for the future, Taiwan-based Great China Airlines has gained landing rights in four Chinese airports. Its ambition is to provide local service to cities on the mainland.

Recently, six Taiwanese contestants wearing ancient Chinese costumes publicized the staging of the First Beauty Contest Across the Taiwan Strait, jointly sponsored by Taiwan and mainland China. In many more substantive ways, the economic and social integration of Taiwan and the mainland continues. In the absence of an official relationship, Taipei's Straits Exchange Foundation and Beijing's Association for Relations Across the Taiwan Straits serve as intermediaries for the two governments. Their first formal meeting occurred, interestingly enough, in a "neutral" Chinese city—Singapore.

Few Taiwanese now seek to proclaim formal independence. The prevailing preference, according to a survey by the *United Daily News*, is for the maintenance of the status quo.[21] Likewise, Taipei no longer talks about reasserting its sovereignty over the mainland. As one government spokesman, Jason C. Hu, puts the matter bluntly, "We are two political entities."[22]

This feeling is emphasized as the leadership of Taiwan increasingly is taken over by native Taiwanese, such as President Lee. In the absence of political upheaval on the mainland, Taiwan will maintain, if not extend, its virtual independence—provided it follows a nonconfrontational mode in dealing with the PRC. Although Taiwan's political independence is clearly unacceptable to the PRC, Beijing has relaxed its objections to Taiwan's economic and cultural relations with other countries, including participation in economic organizations such as the Asia Development Bank and the World Trade Organization. China's President Jiang Zemin has proposed a unification that would allow Taiwan to remain politically and militarily independent.[23]

Aggressive efforts to gain official international acceptance of Taiwan seem doomed to fail. Without a seat at the United Nations, Taiwan will not be recognized as an official national entity by the major nations. And China, as a permanent member of the Security Council, has the power to veto any such attempt, and it surely will.

In the long run, Taiwan's economic future may lie primarily in the Chinese market. According to Professor Charles H. C. Kao of the University of Wisconsin and president of a Taipei publishing company, Taiwan's production could be absorbed fully by the mainland, reducing the island's desire to export to the United States or Europe. In early 1994, the director of the Taiwan Affairs Office of the Beijing municipal government was quoted as saying, "I have seen 71 chairmen of the board of Taiwan's top 100 enterprises."[24] The ultimate impacts of such a close relationship are difficult to forecast.

Despite the rapid expansion of economic and cultural links between Taiwan and the mainland, it is clear that the bamboo network has its limitations. Some Taiwanese companies are scaling back their ambitious investment plans as they discover that, even for them, cracking China's domestic market is difficult. A growing sense of distance from China is reported by some Taiwanese, who are alienated by a country that they increasingly see as brutal, lawless, and corrupt. As a result, Taiwanese entrepreneurs are hedging their bets by placing a rising share of their overseas investment outside of China. Taiwan investments in nearby Southeast Asia are approaching the amount of money already committed to the mainland.

Nevertheless, a substantial array of investments in the mainland continues to be made by Taiwanese and other bamboo network entrepreneurs anxious to participate in the largest business opportunity available to them. In their more optimistic moments, they see Hong Kong in 1997 as a dress rehearsal for Taiwan's eventual union with the mainland. The ease—or difficulty—with which the Hong Kong transition takes place will be crucial in determining the future political climate of Taiwan, and the extent to which bamboo network enterprises continue to make major investments in their ancestral homeland.[25]

MAINLAND CHINA'S ECONOMIC REFORMS

The interaction between the bamboo network and the PRC government has been the driving force behind the economic integration of Greater China. But underlying these social and economic relationships has been massive political change in China itself. Over the last 20 years, the central government of the PRC has fundamentally altered the nation's economic institutions, pursued an ambitious market reform agenda, and opened up large portions of the country to international trade and investment. These changes, in turn, have prompted a massive flow of money from overseas Chinese investors.

According to He Di of the Chinese Academy of Social Sciences in Beijing, Hong Kong and Taiwan have not only become the "windows and partners" of the mainland's economy, but have more importantly come to serve as examples for the mainland's transition to a market economy. He reports that the way of thinking and the lifestyles of Hong Kong and Taiwan are having a tremendous influence on the coastal areas. That lifestyle includes a whole new world of fashion, hairstyles, music, leisure, and desire for self-improvement.[26] Today, the interdependence between the overseas Chinese and mainland China is so great that the fortunes of one have become almost inseparable from those of the other.

The origins of this symbiosis can be traced back to 1976 when, following the death of Mao Tse-tung, a power struggle raged within the senior echelons of China's communist leadership. On one side stood economic hard-liners who wanted to continue Mao's social revolution and reject any capitalist philosophy. On the other side were economic reformers who were alarmed by the persistently underperforming economy. In particular, agricultural productivity remained virtually stagnant during nearly 30 years of communist rule. Unlike the typical capitalist economy, most economic growth in China during this period was due to increases in the sheer number of workers and the amount of capital equipment. Little or no increase had occurred in overall productivity.[27]

Such abysmal economic performance could not easily be explained away by communist rhetoric. The successes of overseas Chinese in nearby Hong Kong and Taiwan served to constantly remind the mainland of socialism's failure to provide even the most basic needs for its citizens. These islands enjoyed none of the natural wealth of the mainland, such as oil and coal reserves, and suffered even more acutely from problems such as dense population. Moreover, they lived under the constant threat of military invasion and political isolation. Nevertheless, Hong Kong and Taiwan possessed the human capital necessary to spur rapid economic development: bankers, traders, entrepreneurs, and skilled workers who had fled the mainland in search of a more hospitable social, political, and business climate.

In 1977, Deng Xiaoping gained control of the Chinese Communist Party (CCP), a move that signaled a strong victory for economic liberals. These reformers set an ambitious agenda to deal with a host of problems endemic to centrally planned economies. The production quality of even the simplest goods was very poor. Prices did not reflect true economic value, resulting in widespread shortages of some goods and massive gluts of other products. China's closed borders protected domestic, state-run monopolies from foreign competition. And, most importantly, workers and enterprises had virtually no incentive to engage in productive activities or to meet the needs of consumers.

From its beginning, the economic reform movement was dependent on the overseas Chinese community. The mainland could begin to rework its backward government bureaucracies, undo decades of socialist propaganda, and establish a market-based economy. However, it needed massive outside assistance—financial, managerial, and technical—in order to develop industries that could compete successfully in world markets.

The bamboo network presented the most obvious source of this economic assistance. First, the geographical proximity of overseas Chinese in Taiwan, Hong Kong, and elsewhere in Southeast Asia minimized the usual costs of foreign trade, such as transportation. Second, the enormous financial wealth of the overseas Chinese community provided a large pool of liquid funds with which to finance new entrepreneurial ventures. Third, Hong Kong and Macao were effectively mainland satellites, reverting as they would to PRC control before the turn of the century. Likewise, Taiwan was considered something of a rebel province, essentially independent but constrained politically by

Beijing. Economic assistance from these regions could therefore be rationalized as not being strictly external, and was thus more palatable to nationalist hard-liners within the CCP.

If the success of economic reforms depended upon the financial resources and business expertise of overseas Chinese, so too did the overseas Chinese community come to depend upon the success of reforms. Many of these investors had already been burned by the communist takeover 30 years earlier. Although they enjoyed certain advantages over other foreign investors—such as a common language, contacts on the mainland, and geographical proximity—the overseas Chinese were not immune from business risk. As capital inflows from Hong Kong, Taiwan, and other Southeast Asian countries grew, so did the vested interest of the bamboo network in ensuring that economic reforms continued to move forward.

By 1978, Deng Xiaoping and other reformers within the PRC had initiated what seemed at the time to be only a modest series of gradual economic changes. But success did breed further change—and further success. Throughout the 1980s, reforms became increasingly ambitious and widespread. The culmination of this profound philosophical change in China's senior leadership occurred in 1992 with the declaration of the Fourteenth National Congress of the Communist Party that the Chinese economy would be converted from central planning to market freedom.

Deng Xiaoping's trip to southeastern China in early 1992 was the catalyst that transformed the popular mood in favor of economic reform. Deng called for all of China to emulate the free-wheeling, Hong Kong-inspired model of Shenzhen in nearby Guangdong province. This highly publicized trip encouraged government-owned enterprises to establish new subsidiaries devoted to earning a profit. Other publicly owned firms were contracted to entrepreneurs who agreed to pay fixed monthly taxes in return for the freedom to manage the enterprises and maximize their profits.

Staff members within state enterprises were allowed to lease and work in joint ventures or to establish their own money-making companies. Some of the new entrepreneurs replaced the photographs of Mao that hung from their rearview mirrors with *fu*, the Chinese symbol for good fortune. Some hedged their bets by attaching the symbol to Mao's picture.

Such dramatic change has not proceeded without opposition. To this day, hard-line factions within the CCP continue to resist economic liberalization. Many old-line Marxists, including Mao himself when he was alive, have openly criticized Deng for his "capitalist" philosophies. Such a characterization has some basis in fact. In 1922, the young Deng opened a profitable grocery store while studying abroad in Paris.[28] Imagine the chagrin of hard-line communist officials when they realized that China's "paramount leader" was, in reality, a former capitalist entrepreneur!

Despite some resistance, Deng has successfully maintained the momentum of economic reform. Massive change has been achieved since the beginning of the "open door policy" less than 20 years ago. China's economic reforms have dramatically improved the productivity of agriculture and industry through increased reliance on market forces and the acquisition of advanced capital and technology from private companies in other nations. The cumulative effects of these policies have directly improved the welfare of hundreds of millions of people, and are likely to shape the future of a billion more.

AGRICULTURE

Agriculture was the first sector of China's economy to undergo fundamental change under Deng's reforms. Before 1978, decisions on food production were highly centralized, being passed down through a strict organizational hierarchy—from communes to brigades to production teams. Although some workers were allowed to maintain limited private plots, most output was produced on state-controlled land. As farmers did not own what they produced, individual pay was not linked to productivity, giving workers a great incentive to shirk. Production increased so slowly that it barely kept up with population growth. Average farm output per worker remained essentially flat from 1957 to

1975. When taking into account the number of hours that laborers worked, productivity actually *declined* during this period.[29]

From 1978 to 1980, widespread agricultural privatization reversed these dismal trends. The central authorities abandoned the policy of "grain self-sufficiency," which required farms to grow enough grain for their own consumption before planting other crops. Instead, the government encouraged farmers to specialize in the production of crops that best suited the regional land and climate. The size of private plots was allowed to increase and restrictions on rural markets were relaxed. Thus, more of the rising production from individual plots was sold privately. Families were increasingly allowed to make their own production decisions and marketing plans. As economic choices were decentralized, the political hierarchy that had formerly directed rural life—called "cadres" by the communists—lost much of its power.

By 1983, the "household responsibility system" had become the standard agricultural production method, adopted by virtually all the farms in China. Plots of land were leased to individual households for a fixed duration (15 years for annual crops). This leasing arrangement typified the Chinese government's desire to move gradually toward market reforms while maintaining ultimate control over economic resources in a type of "market socialism." A fraction of each family's agricultural output was retained by the state. The remainder could be sold in the market or to the government, generally at government-controlled prices. Although falling short of establishing private property rights, this system did provide farmers with the incentive to take care of their land and make better planting and harvesting decisions.

During the mid-1980s, the freedoms granted to farmers were expanded even more dramatically. Individual households were allowed to hire labor, purchase tractors and other capital equipment, and transport their output across administrative boundaries to competing markets. The key was to abolish the agricultural communes. Peasants once again were owners of the land they cultivated. Farm productivity and output skyrocketed. Between 1957 and 1975, China's agricultural output had grown only 1.7 percent a year (roughly the rate of population growth).

During the 12 years following reform (1978–1990) the annual growth rate more than tripled—to 5.6 percent.

Farmers also diversified into more profitable crops, improving the variety and quality of the average diet. Per capita consumption of grain increased more than 20 percent from 1978 to 1990, pork consumption more than doubled, and fresh egg consumption more than tripled. These increases in farm output contributed to a dramatic improvement in the well-being of the citizenry. Per capita daily caloric intake rose from less than 2,000 calories in 1965 to nearly 2,700 calories in 1990. Many fresh fruits and vegetables once considered luxury items became increasingly commonplace in even the most distant northern provinces, due to improvements in farming methods and more widespread use of refrigerated transport.[30]

Although some problems persist, China's agricultural reforms have been extraordinarily successful. Higher productivity has generated increased trade between rural and coastal provinces. Villagers can use the proceeds of their harvests to purchase clothes from Shanghai, cassette recorders from Guangdong, and furs from the Far West.[31] Improved capital, technology, and farming methods have simultaneously increased farm output and decreased labor demand. Redundant farm labor has been released from the inland provinces, providing the people needed for industrial expansion in the coastal provinces. As we will see in Chapter 4, the integration of these unskilled, rural laborers into a modern, urban work force remains one of the central challenges facing China's political leadership.

INDUSTRY

China's industrial reforms have also gone through several distinct stages. Beginning in 1980, firms were allowed to sell goods outside the state plan, keeping a share of the profits they generated and giving bonuses to productive employees. Political commissars were removed from many factories, especially in the southern coastal region. Managers could concentrate on efficiency rather than ideology.

A second wave of reforms in the mid-1980s replaced state planning with "responsibility contracts" that gave firms considerable flexibility in making output decisions after meeting assigned production targets. A dual price system allowed firms to sell their output at market prices after selling their targeted production to the government at low, subsidized prices. This partial deregulation generated substantial competition in a broad range of markets. China's southern provinces took advantage of these new policies by attracting the skills and investment capital of the overseas Chinese.[32] Many of these foreign investors were given substantial freedom to hire and fire workers without political interference, a dramatic departure from traditional communist practice.

These changes fueled the rise of some private businesses and of many more locally controlled "collectives." Chinese collectives are not worker-managed enterprises in the conventional communist sense. Rather, these township and village enterprises (TVEs) constitute an organizational structure unique to the Chinese experience that is not easily classified as either private or public. Local governments own and control them and are deeply involved in strategic management decisions. Community leaders typically appoint the TVE management, whose compensation is based primarily on the growth and profits of the enterprise. Local residents have no rights of membership or ownership, nor do they have any power to participate in managing the TVE. Nevertheless, most of the benefits of TVE growth remain within the community.

Some Chinese economists describe collective industry as the "second state sector."[33] Unlike their state-owned counterparts, however, TVEs may go bankrupt, lay off workers, or change what they produce according to market conditions. The government has shown a strong preference for TVEs by restricting the supply of credit, electricity, public transport, and foreign exchange available to competing private businesses.[34]

The growth of TVEs is a natural response to the government's partial privatization efforts, which continue to prohibit ownership of natural resources such as land, minerals, and oil. Despite such restrictions, local communities do generally possess the right to utilize or extract these resources. Thus, given the absence of property rights in land, TVEs allow communities to reap the economic benefits linked to local resources.[35] The health of these local enterprises also reflects the efforts of Chinese entrepreneurs to capitalize upon new economic freedoms despite a rapidly changing and inadequate system of legal protections.

Yet, despite the success of TVEs and private businesses, state enterprises continue to be the bastions of CCP power. In heavy manufacturing industries such as petroleum, electricity, and steel, state-owned firms control 90 percent or more of national output. These firms suffer from a multitude of inefficiencies that place a drag upon the entire Chinese economy. The financial and corporate governance controls common to most Western enterprises have not yet been developed in China. Lacking the self-discipline of competitive businesses, state enterprises frequently yield to favoritism and unconstrained managerial power. In the absence of management accountability, senior executives treat the enterprise's assets as their own personal property and pass on control to relatives.

China's transition from communism to capitalism has been bumpy and is far from complete. Examining the developing Chinese economy from the vantage point of a Western consumer, one experienced American reporter described Beijing in 1994 as "a laboratory exhibiting every virtue and defect of free-booting, frontier capitalism."[36] Furniture stores are crammed with "antiques" that may not be much more than two weeks old. Ration coupons are still used in much of China, yet in prosperous Guangzhou they are on display in museums.[37]

Increased competition has forced Chinese industry to focus on quality, variety, and customer service. At the same time, a large gap has emerged between the opportunities and incomes available to managers and workers of profitable firms and the returns provided by the unsuccessful ones. Employees of collectives operating at a loss are frequently dismissed and unprofitable state firms have been forced to cut their bonuses and benefits.

In Guangdong, these dramatic changes are described as the

breaking of the "three irons." Workers no longer benefit from the "iron rice bowl," the lifetime employment system that was guaranteed under communism. The rice bowl included housing, medical care, education, pensions, and many other goods and services provided by employers. Likewise, managers have lost their "iron chairs," or tenured positions. Furthermore, employees no longer receive "iron wages," or protection from pay cuts. The rest of China is following suit in an effort to scale back the size of government, which has traditionally financed every dimension of a citizen's welfare from birth to death. Home ownership, which has been gradually introduced in Shanghai, Beijing, and Guangzhou since 1992, is among the more dramatic of these changes.[38]

The theoretical underpinnings of reform frequently appear to be more practical than philosophical: use whatever works to raise the standard of living and do not worry about what to call it. But progress will not come easily as long as arbitrary differentials in pay and benefits affect Chinese work effort. Indeed, many Chinese plan marriages to get the best of both the socialist and capitalist worlds. One partner works for the government to earn housing, medical, and other benefits, while the other partner works for a firm in the private sector to earn a high cash income.[39]

COMMERCE AND TRADE

As China began to reform its domestic agricultural and industrial economy, it also took its first critical steps toward opening up its borders to trade with Southeast Asia and the rest of the world.[40] The policies that brought about this change were implemented in four distinct phases. The first of these phases—and the strategic breakthrough—began in 1979 with the establishment of four Special Economic Zones (SEZs). These zones were intended to mimic the successes of foreign trade and economic activity zones established in other newly industrializing countries. During the second stage, which began in 1984, the liberal economic policies of the zones were partially extended to an additional 14 coastal cities. The third stage was the establishment of Hainan Island as an SEZ in 1988 and the opening of the most ambitious economic development zone—the Pudong New Area in Shanghai—in 1990. The fourth stage, starting in 1992, extended economic reforms to selected cities in the inland provinces and along China's northeastern borders.

Special Economic Zones

Ease of access to foreign markets, particularly to overseas Chinese traders in nearby Hong Kong and Taiwan, was the primary consideration in locating the first four zones. Three were located near Hong Kong in the coastal province of Guangdong (Shenzhen, Zhuhai, and Shantou), while the fourth (Xiamen) was established across from Taiwan in Fujian province. Hainan Island, located off the southern tip of Guangdong, was designated an SEZ in 1988.

The Chinese government originally intended for these SEZs only to produce manufactured exports, facilitate the import of advanced technologies, and attract foreign capital. Over time, the SEZs have come to serve as laboratories for experimentation with market reform. Most investment decisions in the SEZs are outside of the State Plan. Local government authorities offer preferential policies such as tax breaks to foreign investors in order to attract desperately needed capital for infrastructure and other critical projects. Export industries are given particular preference because exports help the central government amass foreign exchange reserves. Also, by exporting goods that are produced in the SEZs, bordering regions can be better isolated from the effects of capitalist reforms.[41]

By opening up to foreign investment, the SEZs provided overseas Chinese traders with opportunities to aggressively expand their business relationships with the mainland and to establish a commerce-oriented bamboo network. Indeed, many overseas Chinese firms were ideally suited to qualify for the tax breaks and investment subsidies offered by the SEZs. While most Western firms sought to sell their products within the mainland, firms in

Hong Kong and Taiwan were seeking to expand their exports to the West. Because of this, investors from these regions found themselves sharing the same strategic goal as Beijing. Without this common goal, the high level of economic synergy between overseas Chinese and the mainland might never have been realized. Indeed, bamboo network members would likely have stayed put or sought opportunities in other regions of Southeast Asia.

Entrepreneurial freedoms unheard of in the inland provinces are openly granted in the SEZs. Enterprises can make their own investment, production, and marketing decisions. Foreign-owned enterprises, including joint ventures, can *generally* choose their own organizational and personnel structures, wage systems, and employment levels. Furthermore, firms are *generally* given the authority to hire and fire employees. We say "generally" because at times the individual firm faces unexpected and arbitrary directives from governmental authorities (Chapter 5 provides numerous examples).

Foreign enterprises do face restrictions, however, that enforce the key original rationale for the SEZs: encouraging the export of manufactured goods. Foreign-funded enterprises are allowed to sell only limited portions of their output in the domestic Chinese market, and then only with the approval of local authorities.

Open Coastal Cities

From 1983 to 1985, encouraged by the success of the four original SEZs, the Chinese government opened Shanghai and 13 other large coastal cities to foreign trade and investment.[42] They were much larger than the original zones in terms of population and geographic size. Like the SEZs, however, their location made them especially suitable for export-oriented industries. Unlike the original SEZs, these cities already possessed relatively high levels of physical and human capital in terms of industry, infrastructure, and managerial expertise. However, the presence of an experienced work force turned out to be a mixed blessing. Many workers had succumbed to the bureaucratic routines of communist society and had difficulty adjusting to the competitive pace of the marketplace.

These coastal cities retain many of the preferential policies and incentives of the SEZs but their performance has been mixed. The new incentives have been more effective in increasing exports than in expanding industrial production, perhaps because of the bureaucratic experience of the work force. Only eight of the 14 have expanded their output at a faster rate than the country as a whole. The other six pulled the aggregate production figures for all 14 cities below the national average.

Pudong New Area

In 1990, China's open door policy progressed further with the selection of the Pudong New Area of Shanghai as an open economic zone. This New Area is strategically located at the opening of the Yangtze River valley, a region that includes other major cities such as Nanjing, Wuhan, and Chongqing. The valley is home to roughly 400 million people—approximately 8 percent of the world's population—and is one of the most economically advanced regions in China. Its combined agricultural and industrial output accounts for 40 percent of the national total.[43]

Pudong benefits from economic policies that are even more flexible than those of the original SEZs. The intent of these liberal policies is to position Pudong as a major trading and financial center, while fostering exports and encouraging the development of high-tech industries. In the process, Shanghai may become a counterweight and competitor to Hong Kong, which many senior Chinese officials fear they may never be able to control effectively.

Large-scale liberalization has created booming growth for Pudong: wages in the area have more than quadrupled since 1985. Two years after its establishment, Pudong attracted 704 foreign-funded projects—mostly high-tech, including electronics, telecommunications, and microbiology ventures—and more than $3 billion in investment. At least 11 foreign banks have opened branches in Pudong, and more than 30 others have applied for permission to do so.

Such rapid growth has necessitated a massive effort to provide the necessary infrastructure. Over $40 billion worth of public works projects are under way in Pudong, including a major international airport, the world's longest cable-stayed bridge, an elevated six-lane road that rings the city, and a brand-new subway system. Despite being home to only 1 percent of China's population, Shanghai now earns over 4 percent of the national income, produces 6 percent of China's industrial output, and raises 8 percent of its fiscal revenue.[44] Clearly, the rise of the Pudong area makes it more likely that Shanghai will regain its earlier commercial and financial eminence serving as a mainland alternative to high-priced Hong Kong.

Inland Provinces

After Deng Xiaoping toured the open coastal cities and SEZs in 1992, Beijing extended some preferential policies to 23 major cities in the inland provinces. Six new "development zones" were established, and 13 cities bordering on neighboring countries were allowed to open their economies to the outside world. Currently, three "open areas" are developing around these border regions: the North Open Area (facing Russia and central Asia), the Western Open Area (facing southern Asia), and the Southern Open Area (facing Thailand, Myanmar, Cambodia, and Vietnam).

Also in 1992, the central government lifted restrictions on foreign firms participating in certain critical service industries, such as banking, insurance, trade, and real estate. Prior to 1992, foreigners were prohibited from entering these markets, or were restricted to operations within the SEZs.[45]

So far, the success of the inland provinces has been very limited, far slower than the gains achieved in Guangdong and Fujian. Most of the foreign investment in these regions has been restricted to a few areas, primarily around Beijing. Given the lack of infrastructure and skilled labor in the interior provinces, there is little incentive for foreign firms to look beyond the glittering success of China's coastal regions. Attempts to penetrate the inland provinces primarily involve natural resource extraction rather than manufacturing. Investment in retail business naturally favors the SEZs and coastal cities, where consumer demand is strongest and the infrastructure is most modern. Ventures outside these areas frequently must wait for government investment in distribution facilities and other infrastructure.[46]

CONCLUSION

The gradual nature of China's open door policy contrasts sharply with the drastic, sudden economic reforms of Poland, Russia, and other Eastern European nations—the so-called "big bang" or "shock therapy" approach. The history of the Chinese movement to a market economy is largely one of experimentation and cautious step-by-step implementation, a process that continues to this day. Perhaps because of this approach, the Chinese central government has been able to maintain much of its political power despite the massive economic change.

A central tenet of China's reform is that a stable political order is a fundamental and necessary condition for economic progress. Many communist officials believe that, if political dissent is allowed or if economic reforms are instituted too quickly, China will experience the type of chaos plaguing the former Soviet Union. Because of this, China has followed a path of "perestroika without glasnost."[47] The uncertainty involved in instituting widespread, drastic change within a society that encompasses one-fifth of the world's population is another reason for caution. The expression "Cross the river by feeling its stones" vividly distills much of the spirit of the reform now under way.[48]

Critics of this incrementalism contend that, if partial reform is good, more reform is better. By experimenting in only certain regions, China has created massive incentives for those living outside these privileged areas to relocate. As we have seen, income inequality within China, a society that historically has been concerned with the general welfare of all its citizenry, is large and growing.

Gradual change also creates economic rewards for corrupt governmental practices: bureaucrats hold tremendous power in determining which new investment projects are allowed under current reform law and which are not. Outrage over widespread corruption, particularly that tied to the relatives of senior Communist Party members—the so-called "princes and princesses"—helped spark the discontent that paved the way to the sad episode at Tiananmen Square in June 1989. Gradual change also gives defenders of the status quo the opportunity to mobilize against reform.[49]

The overall effect of the rapidly evolving economic climate in China today is one of both opportunity and uncertainty. How do private companies identify business opportunities in China and seize them before they disappear under conditions of intense competition? How do firms comply with the requirements of constantly changing, often vague, governmental regulations? These are some of the many challenges confronting foreign investors eager to participate in the enormous potential of the Chinese market. Chapter 5 highlights the problems that confront Western business in China, while Chapter 6 examines the experiences of American companies that deal with these issues as investors. However, before we address these issues, we need to take a deeper look at the unparalleled changes in China's economy.

CHAPTER 4

The Rise of China's Economy

To be rich is glorious.
—Deng Xiaoping

Over 150 years ago, the British calculated that if the Chinese lengthened their shirttails by only an inch, the textile mills of Lancashire could run nonstop for generations to fill the demand. Dreams of this variety have inspired entrepreneurs ever since. Today's marketers speculate that, if the Chinese drank the same amount of Coca-Cola per capita as do Australians, the beverage company would sell about 10 billion cases a year on the mainland (instead of the 100 million reported currently).

All of these forecasts underscore the fact that, in comparisons of China with other countries, the statistic that looms over all others is population. The sheer size of China's population is staggering. With an area roughly equal to that of the United States, mainland China contains more than five times as many people—approximately 1.2 billion. Indeed, its population is slightly more than one-fifth of the world's total, a proportion that has remained relatively constant over the last 25 years. It is difficult to visualize such an enormous number. Consider this: China's population is roughly equal to that of the United States, Brazil, Russia, Japan, Mexico, Germany, Italy, the United Kingdom, France, Spain, Canada, Australia, Belgium, and Sweden—combined.[1]

Some of the mainland's individual provinces are comparable in population to entire European nations. In terms of population, Guangdong province—home to 64 million people—is roughly the size of the United Kingdom. Fujian province, approximately the size of Greece, has 30 million people. China's vastness, both in terms of population and geographical size, makes it the last great multiethnic transcontinental empire left in the world, stretching from Xinjiang's Turkic cities to Manchuria's Korean enclaves, from Tibet's Buddhists to Guangdong's Han Chinese.[2]

THE PERILS AND BENEFITS OF POPULATION

It is this vast number of potential consumers that has compelled so many firms to enter the Chinese market. Indeed, the dreams of the Lancashire textile producers are little changed today. It is the promise of future consumers, hampered for decades by communist inefficiencies, that beckons investors. The Asian Rim—which contains 1.7 billion people, two-thirds of whom are Chinese—is the fastest growing consumer market in the world. The business consulting firm McKinsey & Co. predicts that in this region (excluding Japan) the number of people in households earning more than $10,000 will grow to 110 million by the year 2000. For specific parts of the area, forecasts are even rosier. Some analysts have projected Taiwan's average personal income to reach $13,000 by 2000, or slightly above what countries such as Spain or Ireland have achieved today.[3]

This emerging middle class is attracting many entrepreneurs who are mesmerized by the notion of Southeast Asia generally and China specifically as the newest and largest potential mass buyer of consumer goods. For example, the mainland is estimated to be the world's largest cigarette market, with roughly 300 million smokers. To other businesses, the great Chinese population conjures up visions of an unlimited supply of cheap labor.

Yet while some view the enormous Chinese population as a magnet for foreign investment, others see it as a barrier to China's future economic success. These critics point out that China's population density of 120 people per square kilometer is more than three times the world average, and more than four times the U.S. figure. Their concern is that in such an environment population growth will outstrip economic production, effectively "immiserising" the country.

Such arguments have been made since the era of Thomas Malthus (1766–1834). Malthus is most famous for his theory that unchecked population growth increases geometrically over time, while food production, constrained by a fixed supply of land, increases only arithmetically. Because of these divergent trends, Malthus predicted that population growth would eventually overwhelm economic progress, creating poverty, starvation, and resource scarcity.

History has not been kind to Malthus. Improvements in the technology of food production have consistently resulted in world food supplies that outpace population. Nevertheless, present-day neo-Malthusians see the makings of a doomsday scenario in China. Ironically, rising national income is considered to be as much a culprit as population growth. Higher income levels have dramatically increased consumption of meat and dairy products in China, a trend that has simultaneously increased grain demand. If China's population and grain consumption continue to grow at their current rates, worldwide food shortages are predicted.[4]

Such hypotheses ignore basic economic forces. As demand for food increases, prices rise. This encourages suppliers to expand their production and utilize more advanced technology. Simultaneously, higher prices encourage people to shift their consumption patterns to less expensive types of food. The combination of these forces prevents any shortages from persisting. Furthermore, neo-Malthusians overlook the ultimate irony in their argument.

They worry that a future food crisis will arise because people are eating *too much*, not too little!

Extrapolating future economic performance from population density statistics is chancy and can be misleading. Overcrowding has certainly been—and continues to be—a social and economic problem for Japan (with a population density of over 320 people per square kilometer, nearly three times that of China). Nevertheless, this heavy concentration of people—as well as a notable lack of natural resources such as oil and farmland—has not been an insurmountable barrier to Japan's tremendous economic performance over the last several decades. South Korea's population density stands at 432 people per square kilometer, even greater than Japan's. Despite this, South Korea has enjoyed tremendous economic growth over the past 20 years.

Further evidence in contradiction of the Malthusian hypothesis is provided by flourishing Hong Kong. Albeit more of an extended urban area than a country, Hong Kong's 1,000 square kilometers of land on Hong Kong Island, Kowloon, and the New Territories are home to about 6 million people.[5] This translates into an astonishing 5,500 people per square kilometer! Clearly, there is no observable relationship between a nation's population density (or absolute population level) and its economic prosperity. Some areas of the world with the lowest population density— such as regions of Africa—have difficulty feeding their people and maintaining environmental quality.

This is not to say that China's population pressures are a trivial matter. The point is that other developing nations in Asia have experienced similar pressures and have overcome them. From this perspective, China has room to grow relative to its East Asian neighbors, and there is little reason to expect population density pressures to be a constraint on its economic performance.

This is especially true when we consider the effect of China's draconian measures to reduce its rate of population growth. Couples in most urban areas are limited to only one child, while rural authorities generally allow two children. Frequently, women who have already had children are forced to undergo sterilization.[6] These policies, as well as an increased standard of living in the coastal provinces, have slowed down population growth over the last decade. During the years 1970 to 1980, China's annual population growth rate averaged 1.8 percent. This was high by the standards of high-income countries (many of which averaged less than half that rate over the same period). However, it was below the average in upper-middle income countries, a group that includes South Africa, Brazil, Mexico, and Korea. During the 1980s, China's rate of population growth dropped to 1.5 percent a year, reflecting the continued efforts of the Chinese government to tighten birth control measures. This downward trend has continued into the 1990s.

Despite the rapid decline in China's overall population growth, there is still a substantial disparity in birth rates between urban and rural households. This gap can largely be explained by examining the special nature of agricultural living in China. The lack of private property rights in land has given rise to a system where land is allocated based on family size. This provides a strong incentive for poor rural families to have more children. Furthermore, most rural households, lacking access to formal savings plans, rely heavily on children to provide for their parents in old age.[7]

There are indications that China's population growth may slow even further. In 1994, the growth rate was at its lowest level since the Communist Revolution: 1.1 percent. Compare this figure to Japan's 1.3 percent rate of population growth in the 1970s, a period during which Japanese industry began to penetrate many traditionally Western markets. Likewise, South Korea's annual rate of population growth averaged 1.8 percent over the years 1970 to 1980, before rising incomes accompanied a slowdown to an average rate of 1.1 percent over the following decade.[8] Thus, it seems that the pessimistic Malthusian scenario will be postponed once again, in this case due to a combination of economic incentives and governmental policies.

THE PACE OF ECONOMIC ACTIVITY

Any doubts about the ability of China's economy to grow in spite of its population pressures can be resolved by examining the recent record. China has experienced an astonishingly rapid economic expansion over the last decade, far outstripping population expansion. During the decade from 1984 to 1994, real GDP grew at an average of 10 percent a year, roughly six times the rate of population increase. If this growth rate is sustained, the Chinese economy will double in size roughly every eight years. In contrast, over the same period, the economies of Japan and the United States grew much more slowly—at an average annual rate of 4 percent and less than 3 percent, respectively.[9]

It will be virtually impossible for China to maintain its current rate of economic growth indefinitely. At present, the country is replicating the development of other Asian dragons as they sought to catch up with Western economies, primarily through the use of imported technology and production methods. After such a catch-up phase, Japan made the transition to domestically developed, cutting-edge technologies. As China approaches this more advanced stage of development, its growth will likely slow. Furthermore, China may not be spending enough on schools and universities to ensure that it will have a large supply of technicians in coming decades. If that is so, the economy's growth rate will slow to a less feverish level sometime after the year 2000.

For the immediate future, however, growth predictions for China's economy continue to be extremely robust. Indeed, the Fourteenth Congress of the Chinese Communist Party (CCP) announced in 1992 that 8 to 9 percent annual growth would be China's economic goal through the year 2000. Unlike its former Soviet counterpart, the CCP has a past track record of *underestimating* future economic performance. The goal established in 1980 was to double the size of the economy in the 1980s, and once again in the 1990s. By 1990, however, the economy had already tripled in size as a result of an average 9 percent annual growth rate.[10]

Growth statistics can be misleading when comparing countries of varying size and levels of development. A country can easily grow quickly from a very low level of economic activity as small absolute changes translate into very large growth rates. How does China compare with other countries in terms of its actual level of economic output, as measured by gross domestic product?

This simple question is actually quite difficult to answer precisely. Each nation produces a different combination of goods and services, while its consumers buy a different mix of items. A direct "apples to apples" comparison between countries cannot be made. Furthermore, all of this activity is measured in local currencies, which themselves are not comparable from country to country. Prior to 1993, statistics on the economies of different countries were based on standard international exchange rates: the total value of a nation's GDP was simply converted from its local currency into dollars using the official exchange rate (100 yen = 1 dollar, 1.6 deutsche marks = 1 dollar, etc.). Thus, the estimate of a foreign nation's GDP, computed in dollars, was very sensitive to the international trade and investment patterns that influence foreign exchange rates.

In 1993, the World Bank developed a new method of calculating GDP across nations that eliminated this shortcoming: purchasing power parity (PPP) exchange rates are now used to measure a country's output in dollars. Under this system, a nation's GDP is determined by the amount of local currency necessary to purchase a specified bundle of goods and services. The World Bank uses the United States as the base country in determining these PPP rates. In this calculation, a country's exchange rate is defined as the amount of local currency necessary to buy the same amount of goods and services domestically that a dollar could buy in the United States. Adjusted GDP figures are obtained by dividing a country's GDP, expressed in terms of domestic currency, by this exchange rate. (The appendix to this chapter covers this subject in more detail.)

Under the old system, the production of many goods and services that are not traded internationally had little impact on a nation's foreign exchange rates, and thus were underestimated when computing GDP. Important examples are health care, housing, and local transportation. Although the precise calculations are complicated, the general idea of PPP-adjusted exchange rates is not new. For example, it is common knowledge that it costs more to live in cities such as New York and San Francisco than in Houston, a fact that is often reflected in wages, salaries, and benefit packages.

These PPP adjustments are especially important in China, where many consumer goods are often heavily subsidized by the government. For example, rent accounts for only 1 percent of the average household's expenditures, compared to 20 percent or more in most developed countries.[11] Because of this, traditional measurements substantially *understate* the standard of living of most Chinese.

The difference between PPP and conventional methods of measurement is deceptively subtle. When the World Bank changed its methodology, its estimates of China's 1991 GDP increased overnight more than fourfold (from $0.4 trillion to $1.9 trillion). Under the old system, China's was the tenth largest economy in the world, below those of Germany, France, Italy, Britain, and Canada. Under the PPP system, China vaults to third place, behind only the United States and Japan. (See Figure 7.) Furthermore, the staff of the World Bank predicts that the combined output of China, Hong Kong, and Taiwan will quickly overtake Japan's, rivaling U.S. GDP by the year 2000.[12]

Measuring aggregate economic output is a useful way of gauging the extent of a country's domestic market. It is also a good guide to the amount of financial resources that are available for national defense, foreign aid, and other programs that influence national security. Nevertheless, some analysts contend that *per capita* income is a far better measure of a country's wealth, the technological level its society has achieved, and even the potential quality of its armed forces.[13]

On a per capita basis, Hong Kong—with a 1994 PPP-adjusted per capita GDP of approximately $20,000—is wealthier than its colonial ruler. Britain's comparable figure is $17,000, and the average for all industrialized countries for that year was only $19,000.[14] Mainland China, however, lags far behind these nations. Even when using the World Bank's PPP figures, China's per capita income is still only one-tenth that of the United States, Japan, or Germany. If its per capita income continues to grow at the rapid rate of 7 percent annually, China will take at least 40 years to reach the average standard of living that the United States achieved in 1994. By the year 2035, U.S. per capita income will likely be much higher than at present, so the prospect

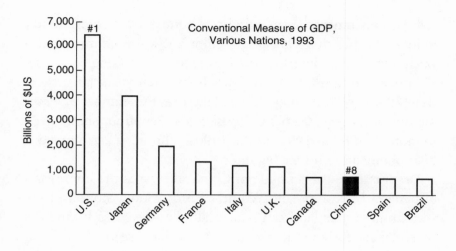

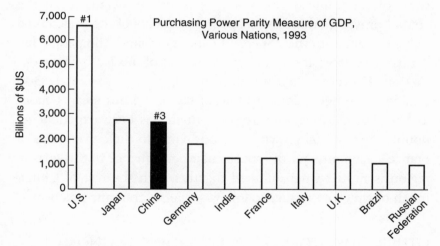

FIGURE 7

of China's catching up with the world's wealthiest nation is distant at best. Nevertheless, China's recent per capita growth rate does imply a steadily rising standard of living. This economic progress is having a tangible impact on the Chinese citizenry. Literally hundreds of millions of people are rising out of poverty. The changes in what constitutes the average consumer's "big three" tell the story vividly. Prior to economic reforms, the three consumer items most sought after by a typical Chinese family were a wristwatch, a bicycle, and a sewing machine. During the

1980s, consumers began purchasing more expensive, luxury items—the big three became a color TV, a refrigerator, and a washing machine. In 1981, there were fewer than one color television set for every 100 city households. Ten years later, there were 70 sets per 100 households. Likewise, the number of washing machines per 100 urban households grew from six in 1981 to more than 80 in 1991. In the 1990s, a house, a car, and a cellular phone make up the big three.[15]

Despite these gains, much of China still leaves the impression of being a backward Third World country. Surely not all of the vast Chinese mainland can realistically be viewed as having the potential for early modernization. As we have seen, the current wave of economic development is primarily occurring in the coastal provinces that have reaped the benefits of the preferential policies granted to their Special Economic Zones. The people living in these areas are only a small fraction of the 1.2 billion population. However, their absolute number—approximately 300 million—is roughly equal to that of the entire European Union! The output of the coastal region, which has been experiencing double-digit annual growth, is about equal to the current size of France's economy. Yet the spectacular performance of this coastal region is muted when lumped together with the rest of China, much of which continues to follow socialist economic practices.

OTHER INDICATORS OF AN EXPANDING ECONOMY

A word of warning is in order: as with other developing nations, statistical reporting in China is primitive by Western standards. The country's statistics are approximate at best and sometimes outright misleading. Gathering data in a nation so vast is a herculean task, compounded by inconsistent accounting methods. Many local bureaucrats are suspected of tinkering with reported data in order to paint a rosy growth picture. In a 1995 survey of the quality of statistical reporting in the emerging economies, China ranked near the bottom of the list, tied with Russia. On the other hand, Hong Kong, Singapore, and Taiwan scored near the top.[16]

Statistical wrangling aside, however, two basic points regarding China's economy cannot be denied: it is big and it is growing very quickly. These two facts are confirmed by evidence beyond calculations of GDP. For example, capital investment has been expanding at unparalleled rates. The flow of direct foreign investment into the economy has jumped from less than $400 million in 1982 to over $33 billion in 1994, an eightyfold increase. In 1994, China ranked second in the world (behind the United States) in inflows of direct investment. The prospects for attracting more foreign investment on a large scale remain very high. In 1994, new foreign commitments to investment in China totaled $81 billion.[17]

As the following table illustrates, however, the majority of these investments have been contributed by Hong Kong and Taiwan. Indeed, the contributions of these two nations are more than three times those of all other nations combined.[18] The role of overseas Chinese investors in the mainland's economic development is even more dramatic when we consider the substantial investments from Thailand, Singapore, and elsewhere in Southeast Asia.

Two qualifying points are worth noting. First, the figures for

Contracted Foreign Investment in China, 1979–1993

Country	Percentage of total
Hong Kong	68
Taiwan	8
Subtotal	76
U.S.	7
Japan	4
All others	13
Subtotal	24
Grand total	100

Hong Kong may be inflated because of the operation of Chinese-owned shell companies in Hong Kong that merely redirect PRC money back to the mainland. These companies do so to take advantage of Chinese regulations that favor "foreign" over domestic investment (Beijing is trying to close this loophole). Second, there is some evidence that the geographical distribution of direct foreign investment is widening. In the early years of market reform, these investments were largely limited to mainland industries that could export via Hong Kong. In recent years, however, China's expanding domestic market has attracted more Western companies.

Another good indicator of China's solid progress on the economic front is that foreign commerce is also booming. Exports rose from $25 billion in 1984 to $120 billion in 1994, a growth rate of 17 percent a year over the decade. In contrast, the comparable figure for the United States and Japan is only 8 percent.[19]

This trade is not occurring solely with other Asian nations. Although official trade statistics report that Hong Kong is the number one destination for Chinese exports, about two-thirds of this is re-exported to the United States. Even official trade statistics that do not include such *entrepôt* trade show that China is America's sixth largest trading partner.

Clearly, international business is of growing importance to China. Its export-to-GDP ratio rose sharply from 8 percent in 1984 to 24 percent in 1994. Over the same time span, the country's share of total world exports grew from 1.5 percent to 2.5 percent. China's current trade volume places it among the world's top ten trading nations, a position previously unheard of for a developing nation.[20] Exports have pushed up foreign exchange reserves throughout Southeast Asia. China's reserves topped $50 billion in 1994, while Hong Kong, Taiwan, and Singapore held combined reserves of $180 billion—equal to those of Japan and Germany together.

The enormous growth in foreign trade and investment has created a burgeoning capital market. Businesspeople traveling in China joke that in the coastal cities a stockbroker seems to be on every block. In Taiwan, the total value of traded securities has ballooned from $8 billion in 1984 to $346 billion in 1993, an average growth rate of 65 percent per year. On the mainland, the rise has been equally dramatic. In 1991, the first full year of trading activity, the value of shares traded in China was only $820 million. Two years later, that figure had jumped fiftyfold, to $43 billion.[21]

Fueling this capital market activity are extremely high saving rates. Since 1990, China's gross saving rate has averaged 37 percent of GDP, the highest in the world. Such high saving rates are the rule in Greater China. Both Taiwan's and Hong Kong's rates are 29 percent, while Singapore's tops 30 percent. In contrast, the United States, Canada, and Britain each save only 15 percent of their GDPs.[22]

High saving rates do not imply an aversion to risky investments. Indeed, the frenzied activity of Chinese stock markets makes Wall Street appear tame by comparison. In February 1992, the Shanghai Composite Index stood at 365. By April 1993, it had nearly quadrupled to 1,358. It then plummeted, losing 75 percent of its value before bottoming out at 334 in July 1994. The Shenzhen stock exchange has experienced similar volatility, dropping 72 percent between its peak in early 1993 and mid-1994. Even the more mature Hong Kong financial markets have displayed tremendous variance. In early 1991, the Heng Seng share index stood at roughly 4,000. By mid-1993, it had tripled in value to over 12,000 before diving to 8,000 in early 1995.[23]

The extreme volatility of Southeast Asian stock markets has frightened many investors away from the region. Some analysts have taken recent declines as evidence that the long-term profitability of companies within the bamboo network may not be as great as once imagined. However, overseas Chinese family firms—with their large reservoirs of investment capital—maintain considerable discretion over which business opportunities are offered to the public and which stay within the family's private holdings.

Most likely, the more attractive investments are reserved for the family or a tight circle of friends. The higher-risk and lower-return opportunities are made available in public offerings through companies listed on stock exchanges but also controlled by the family. Thus, the market performance of these public companies is not necessarily a good indicator of the overall profitability of the array of public and privately held companies controlled by family members.

Moreover, there are several special reasons for the "roller coaster" aspect of China's stock markets. First of all, stock offerings are relatively new to China. The country's first exchange was established in Shanghai in late 1990. Pent-up demand, coupled with a limited number of offerings, has led to high levels of buying pressure. When the Shanghai Securities Exchange first opened, potential investors had to buy applications—at a cost equivalent to roughly two weeks' average wages. The applications merely entered them into a lottery; the winners (10 percent of the applicants) were given the right to purchase shares. The same procedure has been used for the initial public offerings of individual companies. This all-or-nothing rationing contributes to enormous speculation and excess demand.[24]

Uncertainty surrounding the stability of governmental regulation of the securities markets has compounded these problems. Beijing has restricted foreign investors to buying only "B-shares" that are traded in U.S. or Hong Kong dollars. Domestic investors, however, purchase "A-shares" with the local Chinese currency. The purpose of this segmented market for essentially identical shares of stock was to attract foreign investment and hard currency through the B-share market. The effect, however, has been to separate small, individual investors from larger (and more stable) international traders. As a result, A-shares are much more volatile (and generally more expensive) than B-shares. Rumors persist that the Chinese government intends to unify the two types of stock, although this remains unlikely as long as Chinese currency is not freely convertible on world exchange markets.

At times, China's lack of experience with financial markets is dramatically evident. In August 1992, a million people descended on the city of Shenzhen for a two-day sale of stock applications. Many of the potential investors, with money collected from entire villages, came to buy shares in three new public offerings: a soft-drink company, a glass manufacturer, and an electronics producer. People began queuing up 48 hours before the sale was to begin. The day before the opening, riot police used electric cattle prods to control fights that were erupting throughout the crowd. The sale went off as planned, but rumors circulated that bureaucrats had withheld some of the stock applications. In response, more than 50,000 protesters formed outside the Shenzhen government offices. After several government cars were destroyed by the crowd, the protesters were dispersed by riot police and tear gas.[25]

Ironically, because of its poorly developed capital markets, China is less vulnerable than other emerging economies to fluctuations in international exchange rates and capital flows. To date, most investment in China has been direct investment. Mexico, on the other hand, relied largely on portfolio investment (purchases of stocks and bonds) during the early 1990s. When the peso declined in value in 1994, this inflow of funds not only stopped but rapidly reversed as investors took flight. Nevertheless, the benefits that come from a more stable investment base are offset by the reluctance of investors to sink their money into China without guarantees that they will be able to move their money to another location if the business climate turns unfavorable.

INCOME INEQUALITY

Clearly, not all of the economic developments in today's China are positive ones. The dramatic success at modernization of the coastal regions while the inland provinces remain in their traditional mode has created massive social problems throughout the country. Typical urban workers earn roughly three times more than their rural counterparts. Paradoxically, such a wage gap is evidence of a higher degree of income inequality in communist China than in the capitalist nations of Asia. In Japan, the richest fifth of the population earns 38 percent of the national income, lower than China's 42 percent. The poorest fifth in Japan earns 9 percent of that country's income, higher than China's 6 percent.

The legacy of communism is fascinating to behold: the rich are richer and the poor are poorer.[26]

This income inequality highlights the disparity between the coastal provinces that have been opened up to capitalist reforms and the inland regions that remain primarily socialist. By 1993, more than 5,000 joint ventures had been established in each of the coastal provinces of Guangdong, Jiangsu, Fujian, and Shandong. However, only a few hundred foreign joint ventures had been established in the more remote western provinces.[27] As a result, the average per capita income in Guangdong, the wealthiest Chinese province, is over three times that of Guizhou, the poorest province.

Under uniform economic institutions, rising wages in the coastal provinces would be expected to create opportunities for firms to move inland: wage rates between the two areas would narrow. But economic policies in China are far from uniform. Higher labor costs in the coastal zones continue to be offset by the preferential treatment offered to the firms that invest there, coupled with the more desirable geographical location of the port cities and the better transportation and communication services they provide.

These differences in income have created incentives for widespread internal migration. Just as California's economy beckoned American workers from the turn of the century to the end of the Cold War, China's coastline is triggering massive migration eastward. In a manner reminiscent of the American westward migration depicted in John Steinbeck's *The Grapes of Wrath*, the future of the Chinese who seek a better life on the "Golden Coast" often diverges widely from their dreams of success.

The coastal cities do not currently have enough new jobs, housing, or services to sustain the enormous influx of rural, mostly uneducated, workers. This "floating population" of *mang lui* (or wandering migrants) is estimated to range from 80 million to more than 100 million—a phenomenally large number for any country. The ranks of *mang lui* stand to grow as agriculture continues to modernize and rural workers become redundant. The current farm labor force is 450 million, but Chinese officials estimate that nearly half of these people will eventually have to find other work.[28]

These millions of unemployed rural workers have become an unstable and easily exploited population in the crowded and polluted urban areas. Many of the *mang lui* live in migrant slums. Each of the larger coastal cities has a million or more migrants living in shantytowns, dormitories, or public places. Problems of homelessness and unemployment that were supposedly unknown in communist China have begun to openly plague these coastal boomtowns. Disoriented rural migrants often fall prey to urban gangs who recruit them for prostitution, smuggling, and other criminal activities. As long as China's economic growth races ahead at 10 percent a year or more, jobs are made available for many of the migrants. Those who become prosperous by rural standards serve as a magnet, attracting still more migrants. Only severe recession would succeed in changing this situation dramatically.

Meanwhile, the response of the coastal provinces to the migration problem is remarkably similar to the efforts of the United States to stem its tide of illegal aliens from Mexico. Guangdong has passed strict measures to prevent the hiring of migrant labor from outside the province. The Zhuhai Special Economic Zone, next to Macao, has erected a 24-mile fence to prevent migrant labor from crossing its border. Beijing's city government has passed a law to stem the flow of migrants, who are believed to commit the majority of crimes within the capital. The new law requires employers that hire workers from outside the city to pay a penalty of 100,000 yuan—over $11,000—for a residence permit. Individuals can purchase the permit for 50,000 yuan—a prohibitive amount, equal to roughly 16 years of wages for an average factory worker.[29]

Meanwhile, the grievances of the *mang lui* are building up. Many rural workers, lured by the promise of high wages, find out only after relocating to the city that they are victims of a scam. A typical sweatshop requires workers to live in a dormitory within the factory and then deducts room, board, and other expenses from their pay. The vast supply of poor, desperate *mang lui* means that employers have little incentive to treat employees generously.

Urban working conditions are often primitive by Western standards. In Guangdong province alone, 45,000 industrial accidents were reported during 1993, resulting in nearly 9,000 fatalities. China's coal sector is one of the world's most dangerous. In 1993, over 5,000 miners lost their lives in work-related accidents. Frequent tragedies occur due to employer neglect. In 1993, 87 workers died in a fire at a Shenzhen toy factory where government inspectors had accepted bribes to overlook the electrical problems that ultimately caused the blaze. Also overlooked were the barred windows and locked doors that prevented the employees—mostly young women—from escaping their dormitory. In another Shenzhen incident, 76 workers were killed in the collapse of a textile factory. A fire had gutted the building the day before, but workers were ordered back inside to salvage cotton bales.[30]

Such tragedies prompted an investigation in 1994 of seven foreign-funded enterprises in Guangdong province. State health inspectors found levels of benzene in the air eight to ten times higher than allowed by international standards. In three toy factories, 93 workers had been poisoned, four of whom died and eight of whom were permanently disabled. Three-fifths of the employees routinely work seven days a week, and many put in 10 to 12 hours a day.[31] The mass of dislocated workers, glad to get what jobs are available, have little recourse.

To combat these problems, Beijing has passed legislation designed to prevent labor abuse. Among the law's provisions are a minimum worker age of 16, a minimum wage, and a 44-hour maximum average workweek. As in many other areas of government policy, enforcement is uneven at best. Reports of child labor, employee strip searches, and other abuses continue.[32]

Poor labor conditions are not limited to foreign joint ventures, but few official reports of worker accidents surface from Chinese-owned firms. Occasionally, however, Beijing is forced to acknowledge such incidents, as it did in 1993 when 70 workers died in an explosion in Shenzhen. The enormous blast could not be hidden: the resulting mushroom cloud was visible across the border in Hong Kong.[33]

Economic growth and change do not benefit all equally. Reforms in China are creating winners and losers, a fact that statistics on the national economy do not reveal. Despite the great successes of certain regions and a general increase in the standard of living throughout the country, many people still live in absolute poverty. Although the number of people lacking basic necessities such as food, shelter, and clothing is falling, this portion of the population still amounts to roughly 100 million individuals, or one out of every 12 Chinese.[34]

Nevertheless, a large pool of eager laborers does have its positive side. Ex-farmers are the engine of China, providing a virtually inexhaustible supply of cheap labor that is helping to build the country. They are the reason why 5,000 factories can be under construction simultaneously in China's coastal provinces. Meanwhile, the flow of remittances from the migrants to their families is a major new source of income in poor rural areas. In 1993, migrants sent $138 million to one county in Sichuan province, more than the county's total economic output of $115 million.[35]

THE CONTINUING BURDEN OF COMMUNISM

The rapid pace of economic activity could well slow down in the years ahead. The continuing combination of rapid inflation, expanding corruption, and growing inequality may erode political support for the government's economic openness. Such problems could be compounded by the perennial shortcoming of authoritarian leadership: the inability to respond to popular grievances.

The government's difficulty in controlling inflation reflects both the shortcomings of China's political institutions and a reluctance to suffer the inevitable short-term consequences of the austerity typically required by antiinflation efforts. In theory, China's central bank—the People's Bank of China (PBOC)—is supposed to manage inflation by controlling the growth of the money supply. In practice, however, the PBOC has been unable to slow down rampaging money growth, resulting in a 12 percent annual average inflation rate over the decade from 1984 to 1994, and 24 percent inflation in 1994 alone.

The PBOC has been unable to achieve national price stability (or even predictability) because it lacks the basic powers of a modern central bank to control the flow of money and credit. For example, it does not set reserve requirements for individual banks and cannot independently purchase or sell government securities in the open market. Furthermore, the PBOC does not enjoy the autonomy of Western banks. It is required to fund the enormous government deficit through unrestricted loans to the many nationalized enterprises unable to cover their expenses with their own resources. Given the high rate of inflation and the low nominal interest rate (the latter set by government authorities), the real interest rate on PBOC loans is *negative*, further encouraging subsidized borrowers. This situation—coupled with the fact that most of the loans are never repaid—has led to uncontrolled monetary expansion.[36]

Beijing has attempted to increase the authority of the PBOC to control runaway inflation. Standing in the way of these reforms, however, is an entrenched network of several hundred thousand money-losing government-owned enterprises. These compete with privately and locally owned businesses for available resources and create an enormous drag on the economy. Despite the rapid progress of economic privatization in the coastal regions, nationally owned firms continue to produce almost one-half of China's industrial output. Many of these firms are run like government agencies, forced to cope with an extensive array of social responsibilities with no incentive to improve efficiency.

Shanghai Petrochemicals (SPC) is a good example. This refinery is required to provide employment for its 60,000 workers regardless of their performance. Because it is also charged with educating their children, it operates an elementary school, a high school, and a technical college. It is also responsible for employee medical care and maintains a staff of 2,000 medical personnel. SPC police guard the community, which is largely coterminous with the enterprise—and SPC counselors even help with marital disputes. To fund these activities, as well as traditional benefits such as pensions, SPC receives subsidies from the national treasury and loans from the PBOC.[37]

Besides being saddled with social responsibilities, state-owned firms also suffer from a lack of clearly defined property rights. When one of these firms earns profits, it has to decide whether to pay them out to employees or reinvest them in newer, more efficient capital. Unfortunately, lacking ownership of the firm's assets, managers have little incentive to reinvest its profits. Even if their investments succeed, there is no guarantee that the state will not seize the resulting profits.[38]

Even though they frequently purchase raw materials at government-subsidized prices, most of these socialist enterprises are money losers. As such, they rely on the PBOC's low-interest loans to remain solvent. These government-owned firms consume a rising fraction of China's investment capital (70 percent in 1993), despite their shrinking share of industrial output—down to less than 50 percent.[39] This diversion of funds keeps badly needed capital from the small but rapidly growing private sector at a critical stage in its development. By Beijing's own admission, investment in the private sector is twice as productive as investment in the state sector. The reality is probably even worse than that.[40] If the PBOC and other Chinese banks operated on capitalist principles, they would dramatically cut back their lending to these inefficient, state-owned firms. In China, however, the lender and the borrower are both instruments of the government, a situation that makes the profits and losses of each less relevant.

Government-owned firms continue to suffer from a host of traditional socialist ailments. Employee compensation is rarely linked to performance. Managers focus on numerical measures of output rather than on quality or customer needs, which leads to large-scale production of shoddy goods that are difficult to sell.

China's steel industry, in particular, is reeling from enormous stockpiles of low-grade steel products that cannot compete with superior and cheaper imports. As 90 percent of China's iron and steel industry is controlled by the state, Beijing has been forced to impose strict limits on steel imports in order to prevent large-scale bankruptcies.[41] Even the "reformed" state-run steel mills are woefully inefficient by Western standards. Consider Maanshan Iron & Steel Co., which has opened itself up to partial foreign ownership and trades on the Hong Kong stock exchange. Foreign capital has provided new, modernized equipment relative to other state-owned firms. Nevertheless, compared to a Western steel mill, Maanshan employs 11 times as many workers per ton of steel produced.[42]

On the positive side, we occasionally come across a rare example of a successful government-owned enterprise. An almost singular rarity, a PRC-owned firm that is genuinely making the transition is Yizheng Chemical Fiber, located east of Nanjing. Roughly a third of Yizheng's equity trades on the Hong Kong exchange. The company is China's largest maker of polyester, a hot commodity during a time of increasing textile and garment exports. With a market capitalization of over $1 billion, Yizheng has focused on modern production technology while keeping tight control over company credit. In 1994, Yizheng's net earnings were over $100 million, a figure confirmed by a U.S. Big Six accounting firm.

Still, among the thousands of state-owned firms, Yizheng is the exception. And even with its successes, Yizheng is still weighed down by its responsibilities to the local community: health care, law enforcement, education, etc.[43]

CONSTRAINTS ON FUTURE GROWTH

Even if China's government-owned firms successfully manage their transition and are able to cope with market forces, bottlenecks will still arise in key sectors such as agriculture, energy, and transportation if investment does not continue to pour into the region. China is already showing the strain of 15 years of very rapid economic growth. The lack of basic infrastructure is painfully apparent: barely one out of every 50 Chinese had a telephone in 1994, one of the lowest rates in the world. Demand for telecommunications service far outpaces the supply, and available systems are frequently out of order.[44]

Not surprisingly, pent-up consumer demand has caused prices to skyrocket. From 1989 to 1993, installation costs for local telephone service increased by up to 100 percent—to as much as

$1,000 a line. In some cities, installation fees are ten times the yearly income of an average factory worker. Nevertheless, demand is so great that consumers must wait more than six months before they get their turn.

Even if the Ministry of Posts and Telecommunications succeeds in achieving its ambitious goal of 15 percent annual growth in subscribers, only 5 percent of the Chinese population will have telephones by the year 2000. Even the prosperous urban areas will have only a 30 percent "teledensity" rate by this time, compared to virtually universal service in the United States.[45]

Shortages of infrastructure are not limited to telecommunications. Traffic bottlenecks are severe in many locations, raising doubts as to whether the transportation network of many regions can support further rapid growth. In late 1994, one of the authors found the traffic in Guangzhou very slow going—despite having the benefit of a motorcycle police escort. Many parents board their children at school during the week because it takes so long to bring them to school in the morning and pick them up at the end of the day.

The further expansion of production facilities will continue to test the nation's ability to deliver goods and people when and where they are needed. Logistical nightmares are easy to envision: components are involuntarily stockpiled in one city and the production of the end product halts in another city. Energy shortages, along with increasingly polluted air and water, will compound these problems.

Beijing has undertaken a massive effort to improve its infrastructure, but the needs are enormous. It is estimated that by 2004, China will require 20 new or expanded airports, 10,000 miles of rail, 30,000 miles of roads, 200 new port berths, and more than 100,000 megawatts of electric generating capacity. Spending on telecommunications gear in China, Hong Kong, and Taiwan totaled over $11 billion in 1995, more than Mexico, Brazil, India, Thailand, and Indonesia combined. China accounted for $8 billion of that figure, a fourfold increase from 1990.[46]

Despite its large population, China is still an overwhelmingly rural country. It has few equivalents to the huge metropolitan areas of more developed nations, or even those of poorer Third World countries. In a listing of the world's largest cities, mainland China's largest—Shanghai—ranks number 23, far below Tokyo, Seoul, New York, and Moscow, as well as Third World cities such as Calcutta, Karachi, and Lagos. Considering the conditions in some of those cities, China may consider itself fortunate.

However, booming economic growth has spurred a massive influx of foreign businesses into China's underdeveloped urban areas. Excess demand for office accommodations has driven rents sky-high, while geography constrains large-scale construction efforts in Hong Kong. Of the four most expensive places in the world to rent an office, three are located in Greater China: Shanghai, Beijing, and Hong Kong (Tokyo remains the most expensive). Rapidly developing Guangzhou ranks ninth. Rents may ease on the mainland in future years as supply catches up to demand. Until then, many foreign businesses will continue to operate from hotel rooms in order to cut costs.[47]

Many of the booming urban areas in China are unable to cope with a rapidly growing, increasingly wealthy population. The population of the Shenzhen Special Economic Zone rose from 30,000 in 1977 to over 2 million in 1992, and is continuing to expand, although at a slower rate. Cities built to accommodate bicycle and pedestrian traffic are proving incapable of supporting widespread automobile usage. In 1984, fewer than 100,000 vehicles drove on Beijing's streets; by 1994, the figure was 670,000, and it is expected to grow to 1.5 million by the year 2010. State-run postal offices are bureaucratic nightmares, marked by long queues and unreliable service.[48]

Nowhere are the strains of rapid growth more apparent than in the energy sector. Mainland China's energy production grew by nearly 5 percent a year between 1981 and 1991. That seems a brisk rate until we consider that real economic growth grew twice as fast and industrial expansion was almost four times as rapid. This inadequate increase in energy production has resulted in repeated electrical blackouts, especially in the coastal regions with their large amounts of new industrial investment. Coal continues to be China's primary source of energy, yet the rail and road networks needed to transport coal are severely underdeveloped. The mainland's road network is barely larger than it was 30 or 40 years ago, but the freight transported by road has grown by a factor of 250 during the same period.[49]

Perhaps more important than all of these problems is the lack of business infrastructure. As nations grow, the so-called "tertiary" employment sector becomes critical to economic success. This sector includes services such as banking, insurance, accounting, law, consulting, and other professions that do not create physical products but instead facilitate increasingly complex transactions. Three decades of communist rule—which measured its success in sheer physical output—effectively eliminated these services in China. Today, due to the lack of well-trained personnel, Chinese firms often contract out these activities to foreign experts. For example, when a Chinese company prepares to issue stock, U.S. accounting firms are retained to help convert the firm's books from communist era accounting to internationally accepted standards. At the Tsingtao Brewery, the first Chinese state enterprise to be directly listed on the Hong Kong stock exchange, this job took Arthur Andersen 6,000 hours.[50]

CONCLUSION

China's rapid economic growth has been accompanied by a host of problems: rising inflation, growing corruption, and the demand for political liberalization to accompany the economic reforms. The failure to deal with these issues has had such dramatic consequences as the bloodshed at Tiananmen Square. Even if the political pressures are contained, the economic shortcomings will be difficult to deal with.

An unusual combination of opportunities and pitfalls underlies China's future. Beyond the growth statistics lies an authoritarian government that exercises arbitrary power. Economically, China's business environment is treacherous. In the following chapters, we will examine the possibilities for balancing these striking pluses and minuses, particularly from the viewpoint of Western investors.

APPENDIX: MEASURING NATIONAL ECONOMIES

As noted earlier, conventional measures of national economies are being supplemented if not supplanted by purchasing power parity (PPP) measures. This appendix is devoted to detailing how these measurements are made, and their interpretation in the case of China.

The most ambitious effort to compile historical PPP figures of the gross domestic products of various countries is the Penn World Table, constructed by economists Robert Summers and Alan Heston. This table contains PPP-adjusted economic data for over 100 countries over the last 40 years.[51]

However, some controversy exists as to whether PPP figures are entirely accurate. Many economists believe that it is impossible to measure across different countries the precise value of goods that are not traded in world markets. Is a medical checkup by a doctor in the United States the same service as a checkup in Taiwan? Is a house in Britain the same good as a house in Japan?

Despite these complications, most economists consider the logic of PPP measurements to be superior to that of standard exchange rate analysis. Because of this, there have been recent efforts to create a uniform system by which purchasing power across countries can be compared.

One whimsical method of determining PPP exchange rates has been developed by *The Economist* magazine. The starting point is the notion in economic theory that, over the long run, exchange rates should converge to a rate that makes the prices of homogenous goods equal across different countries. *The Economist* examines the international pricing of one particularly well-known homogenous good: the Big Mac. By examining the price of a Big Mac in local currency, rough PPP exchange rates can be determined. Using these rates, the official value of the yuan severely underestimates its equivalent U.S. purchasing power. Applying

The Economist's exchange rate of 3.88 yuan to the dollar to China's GNP figures (2,404 billion yuan in 1992) yields $620 billion, a figure considerably lower than the more detailed PPP estimates developed by the World Bank, but also much higher than GNP figures based on official exchange rates.[52]

PART III

ENTER, WESTERN BUSINESS

CHAPTER 5

Western Investment in China

If you're too honest, you'll always lose out.
—A T-shirt on sale in Beijing

Doing business in a foreign country can be both risky and rewarding. This is especially the case in China, where everything seems to be on a huge scale—including the challenges and opportunities that face Western businesses. The difficulties are numerous, starting with the tremendous differences in language, customs, and the pace of everyday life. These obstacles are compounded by sharp divergences from Western legal systems, which hinder business contracts and transactions.

In the case of China, more so than elsewhere, informal local variations are often far more serious than formal legal hurdles because they cannot be anticipated. The combination of these obstacles creates a formidable—but not impenetrable—barrier to foreign businesses that want to participate in China's rapidly growing economy. Gene Kalhorn, senior vice president of marketing of Watlow, Inc., a St. Louis manufacturer of electronic controls, summed up the difficulties of foreigners doing business in China: "The experience we had in dealing with the Far East and

outside of the United States certainly did not prepare us for dealing with China. China is one of the most complicated business
environments I have ever dealt with".[1]

FOREIGN BUSINESS VENTURES

China began to open its markets to the outside world in 1978.
However, Beijing has adamantly refused to allow unrestricted
foreign investment in the mainland. The traditional fear is that
foreigners may somehow steal away the country's resources. In
this view, foreign investors "take the money and run," exploiting
the host country without adequately sharing the profits that are
generated.

Although naive, such sentiments are found not only in developing nations but also in economic superpowers such as the
United States. Witness the public outrage that surfaced in the
1980s at the news of Japanese purchases of well-known U.S.
real estate. (In retrospect, given the subsequent decline in property values, many Japanese investors may think that *they* were
the ones who were taken—by slick Americans.) On balance,
economists argue that foreign investment is mutually beneficial.
Inflows of foreign capital and new technology allow the host
country to create or expand industries that it would otherwise
have lacked the resources to support. In the process, substantial
local income and employment are created. Likewise, investors
benefit by harnessing inputs of land, labor, or natural resources
that are not present—or are far more expensive—in their native
countries.

Despite the many apparent benefits of foreign investment,
China's reluctance to allow foreign control of businesses is not
surprising in view of its long history of economic, political, and
military exploitation. As a result, Beijing has instituted economic
policies that strongly favor joint ventures—cooperative efforts
linking foreign investors with domestic firms. Usually, a limited
liability company is established in which both partners are responsible for the day-to-day management of the firm's operations. Both partners share the profits of the enterprise in direct

proportion to the amount they invested. Foreigners typically contribute the bulk of the cash and know-how. The Chinese provide tangibles such as the factory and its site, plus the intangible but necessary connections for dealing with the governmental agencies that approve joint venture production.

Equity joint venture contracts are typically designed to last between 10 and 30 years, with all assets reverting to the Chinese at the end of the agreement. Many of the contracts have renewal clauses, and most allow for the foreign partners to be compensated in some form for their assets.[2]

In general—there almost always are exceptions—foreign investors must own at least 25 percent of the equity of any joint venture in China. This policy is intended to ensure that foreigners maintain a serious interest in how the joint venture performs. In theory, foreign partners can own as much as 100 percent of the equity. In practice, the majority of joint ventures are Chinese-controlled, a much smaller percentage are foreign-controlled, and only a very small fraction fall under the classification of wholly foreign-owned enterprises (WFOEs).

Generally, WFOEs are allowed only in high-technology fields or in industries that intend to export all their production. Relative to joint ventures, WFOEs pay higher income taxes. Nevertheless, this form of venture has attracted many foreign investors who are reluctant to give up any control to an outside entity. Between 1989 and 1993, China approved almost 24,000 WFOEs with a combined contracted value of $39 billion.[3]

Like most governmental economic policies, the regulations that promote Chinese majority ownership are subject to what is known colloquially as the "inverse Beijing ratio." That is, they are less strictly enforced the further away one is from the capital.[4] Nevertheless, the guiding philosophy of the Chinese government regarding foreign investment is best summed up by Deng Xiaoping's statement that "in joint ventures with foreigners, 50 percent still belongs to socialism."[5] Mutual ownership and management of joint ventures not only satisfies the cultural desire for equality and fairness, but also allows the government to maintain firm control over foreign investments.

FORMAL RESTRICTIONS

A quintessential example of the Chinese government's desire to attract foreign capital and technology while maintaining ultimate authority over these resources is offered by the rapidly expanding telecommunications market. Virtually every major telecommunications firm in the world is investing heavily in China. All hope to tap into the largest unexploited market for telecommunications services.

Standing in their way is the Ministry of Posts & Telecommunications (MPT), the arm of the central government responsible for telecommunications development. The MPT has adamantly refused to allow foreign firms to operate local networks, warning that foreign control of telecommunications networks would endanger national security. Because of these concerns, foreign involvement has been restricted to sales of hardware and switching equipment (high-technology items that China cannot yet produce on its own) or to joint ventures that manufacture for export. Although the market for these items is potentially lucrative, the truly large-scale profits are to be made in system management. However, foreign command of this infrastructure would present a loss of political and social control that Beijing is unwilling to permit.

Rapidly changing technologies have allowed some Western firms to nibble away at the edges of the MPT monopoly. Shanghai's breakneck growth, particularly in the financial district of Pudong, has forced Beijing to consider foreign bids to operate telecommunications networks, including one from AT&T. Two other firms, SC&M International and Brooks Telecommunications, have teamed up with a Chinese company controlled by the army to construct a prototype fiber-optic network in Guangzhou.

In theory, foreign firms doing business in China are treated in about the same fashion as their domestic counterparts. In practice, foreigners pay more for services ranging from rental apartments to telephone bills to hotel rooms. Domestic airline tickets cost foreigners 50 to 60 percent more than they do Chinese citizens. Foreign joint venture advertising agencies must routinely pay 30 to 60 percent more than their domestic counterparts. Advertisements that promote foreign-made products can cost up to five times as much as advertisements for equivalent products that are manufactured locally.

Foreign companies are generally required to recruit their personnel through the Foreign Enterprise Service Company (FESCO), a state-run employment agency, and thus must pay higher salaries than their local competitors. Most of the prospective employees offered by FESCO are former state workers who lack sound work skills and have no foreign language ability. Joint ventures can circumvent this obstacle by recruiting at job fairs and local universities, but retaining good employees is difficult. Many companies offer extremely comprehensive benefit packages to hang onto qualified labor. Some offer beverage, lunch, clothing, laundry, transportation, and housing allowances—in addition to the standard medical and retirement contributions.[6]

Another restriction stipulates that foreign enterprises exporting goods to China must sell through a state-owned import-export company. While local customers pay that middleman in local currency, the import-export company's bank is supposed to remit the money to the foreign supplier in foreign exchange. However, the banks often find themselves short of funds, forcing some exporters to wait as long as six months. Companies try to get around the problem by obtaining a letter of credit. According to international practice, banks are supposed to pay when a letter of credit is presented. That happy state of affairs is not universally the case in China.[7]

Trade barriers contribute to a large and rapidly growing U.S. trade deficit with China. Since 1989, the U.S. excess of imports over exports has grown at the staggering rate of 40 percent a year, reaching $30 billion (or one-fifth of the total U.S. trade deficit) in 1994. In absolute terms, the trade deficit with China is second only to the deficit with Japan. In proportional terms, the imbalance is more severe. Japanese exports to the United States are double their imports from this country. In the case of China, exports to the United States outnumber imports by a ratio of three to one.

Foreign companies trying to export to China face serious impediments. Taxes on imports into China average a stiff 35 percent, customs requirements are vague, and potential competitors in the form of domestic nationalized industries are heavily subsidized. Indirectly, barriers to imports are an incentive for Western companies to invest directly in the Chinese market by establishing local manufacturing facilities—and thereby providing employment for local residents.

Import restrictions are not only severe but are also—like most laws in China—highly unpredictable. For example, Chinese tariffs on the same product may vary, depending on whether the product is eligible for a special exemption. If an item—notably one that involves advanced technology—is included in the government's economic plan, the tariff actually levied may be much lower than the published rate. Rates also differ from entry port to entry port. Local officials often negotiate special rates with Chinese customs officers. Increasingly powerful local bureaucrats who want to maximize their flexibility are less apt to publish local trade regulations.

As noted earlier, one rule of thumb holds: the farther away you are from Beijing, the greater the variability in the interpretation and enforcement of laws and regulations. The ability to obtain an import license, for example, may depend on the desire to protect local industry or the availability of foreign currency or the interest in technology transfer—and especially on the personal relationships between the enterprise doing the importing and a host of government officials.

Even foreign ventures that export from China are beginning to fall prey to Beijing's shifting loyalties. Once nurtured by special tax breaks, these ventures are now subject to a value-added tax. Furthermore, Beijing has repeatedly stated that the incentives offered to foreign investment in the Special Economic Zones will eventually be phased out. The rationale behind these changes is to push more industry and investment into the interior. This may be a worthy goal, but foreign investors are becoming increasingly nervous about committing their funds to a country where the rules of the game change without warning.[8]

Along these lines, a recent shift in import taxation policy

caused the price of some Toyota automobiles to triple. Despite a drastic reduction in sales, Toyota plans to open its first show-room on the mainland to illustrate its long-term commitment to the Chinese market.[9] Toyota's experience parallels that of many firms flocking to China that are making a long-term bet that China will eventually relax its restrictions on imports. If that does not occur, many firms may pack up and head home.

LANGUAGE BARRIERS

Other obstacles faced by Western businesses, although not for-mal, can be equally daunting. The language problems that U.S. firms must overcome to compete successfully in Chinese markets cannot be overemphasized. Of course, language differences are an obstacle to trade with most foreign countries. But the linguis-tic barrier is especially severe in Asia. Oriental languages are ex-tremely difficult for Westerners to learn. Compared to Chinese or Japanese, Russian is a close cousin of English. Western languages are based on the ancient Phoenician alphabet. Oriental lan-guages, in contrast, contain tens of thousands of characters, even though the spoken language has far fewer syllabic tones. Because of this, one sound can represent more than 100 characters, de-pending upon the inflection and tone of the speaker. This is a dif-ficult skill for foreigners to master.

Furthermore, Chinese is not so much a language as a *family* of languages. Mandarin is the mainland's official language, but liter-ally hundreds of dialects—including Cantonese and Fujianese—are spoken by China's different ethnic groups. This is not simply a matter of varying accents and local slang, as in the United States. If you speak only Mandarin, you cannot understand Can-tonese—and vice versa (even though the written versions are the same).

Relatively few Americans and Europeans are educated in Asian languages. Those fortunate enough to have some fluency in Chi-nese can capitalize on their knowledge, often vaulting over their peers. Ethnic Chinese with Western education are a hot com-modity in Western firms. Hong Kong in particular has seen a wave of "ABCs" (American-born Chinese) in recent years, sporting M.B.A.s from top U.S. schools. Nevertheless, these ABCs may still lack command of the local dialect.[10]

The language barrier facing Western business is further exacerbated by China's communist vocabulary, which lacks the specialized capitalist terminology necessary for complex business transactions. At the initiation of business meetings between Westerners and Chinese, days can be spent conveying the meaning of everyday business terms (such as profit and loss statements) or business protocols. Many English words, especially high-tech jargon, are extremely difficult to translate. Interpreters who can translate both technical terms and more colloquial language are rare.[11]

While it is hard to find qualified U.S. business executives trained in Chinese languages, it is also difficult for foreign-financed joint ventures to hire local citizens fluent in English. Because the Chinese typically work at the same firm for their entire career, there is little incentive for English speakers to jump ship for work at a riskier foreign venture. Even if they do, the probability that such employees will have any high-technology or management experience is small.

Even the largest U.S. firms find themselves unprepared for the language gap. In 1987, IBM commanded a large share of the personal computer market in China, but things quickly went sour when the firm discontinued its old PC line in favor of the newer PS/2. The new line was a disaster because it lacked the capability to easily connect with hardware that would allow it to understand and display Chinese characters. Competitors Compaq and AST Research Inc., whose computers supported Chinese language hardware, grabbed the market. These two companies continue to dominate sales of personal computers in China.[12]

CULTURAL BARRIERS

Cultural differences, although less concrete than language barriers, can also create an atmosphere that is hostile to foreigners. Southeast Asian culture, protocol, and modes of behavior differ greatly from those of Western nations. Language mastery is not sufficient to ensure the level of cultural fluency necessary to engage in successful business transactions, a fact often noted by Americans who deal in the region. A former U.S. trade negotiator recalls a Chinese banquet, where he was served fried scorpions with stingers intact: "It was both a joke and a test. You had to laugh and pass the test to maintain the fiction of cordiality."[13]

Such cultural differences are daunting to many foreigners, especially when formalized by governmental regulation. For example, the Chinese government periodically cracks down on Western religions, sharply limiting the religious activities of foreigners and forbidding churches to engage in unauthorized activities or ones financed from overseas. Government officials fear that informal religious activities may replace the official, state-sponsored religions—Buddhism, Taoism, some Protestant denominations, Roman Catholicism, and Islam. Many people consider the government-approved churches to be, in effect, extensions of the Communist Party.

The formal government rules concerning religion are strict. Foreigners must not establish religious organizations or schools, recruit followers, or conduct any other proselytizing activities among the Chinese people. In early 1994, a delegation of Christians in the village of Tong Zhuang in Fang Cheng county was detained for four days. All their valuables and more than $5,000 in cash were confiscated.[14] As a result of such incidents, foreigners usually hold their own, very private services.

Government actions that seem unnecessarily harsh and arbitrary, such as those that took place in Tong Zhuang, must be viewed in a larger context. China's xenophobia reflects a fear that has considerable justification in historical experience. At a time when most governments are trying so hard to combat international drug trafficking, we must remind ourselves that, from 1839 to 1842, Britain battled China in the first Opium War. Back then, "enlightened" England was willing to go to war in order to break China's restrictions on trade imports, including its ban on the importation of opium, much of which was produced in British India. The Treaty of Nanjing ended the war by forcing the cession of Hong Kong Island and the opening of five ports to trade (Guangzhou, Xiamen, Fuzhou, Ningbo, and Shanghai). The second Opium War, fought from 1856 to 1860, pitted China against both Britain and France. The terms of settlement followed a familiar pattern of trade concessions and large indemnities, including the loss of the Kowloon Peninsula.

In 1894–1895, China suffered a crushing defeat in the Sino-Japanese War. The Treaty of Shimonoseki, which settled the conflict, called for ceding Taiwan, the Pescadore Islands, and the Liaodong Peninsula to Japan. A few years later, the Boxer Rebellion (1898–1901) was essentially a reaction against the imposition of foreign religions and culture, with attacks made mostly on churches and missionaries.

Foreign aggression continued into the twentieth century. In 1907, secret treaties signed by the Russians and Japanese carved Manchuria into spheres of influence. In 1931, Japan invaded and occupied Manchuria. After World War II, the United States, Britain, and the Soviet Union signed the Yalta Pact, which legitimized for a time the Soviet occupation of Manchuria.

Such humiliations have imprinted themselves indelibly upon the minds of most Chinese. During Deng Xiaoping's negotiations with Margaret Thatcher in 1982 over the future status of Hong Kong, he made it clear that China would not accept "another Li Hongzhang." This was a reference to the Chinese official who, in 1898, signed away the remainder of the Hong Kong area (including the "New Territories") to the British.[15]

This fear of exploitation has been the rationale behind many formal regulations that restrict foreign investors. Beijing has set an arbitrary 12 to 15 percent maximum rate of return on equity in new power production investments funded by foreigners, despite the country's growing need for new sources of energy. The government has also shown an extreme reluctance to approve new joint venture power plants. These policies stem from the belief that foreigners have been making too much money on power projects, presumably at China's expense. Foreigners take the opposite view: investing there is a high-risk proposition and should therefore earn an equally high return. Only after several major providers of capital threatened to withdraw from the mainland to seek more profitable opportunities in other Southeast Asian countries did Beijing ease its maximum return policy a bit. Some investors are now allowed to earn up to 20 percent. Nevertheless, the fact that any such restrictions exist *at all* is troubling, particularly when they can change so dramatically in such a short period of time.

If the Chinese are wary of foreign intentions, Westerners are often baffled by the invasion of Chinese culture into business transactions. The practice of *feng shui* illustrates the cultural chasm separating Western business managers from their Chinese counterparts. Somewhat like astrology, *feng shui* attempts to divine future outcomes from natural occurrences—such as lunar cycles or numerical patterns. Many of the largest firms in Taiwan, Hong Kong, and China employ mystic experts to identify propitious times for making investments, opening new businesses, and making other strategic decisions. More practically, *feng shui* can provide an "out" from an awkward business situation or a scapegoat for a deal that goes sour.

Even the most powerful and successful Chinese business entrepreneurs do not ignore the divinations of *feng shui* and other mystical practices. Ethnic Chinese magnate Liem Sioe Liong, whose Indonesian-based trade and finance empire has placed him among the richest people in the world, continues to live in a modest home in an unfashionable neighborhood in Jakarta. Liem believes the house has brought him luck, and he has bought up other properties along the street for his children.[16]

In Hong Kong, as elsewhere, personalized license plates are widely sought after. The Hong Kong government began auctioning off lifetime rights to plates in 1973, a process that has netted it over HK$300 million. In 1994, tycoon Albert Yeung broke the record by paying HK$13 million for a single-digit plate. Although in the United States one would expect the number 1 to be the record breaker, Yeung's plate reads "9," the number that signifies "eternity" in China. Furthermore, the Cantonese pronunciation of "nine" sounds like "dog," extra good luck in the year of the dog.[17]

U.S. architectural firms attempting to crack the booming sky-scraper market in cities such as Shanghai, Hong Kong, and Taipei have had to work around not only administrative mazes—building designs can require over 100 jurisdictional approvals, or "chops"—but also the cultural nuances of doing business in Greater China. The $400 million Jin Mao hotel and office tower designed by Skidmore, Owings & Merrill for the financial district of Shanghai has incorporated numerology into its basic design. The lucky number 8 surfaces in the building's 88 floors and in the mathematical ratio 1:8, which repeats itself throughout the structure. The Bank of China in Hong Kong opened on August 8, 1988—that is, on 8/8/88.[18] (The careful reader will note that there are eight chapters in this book as well!)

It is easy to dismiss such practices as cultural backwardness, but Westerners tend to overlook their own superstitions. Many Western hotels, for example, avoid identifying a thirteenth floor. Airlines do not label a thirteenth row of seats. In any event, practices such as *feng shui* are an integral part of Chinese business culture and even large international firms treat them with respect. When one American bank listed "geomancy fees" of several thousand U.S. dollars on its expense sheet for a new office in Hong Kong, its headquarters complained. Only after the paramount importance of *feng shui* was explained was the payment approved.[19]

LEGAL UNCERTAINTY

Other barriers to doing business in China arise from shortcomings in its still primitive legal system, which is rarely able to cope with the major disputes that arise between companies and government—or simply between companies—in a market society. The lack of "transparency" in the labyrinth of governmental regulations is especially discouraging to foreign firms trying to do business in China. Western businesses find that many rules and regulations are not published or have been changed without warning. In 1994, the General Accounting Office reported that its in-depth interviews of 33 U.S. companies revealed that "lack of transparency" was the most frequently expressed concern about doing business in China.

Along these lines, China maintains hidden quotas and obscure regulations that effectively keep out Western intellectual property products such as films, records, and tapes. In 1994, the International Intellectual Property Alliance claimed that China maintained an informal quota on foreign recordings of approximately 120 foreign record releases a year. The effect of these quotas is compounded by an apparent ban on foreigners participating in joint ventures to produce and distribute recorded music in China.

Western firms must also negotiate a constantly changing maze of government regulations. In 1994, after pursuing negotiations for two major joint ventures, General Electric was informed by Beijing that foreigners would no longer be allowed majority ownership in any power generation venture. Inconsistent tax policies are another hazard to foreign business. In 1994, the Finance Ministry issued a ruling that prevented some foreign-funded companies (those set up after 1993) from getting refunds on the taxes paid on raw materials used for exports. Numerous complaints were made that this unfairly favored local companies, which would continue to receive the refunds. Later in the year, a recision of the ruling was announced.[20]

China's hunger for technology has helped to create a system of constantly shifting regulations that prevent many Western firms from making long-range plans. The automotive industry is a good example of Beijing's tendency to welcome foreign investment when the domestic industry is clearly inadequate, but then to steadily force an increase in the local content of production. China's auto industry is perhaps the most fragmented in the world. Its more than 200 assembly plants have an annual production capacity ranging from 100 vehicles in small garage factories to 150,000 vehicles in modern joint venture facilities. The component producers are even more widely scattered, numbering in the thousands.

In the mid-1980s, aware that the domestic industry was unlikely to meet the rising demand anticipated for the near future, government authorities permitted investments by Volkswagen and American Motors (the latter since taken over by Chrysler). To protect domestic production and to minimize the outflow of foreign exchange, Beijing imposed a system of import licenses, quotas, and high tariffs. China's tariff on full-sized passenger cars is now a whopping 220 percent.

The China National Automotive Industry Corporation (a branch of the Ministry of Machine-Building Industry) expects each auto assembler to reach 40 percent local content by the third year of production and 60 percent by the fourth year. All domestic assemblers are expected to achieve 80 percent local content by their eighth year of production. As an incentive, a vehicle manufacturer that meets the 80 percent local content target pays a duty of 32 percent on its imported components rather than the normal 50 percent. Although the newest joint ventures have virtually no domestic content, some of the older enterprises report substantial proportions—58 percent in the case of Chrysler's Beijing Jeep, 53 percent for the Guangzhou Peugeot, 47 percent for the Tianjin Daihatsu, and 37 percent for the First Autoworks Audi.

Enforcement of local content regulations has been, to put it mildly, uneven. Some foreign auto ventures are allowed to count components purchased in China toward their local content requirement—even if the item is an import bought from a trading company.[21] This, of course, is another example of the ability of Chinese government officials to cut corners—when they want to.

Beijing has also declared that it will not approve any new foreign joint venture automobile plants until 1997, so that the local car industry can receive preferential government support. Even after that date, Beijing insists that local businesses will maintain majority control over all new automobile assembly plants. Companies such as General Motors, Ford, Chrysler, and Toyota have been informed that they will not be granted any additional production licenses until they begin manufacturing their parts on the mainland. Among the established companies that will benefit from this lack of competition is Volkswagen, which has shifted to locally manufactured parts.

In early 1995, Beijing began an effort to formalize rules on foreign investment by means of a catalogue entitled *Guiding Foreign Investment in Industries*. The result may be akin to industrial policy in Western countries. In both instances, the central government determines the sectors of the economy in which it wants private companies to invest. In the case of China, the proposed guidelines focus on agriculture, infrastructure, and high technology as the sectors of the economy to be favored with tax incentives and easier approval procedures. In essence, the catalogue makes official and open some of the informal policies that Beijing has been following in recent years.

Likewise, foreign businesses will continue to be barred from investing in such strategic areas as telecommunications services, media, and weapons production. In many other cases, the rules will continue to leave ample room for the ambiguity so beloved by bureaucrats involved in the approval process. Refrigerator manufacturing, for example, would probably be turned down in view of the general glut, but refrigerators with new technology might pass muster.[22]

PROPERTY RIGHTS AND CONTRACT LAW

Fundamental property rights in China are weak and sporadically enforced. Under China's constitution, land, factories, natural resources, and other physical assets belong to the state. The decentralization of government in recent years raises doubts as to whether ultimate ownership of individual assets rests with the central government or with increasingly powerful regional units. This state of affairs leads to frequent battles among government agencies over which one has the right to enter into a particular joint venture with a foreign company.

Asia Minerals Corporation of Canada, for example, signed a letter of intent in 1993 to invest in a lead, zinc, and silver mine in Shaanxi province, believing that it had a clear go-ahead. After all, it was dealing with a provincial enterprise that supposedly represented the interests of the provincial government, the China National Nonferrous Metal Industry Corporation of Beijing

(CNNMC), and its local affiliate. But, in 1994, CNNMC claimed control of the mine and asserted its sole right to negotiate with potential foreign partners, introducing new uncertainty into the entire enterprise.

This example illustrates the wide differences between the formal provisions of Chinese law and its actual practice. Many regulations are unwritten and frequently can be waived by local officials. But how can Western investors *know* when regulations can be waived and when they cannot? If they bet wrong, their agreements may be null and void later on in the negotiating process.

Differences in the administration of contract law vividly illustrate the difficulties Westerners confront when making business deals in China. In the United States, a signed contract (unless coerced) is legally binding. In China, most major contracts must be approved by the government. For example, the Association of Light Industries approves contracts signed in the leather, furniture, and clothing industries. Failure to obtain this approval makes a signed contract null and void. This type of governmental approval is not unheard of in some U.S. markets: defense contractors are routinely required to obtain approval from the government before selling weapon systems to foreign firms. In the great majority of U.S. markets, however, sellers do not face such constraints.

Horror stories abound of foreign business deals in China that are closed with signed contracts, only to be voided later by government officials that offer neither explanation nor compensation. Because of these uncertainties, negotiating with potential joint venture partners can be extraordinarily difficult. Foreigners are never certain that a contract provision once agreed upon will not be amended unilaterally by the Chinese partner.

This situation arises largely because of fundamentally different attitudes toward a business contract. The Westerner views it as a future commitment. The Chinese counterpart sees it as a description of the current situation and merely a plan for the future. According to the latter, the contract needs to be updated and modified as the situation changes. The problems arising from this basic difference in conception are compounded by the fact that, as a practical matter, foreigners have little effective recourse in Chinese courts.

All these factors contribute to the dilemma facing even the largest, most important investors in China: how to develop a long-term corporate strategy in a business climate where contracts can be overturned at the whim of the central authorities, and where overtly preferential treatment is given to investors with the best *guanxi*.

Efforts by Beijing to tighten up the rules that govern business transactions are often precise on paper but vague in implementation. In 1994, China's first Company Law took effect. This law establishes regulation of securities, accounting rules, and enforcement of judicial decisions. It also provides for limited liability. This is surely a step in the right direction, but the absence of a body of case law makes it only a modest start. According to attorney James D. Zirin, who has lectured to Chinese lawyers at Shanghai University, the Chinese court system is capricious and, he adds ominously, "presumptively corrupt."[23]

Even viewed in the most favorable light, much of the new law is so fresh that it is untested in any real-world case. If a foreign investor holds stock in a publicly traded Chinese firm that goes bankrupt, that individual holds—in theory—partial claim to the firm's assets. In reality, such a claim has yet to be made. Many fear that central or local authorities would simply seize the assets. Even more nettlesome is the possibility of a contract dispute between a foreign firm and a state-owned (or military-owned) enterprise. The Palace Hotel in Beijing is managed by a joint venture consisting of a foreign consortium and the People's Liberation Army. If a dispute arises, which army general do the investors sue? And even if they succeed, how do they collect? In the final analysis, a foreigner must rely primarily on trust and negotiation, rather than on litigation, when disputes arise.

Such uncertainty in the business climate is especially treacherous for foreigners, who lack the language and cultural skills necessary to negotiate creatively with their Chinese partners. Contracts between foreigners and mainland Chinese investors do not possess the implicit guarantees of performance contained in those signed by members of the bamboo network, among whom repeated interaction facilitates trust. Because of this, Western firms are strongly inclined to invest in short-term, lower-risk projects, a fact that creates a further advantage for overseas Chinese entrepreneurs.

The juxtaposition of rigid formal law and its very personalized administration creates great complexity for foreign investors. The effort to privatize real estate illustrates the importance of personal and political connections. Technically, there is no real estate market in China, at least not in the Western sense of the word. Land belongs to "all the people." However, in a creative sidestepping of formal law, the government allows its citizens to trade in the right to *use* the land, sometimes in perpetuity. These property rights are often transferred to private citizens in a disturbingly arbitrary manner. The price system has much less to do with these allocations than do *guanxi* and political favoritism. The overall goal of land privatization is a noble one, but the allocation process reeks of corruption as entrepreneurs grease the palms of government bureaucrats with expensive gifts.

Most Western firms missed the boom in the real estate market of the late 1980s, when Beijing first began issuing long-term land leases to developers. Despite governmental assurances, American and European investors were wary of sinking large amounts of fixed capital in China. Questions regarding foreclosure, land ownership, and political stability were left unanswered, causing many Western firms to wait while investors from Hong Kong and Taiwan flooded the market with new buildings. Today, more Western firms are entering the market, but they may be too late: many analysts warn of looming oversupply as earlier projects near completion.[24]

Some analysts believe that, were it not for the presence of the bamboo network, the lack of property rights protection and enforcement of contracts would limit foreign investment in China to all but a trickle.

PROTECTING INTELLECTUAL PROPERTY RIGHTS

Intellectual property protection such as trademarks and copyrights is flagrantly violated in the PRC. Imitation Bausch & Lomb

Ray Ban sunglasses are sold as "Ran Bans." The packaging of Kellogg's Corn Flakes is mimicked on boxes of "Kongalu Corn Strips" by means of identical type fonts, color layout, and the use of the widely recognized Kellogg rooster. Near-exact copies of other consumption goods, such as "Cologate" toothpaste, are widespread. Lux brand soap is so popular that there are many copies, all with the same colored wrapper and named "Lix" or "Lud." Even Chrysler, one of the first Western firms to establish itself in the Chinese market, continues to be burned by piracy of its Jeep copyright and technology. More bizarrely, some Chinese firms use internationally known names on products that do not correspond to the trademarks: for example, "Rambo" brand facial tissues or "Pepsi-Cola" biscuits.[25]

One reason such problems persist is that China's trademark law is not well suited to deal with many popular Western products. When foreign trademarks are translated into Chinese, the firm can use either a phonetic or a conceptual method. The phonetic method uses Chinese characters that mimic the sound of the foreign word. The Chinese version of McDonald's is pronounced *mac-don-lo*. In contrast, the conceptual method of trademark translation uses Chinese characters to convey the meaning of the foreign name. Thus, the Eveready brand name is translated into characters meaning "perpetual ready cat brand."

Both types of translation pose difficulties for Western firms. Phonetic translations run the risk of confusion or negative imagery. The three characters that represent McDonald's literally mean "wheat," "when," and "labor," words that are nonsensical in describing the product. Different dialects within China compound the problem. The brand of watercolors called Chillo, if phonetically translated into the characters pronounced *chi-lo* in Mandarin, would mean "seventh floor," which is nonsensical but at least does not bear any negative connotation. When spoken, however, the sound "chi-lo" carries a different meaning in Cantonese: "crazy guy."[26]

Occasionally, firms enjoy the good fortune of marketing a product whose name can be translated phonetically *and* conceptually. In the 1920s, Coca-Cola was introduced in China as *kou-*

ke-kou-la, which roughly translated as "a thirsty mouth and a mouth of candle wax." The name was later changed to *ke-kou-ke-le*, meaning "a joyful taste and happiness." The change significantly improved Coca-Cola's Chinese sales.[27]

The difficulties associated with trademark translations are compounded by product nicknames. Quaker Oats products are known by consumers as "old man brand." Toblerone chocolate is called "triangle brand" because of its distinctive packaging. Wrigley chewing gum is known as "white arrow brand." Western companies like to obtain trademark rights to these nicknames, in order to prevent the marketing of copycat products. In the United States, such nicknames become common-law trademarks. Under Chinese law, however, the first company to register the nickname receives trademark protection. Western companies rarely learn of their product's nickname until it is too late—local distributors and retailers have already registered it preemptively.[28]

Many American firms have been hit hard by the lack of intellectual property protection in China. Only one out of 12 companies surveyed by the General Accounting Office in 1994 reported a satisfactory experience when trying to secure the enforcement of their property rights. In 1991, DuPont opened a factory in Shanghai to produce agricultural chemicals. Local businesses filched the formula for DuPont's rice herbicide and produced it without paying any royalties. Nevertheless, DuPont is persevering, entering into a joint venture with a local partner in Shanghai. The chairman of the company has also met with China's president Jiang Zemin to stress the importance of safeguarding the patents of foreign manufacturers.

The risk of losing patent secrets is heightened by Chinese demands that foreign firms share their know-how as a condition for doing business in the country. Whether forced by government or not, the shift of technology from the West to Southeast Asia is perhaps inevitable in the years ahead. The underlying skills in China are so great that Western firms are likely to create rivals, even while they are developing the world's major new market. In a dynamic sense, a firm's best response is to develop new technology at a faster pace than its Chinese competitors can assimilate the existing technology.

However, this strategy may be of little use to firms that discover Chinese counterfeiters producing *identical* copies of Western technology with very little, if any, delay. Taped copies of the hit movie *The Lion King* were sold in Beijing long before the film's official release on videotape in the United States. Virtually all the computer software used in China is copied and distributed illegally. Some of the problems are truly fundamental and their solutions quite elusive. Although other Asian nations are also major offenders, China is a particularly troublesome case. According to William P. Alford, director of East Asian Legal Studies at Harvard Law School, government officials in China do not have a basic respect for the rule of law. They lack a consciousness of the rights of people and maintain a weak court system. Widespread governmental corruption also prevents strict enforcement of patent and copyright laws.[29]

The high level of corruption is underscored by the fact that, though the identities of the companies that produce these illegal goods is common knowledge, most of the perpetrators continue to go unpunished. U.S. trade officials have visited some of the larger counterfeit operations to evaluate the situation firsthand. The names and addresses of the major manufacturers of counterfeit compact discs have been given to the Chinese government, but little action has been taken. Many of these factories are owned by overseas Chinese investors who bring in relatives of Communist Party members as partners. The bulk of enforcement has been in the form of crackdowns on the politically weak street vendors—not on the far more important factories that produce the counterfeits. A dramatic exception to such lax enforcement occurred in early 1995, in an effort to head off retaliatory sanctions by the United States (see Chapter 6).

Meanwhile, compact disc factories in southern China produce up to 80 million counterfeits a year, most of which are believed to be exported throughout Asia. Digital recording technology helps make nearly perfect copies of the most popular Western recordings. These copies sell on the street for only $2 in a matter of days after the original's release.[30]

Microsoft contends that the vast majority of its products in use in China, even those used by the government, are counterfeits. Of far greater concern is the fact that high-quality fakes—those that come in look-alike packaging, sometimes even bearing a counterfeit Microsoft hologram—are being exported from China to other countries. Such unauthorized exports erode sales in other markets throughout the world. Microsoft has pressed Beijing to crack down on such rampant piracy, with little success. Even when counterfeiters are arrested, the usual practice is for them to pay modest fines that do not deter them or others.

Some companies find themselves in a technological race against copyright violators. Because of the proliferation of counterfeit holograms, 3M has attached light-sensitive stickers that display the company's logo on boxes of computer discs sold in China. 3M credits the new technology with reducing piracy of its products from 50 percent to less than 20 percent.[31]

In response to continuing government and business complaints from Western countries, China has tried to improve its rudimentary legal system. Since 1991, it has instituted its first Copyright Law and adopted the Regulation on Punishing Copyright Violators, and it has joined the Bern Convention on Protecting Literature and Artistic Works, the World Copyright Convention, and the Convention on Protecting Recording Products from Unauthorized Duplication. Copyright tribunals have been established in Shanghai, as well as in Guangdong, Fujian, and Hainan provinces. From a formal standpoint, China has rapidly established a system of intellectual property rights that it took Western nations decades to develop.[32] Implementation is quite another matter.

The administration of law is increasingly being pushed down to the level of provincial and city court systems. However, many provinces do not enforce the laws passed by Beijing, while others lack qualified judges who fully understand the subtleties of complex legal arguments. Furthermore, since legal decisions are not published, there is little consistency among rulings. This problem is exacerbated by a bureaucratic leviathan that often seems to be biased against foreigners. Westerners seeking redress can wait months for an initial court hearing. The Chinese government blames these delays on a lack of manpower. American authorities suspect otherwise, pointing to the Ministry of Internal Trade's 600,000 employees.[33] Reluctant to trust the Chinese court system, foreigners frequently demand that an arbitration clause be inserted into any joint venture contract. However, local courts often overturn these arbitration agreements.

Some modest progress is being made. The Beijing People's Intermediate Court has accepted lawsuits by several major U.S. software companies—including Microsoft and Lotus—that accuse Chinese companies of illegal copying, distribution, and sale of software. Beijing's crackdown on distributors of pirated compact discs is beginning to pay off. One spectacular raid in a Guangzhou shopping mall netted a million counterfeit CDs.[34]

CORRUPTION AND CONFUSION

The toughest obstacle encountered by foreign business executives is the pervasive influence of personal relationships. As noted in Chapter 2, one of the durable aspects of Chinese life is the important role of the family, including friends and relatives who are part of the extended family or clan. From the viewpoint of competitive private enterprise, there is a darker side to this bonding. Deals, particularly the more lucrative ones, are made mainly with family and friends.

A sobering view of this phenomenon is provided by Harvard Professor Ezra Vogel, who studied the Special Economic Zones for a 1989 book on Guangdong.[35] More recently, he revisited that province and came away with a cluster of negative impressions: pervasive official favoritism, inside deals (often involving the children of Communist Party chieftains), and outright bribery. Opening China to foreign investment has given tremendous authority to "gatekeepers." These are officials with the ability to either ease or obstruct access to employees, markets, facilities, and a host of special governmental approvals.

When property rights are unclear, local government officials wield enormous arbitrary power in granting land-use rights, approving joint ventures, or simply controlling the local police force. Judicial authorities lack the ability to arbitrate disputes between parties or to rule on complaints against government officials. Corruption is unavoidable. Bribes grease the wheel of bureaucracy and business–government transactions reek of favoritism. A climate of corruption and insider dealing is pervasive.

Because the communists are still manning the political engine of China, many party members profit from rapid economic change by using their political power to approve or deny requests from private enterprises. Gaps between controlled and market prices tempt state officials to profiteer. For example, the state price for coal was recently listed at 70 yuan/ton, while the free market price was 180 yuan.[36] Government bureaucrats with the necessary authority or *guanxi* exploit these price differentials to earn massive, quick profits.

Even when private companies are allowed to establish a presence in China, most of their resources—employees, raw materials, credit, and housing—remain firmly in the control of the government and the Communist Party bureaucracy. This creates opportunities for delay, confusion, misunderstanding, and corruption. These problems often can be "fixed" by members of the families of senior party leaders who act as go-betweens. However, many more government departments claim to have authority over any given area than actually do. In the event of disputes, legal procedures are of limited effectiveness.

The degree of corruption is exemplified in one of the poorest provinces, Anhui. In 1994, the Chinese government announced that more than 300,000 officials, about one-fifth of all Anhui public officials, had been caught siphoning off or misusing a total of 826 million yuan ($143 million). Few of these individuals have been prosecuted, however.

More recently, however, there has been a wave of corruption crackdowns on even top-level officials. In one widely publicized case, Zhou Guanwu, chairman of Capital Iron and Steel Corporation and a close friend of Deng Xiaoping, resigned in 1995 under pressure from anticorruption authorities. Zhou's son was subsequently arrested on charges of economic and commercial crimes, illustrating that even the best-connected businesspeople can fall prey to the shifting alliances of China's Communist Party.

In another case involving father and son, Beijing's CCP chief Chen Xitong was fined and arrested on corruption charges following the suicide of Wang Baosen, Beijing's vice mayor, who had been accused of siphoning off more than $25 million in public money for himself, his younger brother, his mistress, and others. Chen's son, once considered a CCP "princeling," was also arrested in the investigation of shady real estate deals.

The aging of Deng and the resultant jockeying for position on the part of potential successors helps to explain the more activist policy. In any event, corruption continues to rank at the top of the complaints of Chinese citizens.[37]

In a more technical area, China's quest to amass foreign exchange reserves—combined with its reluctance to allow foreign firms to enter domestic markets—has created a massive system of trade subsidies to domestic firms and barriers to foreign companies. Tariff rates on consumer goods are very high: 150 percent for cigarettes, 120 percent for beer and cosmetics, and 100 percent for cassette players, refrigerators, TVs, and video games.[38]

Predictably, such high tariffs have created a large and prosperous smuggling trade, particularly between Hong Kong and Guangdong. Nearly half the consumer electronic goods sold in Hong Kong—TVs, VCRs, and air conditioners—are believed to have been smuggled into the mainland. The smugglers are well organized and high-tech, often utilizing radar and night-vision equipment to avoid customs authorities. Some are rumored to operate with the cooperation of Guangdong law enforcement officials.[39]

All governments suffer from corruption to some degree, but in China the problem is particularly prevalent. During the summer of 1994, officials in the inland province of Hubei diverted over $2 million in government funds intended for flood relief to the purchase of smuggled luxury sedans. The relative importance of these "transactions" can be appreciated when we note that the average income of a rural Chinese citizen is only a little over $100 a year. Despite severe penalties—embezzlers are routinely executed—corruption continues on a large scale. Since 1992, three major Chinese banks have discovered internal computer embezzlement operations that illegally disbursed over $8 million to private accounts throughout China. All eight conspirators were sentenced to death. In 1994, the chairman of a state-owned firm was executed for embezzling over $326,000 to pay off gambling debts in Macao.[40]

Smugglers continue to develop ingenious methods to skirt the letter of the law. Chinese regulations allow travelers to bring in small, duty-free quantities of consumer goods such as beer, soft drinks, and soap. Trading companies have cropped up at high-volume border crossings to exploit this loophole. Imported products are shipped in bulk to Macao and unloaded literally yards from the mainland border. There the large shipments are broken down and distributed among waiting travelers, who pay a deposit equal to the retail value of the products. After crossing the border, they report to a collection site where they exchange the products for their deposit plus a small fee. Some Macanese make this a full-time profession.[41]

Smuggling has become so pervasive that it has encouraged the development of market forces in the coastal areas. Competition from illicit traders who offer such relatively sophisticated products as air conditioners and refrigerators has pushed mainland manufacturers to improve their product lines.[42]

Ironically, Western firms that set up shop on the mainland find that their stiffest competition comes not from local competitors but from their own products smuggled across China's notoriously loose borders. Beijing's complex system of tariffs, taxes, and export incentives makes it more expensive to sell domestically produced goods then to smuggle in products from overseas. For example, there are stiff duties on imported parts and raw materials used to produce goods for the domestic Chinese market. As a result, many firms "export" to Hong Kong, where their goods are promptly smuggled back to the mainland. Such roundabout transactions are not only a hassle for U.S. firms that want to sell to China's domestic market. They also cost Beijing tax revenue and force payment of foreign currency for products that are actually produced domestically.[43]

ADVANTAGES ENJOYED BY THE BAMBOO NETWORK

Many Western firms are unwilling or unable to overcome the language, cultural, and legal barriers to doing business in China. While recognizing the ultimate potential of the Chinese market, these companies are taking a "wait and see" attitude, delaying until further market reforms are made and a more westernized business climate is created. Overseas Chinese entrepreneurs, in contrast, have not been as cautious. They have managed to circumvent many of the problems facing Western business. On occasion, members of the bamboo network have actually turned China's treacherous business environment to their advantage, helping them maintain an advantage over their Western counterparts.

A prime example of this phenomenon is McDonald's recent contract dispute with Beijing. In 1992, McDonald's opened what would become its busiest restaurant only two blocks away from Tiananmen Square at one of Beijing's most heavily traveled intersections. McDonald's had secured a 20-year lease on this prime location. In November 1994, however, McDonald's was informed that it would have to vacate the site so that Hong Kong real estate magnate Li Ka-shing could erect his $1.2 billion Oriental Plaza complex of commercial, office, and residential properties (as a consolation, McDonald's was "guaranteed" a spot in Mr. Li's plaza after its completion in 1998).

That a powerful Western corporation such as McDonald's could experience such difficulty is proof of the bamboo network's influence within the region. In addition to cultural and linguistic factors, the maze of formal and informal barriers to doing business in China confers significant advantages on those with the proper *guanxi*—or business connections. Thus, the children of Beijing leaders (the "princelings") develop close business relationships with foreign businesses. They do have a substantial amount of influence to offer.

The youngest son of Deng Xiaoping, Deng Zhifang, controls a Hong Kong company that builds shopping centers across China (a business that requires many governmental permissions). A son-in-law, He Ping, is a director of two companies in Hong Kong specializing in property and insurance. Another son-in-law, Wu Jian Chang, is the chairman of two Hong Kong property companies.

The term *guanxi* goes beyond Western ideas of networking or business favoritism. Rather, *guanxi* implies the sidestepping of traditional regulatory or contractual processes to seize a business opportunity. For example, it can take months for an outsider to accomplish even the most mundane business activity in China. The simple act of installing a phone can require half a year to obtain numerous approvals from local officials. But for somebody with the proper *guanxi*, approval can be obtained in a matter of days. In an uncertain business climate, personal relationships take precedence over formal procedures. The benefit to Chinese family and clan members—compared to Western foreigners—is obvious.

This is not to say that overseas Chinese businesses do not face difficulties in China's treacherous business environment. Nevertheless, they are accustomed to it and have discovered ways to deal with it effectively. For example, Hong Kong entrepreneurs have already gained a painful and costly education in government corruption. In the process, they have learned that old family connections, plus some hard currency, can help penetrate the labyrinth of official bureaucracy. Consider the Hong Kong investor who manages a factory on the outskirts of Guangzhou. The facility turns out magnetic heads for computer disk drives that are exported to American companies. The investor-manager runs the factory with minimum interference. The secret: he was born in a nearby village, pays a monthly fee to the local authorities—and is pretty much left alone.[44]

Likewise, Guangdong government officials have learned the distinction between property ownership and theft—and the value of good-faith negotiations. It is because of such mutual arrangements that investments by overseas Chinese have succeeded at a time when many Western ventures in China have failed.[45]

In many cases, members of the network target the provinces they grew up in, taking advantage of their extremely detailed knowledge of the local economy. Oei Ek Tjhong fled his hometown of Quanzhou (located on the coast of Fujian) for Indonesia in 1930. There he became a successful commodities trader before diversifying into banking and real estate. Following anti-Chinese riots in 1968, he took the Indonesian name Eka Tjipta Widjaja. By the early 1990s, his Sinar Mas Group had become Indonesia's third largest conglomerate. Yet, despite this success, Tjhong continued to look to the mainland for business opportunities. In 1992, he acquired controlling stakes in 41 state-owned factories located in his hometown.[46]

Likewise, Liem Sioe Liong has constructed the Yuan Hong industrial park in his hometown of Fuqing. Mochtar Riady has contracted infrastructure and tourism projects in his native city of Putian. Li Ka-shing has donated funds for a medical university to his hometown of Shantou.[47]

At times, the mainland overtly offers special treatment to overseas Chinese businesses. Hong Kong businesspeople do not need visas to enter China (although Chinese nationals do not yet have free entry into Hong Kong). Hong Kong investors secure more favorable concessions from the Guangdong local authorities than other "foreigners."

In some respects, business executives and investors from Taiwan are not treated as foreigners. In 1980, China abolished all tariffs on imports of goods with Taiwanese certificates of origin on the grounds that such movement constitutes internal trade rather than foreign commerce. However, this concession had to be modified when goods with fake certificates of origin began to flood the Chinese market. As a substitute, China levied adjustment taxes on Taiwanese goods at less than the prevailing import tariffs. Import controls on goods of Taiwanese origin are also less stringent than on those from other sources. Taiwanese investors are given preferential treatment, including permission to develop land and a longer period before divestiture of equity joint ventures is required. Local authorities also tend to give Taiwanese investors special consideration, such as speedier approval of investment applications and better support services.[48]

Not surprisingly, special treatment of overseas Chinese has fueled some resentment on the part of mainlanders. Some blame the overseas Chinese for the rampant corruption and bribery. More likely, it is the wealth they have created that has generated new opportunities for corruption and bribery.

CONCLUSION

China's efforts to open up its economy to the world have been far more successful than most people (including the Chinese themselves) expected when the open door policy was first unveiled. Foreign investment is pouring into the mainland, particularly into the coastal regions and Special Economic Zones. The resulting business ventures have enabled overseas Chinese investors to exploit their comparative advantages in technology, entrepreneurial ability, and culture, while mainlanders are enjoying dramatic increases in wages and standard of living. In 1994, there were 328,000 registered private enterprises in China employing over 5 million people.

However, 5 million is a small fraction of 1.2 billion. China still remains an enormous distance away from the capitalist ideal. Land is not owned by individuals but is leased by the state. The capital and technology of foreign companies are welcomed, but only conditionally. The Chinese consumer market continues to be largely off-limits to foreign firms that do not contribute either high technology or hard foreign currency. The term "market socialism" is quite apt: a style of hypercapitalism is evolving in some of the coastal areas, but always with a large, and still powerful, government overseeing industrial transactions. To do business in China today, one must—one way or another—have the government as a partner.

Some foreign companies read too much into reports that Beijing has reduced its power over the Chinese economy. While accurate, such a description is incomplete. Officials at provincial and local levels of government have replaced much of the central government's control over business with their own power to tax, levy fees, and grant permits. As a consequence, taxes frequently become a matter of bargaining, permits often require substantial bribes, and fees are unpredictable. The cost of operating in China varies considerably among regions but seems to be rising generally.

Gene Kalhorn, whose company operates six plants in such overseas locations as Singapore and Taiwan, offers a combination of wisecracks and serious advice on the basis of his experience in China. These observation can be summarized as follows:

- Find a good interpreter.
- Expect negotiations to take time. Start off with a long estimate and then double or triple it.
- Laws in China—when they exist—are made to be broken.
- Practice being patient.[49]

A more generic response to the range of problems encountered when doing business in China was given by William E. O'Brien, general manager of H.B. Fuller's Chinese operations and an old China hand: "I think we've found ways to beat the system. But there is no system. It's a lack of system."[50] In that narrow sense, the challenge to entrepreneurs is to learn which laws are enforced and which to finesse—and how.

But, far more fundamentally, doing business successfully in China means meeting the needs of the customer. Although that sounds familiar to business executives around the world, in one fundamental regard the challenge to business in the PRC is very different from that in most Western markets: directly or indirectly, that customer is often the government. The needs of the governmental "customer" in a rapidly growing but still authoritarian society are a shifting combination of citizen desires and state priorities.

CHAPTER 6

Experiences of U.S. Businesses, Good and Bad

There's a foreigner born every minute.
—Attributed to a mythical P.T. Wang

Impressive signs of U.S. capitalism are surfacing throughout many parts of China: Marlboro Man billboards, Kentucky Fried Chicken restaurants, Motorola cellular phones, Elizabeth Arden cosmetics, and Nike shoes. Nevertheless, quite a few successful American companies have stubbed their toes badly trying to penetrate the exotic Chinese market. In this chapter, we examine the unique problems that confront American firms in China, as well as the favorable experiences of some of them, and then draw some useful lessons.

Although there are no simple explanations as to why some firms succeed while others fail, it is not too surprising that the bamboo network turns out to be a positive force in this regard. Surely, the immensely successful overseas Chinese conglomerates hold some lessons for U.S. firms that hope to take the plunge in search of 1.2 billion consumers.

INITIAL PITFALLS

It is useful to start with some of the toe-stubbing experiences. In 1984, Honeywell Inc. was attracted to China by the promise of a huge and untapped market for its industrial controls equipment—the computer systems that run oil refineries and various manufacturing processes. Playing by the rules, the company took on a partner duly designated by China's Bureau of Instrumentation Industry, the Sichuan Instrument Complex in Chongqing. That enterprise seemed ideal: it was well situated politically and it had a thorough knowledge of the local market.

As it turned out to Honeywell's misfortune, Sichuan Instrument was a notorious money loser. It was positioned in an isolated inland location surrounded by mountains far from the rest of China's industry and thus from its potential customers. The Chinese firm was also a failure at marketing Honeywell's systems. In the blunt words of Ted Smith, Honeywell's general manager for China, "They had no selling skills."[1]

Other foreign firms producing industrial controls did better by not going strictly by the book. Honeywell's competitors began making direct sales in China, bypassing mainland Chinese partners altogether. Shaking free of its Chinese associate, however, was not easy for Honeywell. Pressured by the government, Honeywell brought Sichuan Instrument into some deals even when the local firm had little to contribute. Honeywell has since recovered and is now working with a more effective partner, the state-owned China Petrochemical Company, centrally located in Beijing.

Honeywell's experience is indicative of the serious problems U.S. businesses face in cracking the Chinese market. Indeed, most firms that have leapt into the mainland have yet to enjoy substantial profits. Many companies have suffered outright losses. Motorola, one of the most frequently cited examples of successful American entry into the China market, is reported to lose money on all of the mainstay cellular telephones produced in its Tianjin factory.

Doing business in China is very expensive: sky-high office rents, stiff import tariffs, and expensive transportation offset the expected economies in labor and raw materials. Compounding these problems is the enormous competition from companies that want to get their foot in the door at almost any cost. Competition from other capitalist nations is particularly fierce. The Europeans, notably Volkswagen, dominate China's automobile industry, and the Japanese lead in consumer electronics and household appliances. Alcatel (France), Ericsson (Sweden), NEC (Japan), Northern Telecom (Canada), and Siemens (Germany) are all major competitors in the burgeoning Chinese telecommunications market.

Manufacturing firms, with their large start-up expenses, are accustomed to waiting years before turning a profit. However, even the least capital-intensive enterprises have suffered losses in China. Pepper International Associates, a law firm that represents Western companies, started its China practice in 1988 and spent six years in the red before breaking even. U.S. companies are not alone: a survey of Japanese firms that have invested in China found that more than 90 percent have yet to earn any profits from these overseas operations.[2]

Investment banks such as Goldman Sachs and Merrill Lynch have experienced tremendous growth in China—but not without considerable grief on individual transactions. Many analysts believe that these firms are underpricing their services in order to build market share, foster *guanxi*, and establish a presence on the mainland. The result has been lots of business, but little profit. In the highly technical (and highly speculative) derivatives area, some spectacular reneging on the part of Chinese customers has been reported by American firms, to their financial disadvantage.

Visa and Mastercard are also taking a long-term approach. The rapid proliferation of bank cards in China is symbolic of the nation's economic progress. By 1995, more than 10 million cards—most of them Mastercard or Visa—had been issued by state-run banks. Despite this volume, both companies have had limited financial success. Almost all of the cards issued to date are debit cards that, unlike conventional credit cards, draw upon money deposited into savings or checking accounts. Because of this, most card transactions are cash transfers, which earn no fees for the issuing company. Furthermore, Beijing has severely restricted the operation of authorization systems that allow companies to charge fees for domestic transactions. All of this raises the question: why are these companies so interested in cracking the

China market? The answer is that they hope Beijing will eventually change the rules of the game.[3]

CATERING TO THE CHINESE MARKET

Even the largest and most capable Western firms have stumbled when first penetrating the China market. In the early 1980s, when China began shopping for advanced digital switching equipment to upgrade its telephone network, AT&T brushed it off. Ma Bell was still a protected monopoly at home and was not anxious to transfer its top-of-the-line technology to a primitive, albeit emerging market. Its competitors were not so reluctant. Germany's Siemens, France's Alcatel, and Japan's NEC became China's primary suppliers of telecommunications equipment.

Eventually, in the mid-1980s, AT&T sold some switching equipment to China—after the company had been broken up by a court decree resulting from a Justice Department antitrust action. But the corporation at the time was still so oriented to the U.S. market that it did not thoroughly examine Chinese telephone habits. Excess demand for telephone service creates high levels of traffic per line. Furthermore, Chinese callers tend to talk for much longer periods than do Americans. Both of these simple facts necessitate special switching equipment. But AT&T shipped in off-the-shelf units that were not up to the task. Its first switch, used in Wuhan, could not handle the heavy traffic, resulting in malfunctions, delays, and complete breakdowns of the system. Calls would not go through and, in some cases, people could not even get a dial tone.

While its understaffed team was working on repairing the Wuhan system, AT&T switches in other provinces began to malfunction as well. These technical problems were compounded when the PRC's Ministry of Post and Telecommunications complained and found that it had to deal with a branch in Hong Kong: AT&T did not even have an office in China.

Alcatel, in contrast, had large teams stationed in the country and was installing new switches with little difficulty. In the late 1980s, China stopped purchasing switches from AT&T altogether. The American company found itself essentially shut out of the Chinese market. The situation did not improve until 1992, when AT&T persuaded Washington lawmakers to insert a provision into a U.S.–China trade agreement that required the purchase of U.S. digital switching equipment. Meanwhile, a vice chairman of AT&T spent considerable time patching up relations with the Chinese authorities. Trying to learn from experience, AT&T entered into a joint venture to manufacture digital switches in China. The company now has more than 400 employees stationed on the mainland, who can respond quickly when problems arise.

In the 1990s, as a result of their new methods of doing business, AT&T is having considerably more success. It has sold telecommunications equipment for a fiber-optic network linking Beijing and three other cities, as well as switching equipment to Changchun and mobile equipment to other regions. AT&T has also entered into several joint ventures with Chinese partners, including the Beijing Fiber Optic Cable Company and the China American Telephone and Telegraph Communications Company.[4] In 1993, China began negotiating the purchase of switching and transmission equipment, cellular phones, and computer networks from AT&T. Today, the company's annual sales to China exceed $100 million and its prospects seem bright.

Many of the initial difficulties faced by AT&T and other U.S. firms can be attributed to a failure to adapt to *guo qing*, or unique Chinese characteristics. This term is widely used by the Chinese when referring to foreign governments and corporations that blindly impose Western values, norms, and business methods on their society. The concept of *guo qing* is consistent with Deng Xiaoping's frequently stated desire to control the entry of foreign businesses and their alien ideas—to "open up China's windows without allowing too many flies inside." As Deng stated in a 1984 CCP directive, "Western cultures and ideas should be adopted only if they fit *guo qing*."[5]

One practical example of *guo qing* is provided by Chinese demographics. Strict family control measures limit each urban family to one child. This has created incentives for many parents to ensure that their only offspring has the best of everything (education, apparel, toys, etc.). It is estimated that half the premium consumer goods purchased in China are for these "little emperors." Western marketers must understand the implications of Chinese demography when deciding which products to sell in the PRC, as well as how they should be advertised.

Moreover, the desire of many Chinese to pass their fortunes down through family lines puts tremendous pressure on Chinese women to give birth to boys (who can run the business). Dissemination of medical technology such as ultrasound has enabled women to abort unwanted female children, a situation reflected in the ratio of newborn boys to girls (China's ratio is 120:100, compared to a world average of 105:100).[6] Such strong cultural trends cannot be ignored by Western business.

SUCCESSFUL VENTURES

Because entrance into many Chinese markets is tightly regulated by the government, substantial time, money, and effort are required for American firms to penetrate those sectors of the economy. However, the heavyhanded government role may on occasion unintentionally benefit an American firm. The Chinese Ministry of Foreign Trade and Economic Cooperation is proud of the fact that, in late 1993, it licensed Gallup to be the first foreign market research company to do business in the country. Gallup China is a joint venture of the well-known Gallup Organization of the United States and Carrie Enterprises Ltd., a leading Chinese import and export firm.

Headquartered in Beijing, the joint venture opened satellite offices in 19 cities in its first year. Although Gallup China is gaining a large share of the domestic market for surveys and other market research, Chinese authorities hope that its presence will enhance the quality and professional ranks of its domestic rivals. The company is still the only foreign market research firm authorized to do business in China.[7]

Many firms that succeed in adapting to *guo qing* rely on a Chinese partner for cultural expertise and critical *guanxi*. General

Electric owns 65 percent of Beijing-based GE Medical Systems China. Its partners are two state enterprises, one run by the Ministry of Aerospace Industries and the other by the Ministry of Public Health. Baskin-Robbins relies on China Satellite and Launching Control (an affiliate of the Commission of Science, Technology and Industry for National Defense) to sell ice cream products throughout the country.[8] The Beijing Jeep Corporation, a joint venture funded by Chrysler, is the second largest foreign manufacturing investment in China. Citicorp (the U.S. bank holding company) owns an equity stake in a pharmaceutical factory that is part of the San Jiu Enterprise Group of the Chinese army.[9]

Many U.S. firms report happy experiences when they make a special effort to adapt their products to the Chinese market. Hasbro Inc. has been successful in selling its GI Joe doll—but only since it gave the doll a new identity as an "international hero" complete with the colors of the Chinese People's Liberation Army: camouflage green and Communist Party red. Minneapolis-based H.B. Fuller Company, a successful medium-size U.S. firm doing business in Guangdong, follows the local custom of handing out red envelopes with token amounts of cash to employees at the lunar New Year. Philip Morris's Maxwell House does not take for granted the staples of the typical Chinese kitchen. The company sells its instant coffee in premixed packets that include cream and sugar.

Successful American firms have capitalized on international brand-name recognition. Guangdong is Procter & Gamble's largest foreign market for Rejoice shampoo. McDonald's new venture in Guangdong set the world record, with over 14,000 customers in a single day. When 7-Eleven stores opened in China in 1992, the riot police had to be called out in full battle gear to control the huge crowds of customers.

The Coca-Cola Company has managed to penetrate the Chinese consumer market and realize the dream of most Western businesses eager to sell to the masses. Coca-Cola now sells 2.4 billion cans a year—two for each man, woman, and child—winning over 15 percent of China's soft drink market. Production takes place in 13 mainland bottling factories using local supplies (except for beverage concentrate, which is still largely imported). Coca-Cola's current investment of about $100 million is expected to grow to $500 million by 1996 as production expands to an additional ten factories.[10] Coca-Cola's success arises in part from its use of local raw materials and production facilities. It also uses locally made television ads, complete with a Chinese family drinking Coke. Rival Pepsi, with only a 6 percent market share, has been less successful in finding solid local partners.

U.S. beer manufacturers have also had difficulties, despite China's enormous market potential. Currently, China's beer production is greater than Germany's and second only to that of the United States, and it is growing by about 25 percent annually. If this pace continues, China will surpass the United States as the world's number one beer market by the year 2000.

Yet the major American brewers—Anheuser-Busch and Miller—have been unable to establish a significant presence on the mainland. The very strength of these companies in the United States—large-scale production at a small number of very efficient breweries—is a handicap in China. A nationwide market does not exist, at least not yet. Language, culture, and tastes differ dramatically from province to province. Regional and provincial protectionism is substantial and antiquated transportation infrastructure hampers distribution. Given these problems, it is no surprise that the China beer market is highly fragmented and dominated by small, local brands. Tsingtao Brewing Co., the largest brewer, has only a 2 percent market share (compared to Anheuser-Busch's 47 percent share of the U.S. market).

Ironically, the very firms that have found themselves virtually squeezed out of the U.S. brewing market—Pabst and Heileman—are enjoying greater success in China. Both companies are more experienced in small-scale localized operations than their larger U.S. competitors. Pabst sold 2.8 million barrels in China in 1993, 40 percent more than its U.S. sales in the same year. Heileman has been able to capitalize on Chinese perceptions of American quality and the fondness for Western imagery with its heavily marketed Lone Star label. Despite its success, Heileman has been reluctant to sink financial and physical capital into the mainland. Instead, the company earns royalties on local production of Lone Star.[11]

American products that successfully adapt to *guo qing* can enjoy a competitive advantage over similar products marketed by other countries, and even over identical products manufactured domestically. Just as Japanese manufactured goods—particularly electronics and automobiles—have a reputation for high quality in the United States, so do some U.S.-made goods in China. Chinese consumers also appreciate the status they acquire by purchasing American products, often preferring goods that prominently display the logo or brand name of an internationally recognized producer.

Thus, American pharmaceutical firms, with their new, high-quality products, have been able to exploit their reputation for safety and quality to carve out a sizable niche in the Chinese health care system. Furthermore, their products are delivered in tamper-proof packaging with clear dosage instructions. Local products, on the other hand, have short shelf lives and are often packaged in easily damaged bottles that are poorly labeled.

Yet even with this quality advantage, many pharmaceutical companies continue to struggle in the Chinese market. As Beijing attempts to reduce its fiscal burden, it is shifting health care costs from the state to the individual. In 1993, the Ministry of Public Health began to prepare a list of drugs eligible for reimbursement by state-sponsored health care plans. Western manufacturers must now scramble to develop the *guanxi* necessary to ensure that their products are included on these lists. Products that are not included will be limited to over-the-counter sales, which will be severely hampered by the lack of retail pharmacies. Most Chinese are still too poor to purchase Western drugs without state subsidies.

Even large Western pharmaceutical firms—both European and American—have fallen prey to Beijing's shifting, arbitrary regulations. After beginning production at its joint venture antibiotics company, Pfizer faced state-imposed price controls that prevented it from raising prices along with inflation (which topped

20 percent in 1994). Pharmacia, a Swedish firm, had been in China for 13 years before beginning to recoup its investment. However, its contract (like most joint venture agreements) lasts only 20 years, after which ownership will be transferred to the Chinese partner.[12]

THE SPECIAL CASE OF HIGH TECHNOLOGY

Because Chinese companies—both on the mainland and off-shore—focus mainly on low-technology investments in the light industrial and service sectors, U.S. firms have the opportunity to significantly increase their market share by means of large advanced-technology projects. The government of China itself represents an important market, especially in the high-tech arena. One of the first contracts between the PRC and a major American company was signed in January 1972, when RCA agreed to install a $3 million satellite communications earth station. The 33-foot antenna was put in place at a station near Shanghai in time to provide communications for President Nixon's impending visit to China. Disputes were settled through "friendly consultation." The success of this venture encouraged Chinese officials to import more American technology.[13]

It is not surprising that such a high-technology venture was among the first to succeed on the mainland. Beijing has always stipulated that it would show a preference for business deals that augmented China's modest industrial capabilities. Furthermore, if Beijing is going to be successful in developing an effective business infrastructure, local enterprises—private and governmental—must be allowed to procure high-tech equipment that China cannot produce on its own.

The first U.S.–China electronics joint venture began in 1985 with the founding of China Hewlett-Packard Company. The company serves as both a distributor of HP products and an exporter of its own output. It generates over $60 million in annual sales, of which $50 million is domestic and $10 million is export earnings. HP must abide by three principles that virtually guarantee that all its operations in China will benefit the domestic economy. The products that HP provides to the joint venture must be "technologically advanced," they must have the potential to generate foreign currency earnings, and they must be urgently needed but not able to be produced by China itself.[14]

Today, many of the most successful American companies doing business in China manufacture technologically advanced products. The U.S. Department of Commerce has identified ten major markets in the PRC that are especially receptive to imports from the United States.[15] All ten rate high in the level of technology embodied in their products:

	Size of China Market (in millions)	Annual Growth of Imports from United States
Avionics equipment	$ 375	30%
Computers	1,300	20
Aircraft	3,000	15
Mining equipment	1,800	10
Agricultural chemicals	7,350	10
Oil field machinery	5,000	10
Electric power systems	11,000	7
Industrial chemicals	12,000	6
Telecommunications	1,800	5
Agricultural machinery	6,000	5

The Boeing Company, for example, has seized opportunities in the industries near the top of this list: avionics equipment and aircraft. Since its first sale of a 707 in 1973, Boeing has sold or leased 234 aircraft to Chinese airlines at a total outlay of $10 billion. In 1994, unfilled announced orders for 64 Boeing aircraft were valued at $3.9 billion. China is now the largest overseas market for Boeing: 14 percent of the company's commercial airline production is going to airlines in the PRC.[16]

The flow of products is in both directions. Boeing has purchased from local sources in China since 1980. Chinese suppliers have produced over 300 sets of horizontal fins for Boeing's 737, as well as vertical stabilizers for the 737 and cargo doors for the 757. Chinese-made parts are now installed in every 737, 747, and 757 coming off the Seattle-area assembly line. The company's other efforts in China include a flight training center in Zhuhai for 737 and 757 crews and an aircraft maintenance course at Tianjin Civil Aviation Academy (run jointly with the PRC's Civil Aviation Administration).[17]

The McDonnell-Douglas Corporation has also enjoyed considerable success in penetrating China's aviation market, although not without some trial and error. At first, the company planned to manufacture complete aircraft. That effort failed. Then, in 1980, it tried something far less ambitious. It awarded a subcontract to the Shanghai Aircraft Company to fabricate landing-gear doors, a vital but small part of a jetliner. This modest effort succeeded, in the meantime building up a business relationship with China. In 1983, McDonnell-Douglas succeeded in selling China two DC-9s. Since then, China has become an important customer of the American firm, as well as one of its suppliers.

Currently, the McDonnell-Douglas Corporation reports that its coproduction program with the PRC is the largest single U.S.–China technology transfer program, both in the dollar value of goods produced (over $1 billion) and in their technology content. The Shanghai Aviation Industrial Corporation has assembled 28 MD-80 jet airliners from parts and subassemblies provided by McDonnell-Douglas. In the other direction, the Shanghai Enterprise and Chengdu Aircraft Corporation is producing a large volume of components and subassemblies for the American firm's twin-jet assembly line in California. The parts made in China include vital components such as doors, horizontal stabilizers, and nose sections.[18]

Soaring demand for air travel continues to make China a major market for new aircraft. Domestic air travel has grown at an average annual rate of 22 percent over the past 17 years. Chinese officials estimate a need for 800 new aircraft over the next 15 years: a potential $40 billion market. Industry forecasts show that, within 20 years, China will become the world's third largest civilian aircraft market (after the United States and Japan).

Nevertheless, risks abound even in this high-tech market. In

1994, the Chinese airlines postponed billions of dollars of aircraft orders following a series of crashes and near misses. According to the International Airline Passengers Association, Chinese carriers have one of the worst safety records in the world, with a fatal accident rate 40 times greater than North American airlines. Such safety problems are the result of a severe shortage of pilots experienced in flying large, high-performance aircraft. To remedy this problem, the largest aviation contract signed by the Chinese in 1994 was for flight simulators and other flight-training equipment.[19]

A more basic constraint on the Chinese market for jet airliners is the lack of a supporting infrastructure for the operations of the airlines. One-half of the country's 20 major airports already operate at full capacity. Others are too close to major population centers to permit substantial expansion.[20] Shortages of maintenance crews, air control personnel, and even passenger ticketing facilities are all limiting expansion of the country's airline industry. Such barriers are likely to be overcome in the years ahead, but they will definitely have an impact on short-term sales forecasts.

A longer-term concern is far more fundamental and transcends aviation. Many American firms worry that their superior technology and manufacturing expertise are viewed by the Chinese as merely a means to developing their own competitive industrial capacity. Most joint venture contracts contain a provision to systematically replace foreign employees with native Chinese trained in the new technology. Some firms fear that, after the Chinese have learned to utilize advanced Western technologies, they will expel the foreign companies. Then, on their own, they will launch substitute enterprises that will compete in markets now dominated by U.S., European, and Japanese firms. For example, China's joint ventures with Boeing, McDonnell-Douglas, and Airbus may be precursors to Beijing's own effort to develop a passenger aircraft that meets international standards.

For American companies, this is a very difficult issue. If one U.S. company refuses to provide China with technical and manufacturing know-how, will another American competitor do so and claim the vast Chinese market? If all American firms keep the know-how to themselves, will European or Japanese competitors deal with the Chinese instead, favoring short-term gains over longer-term worries? There is no set answer to these tough questions. Each company must make its own evaluation of the potential risks and rewards.

There are indications that most Japanese firms are erring on the side of caution. The heavy industries in which Japan excels—particularly automobile manufacturing—require massive amounts of fixed investment. Furthermore, Japanese negotiators have faced great difficulties in securing guarantees over technology transfer. Japanese companies are extremely reluctant to hand over their superior technology to what they view as a potential competitor within their home region. Indeed, there is little need to do so when China's loose borders prevent strict import controls. Unofficial imports of automobiles are estimated to exceed official imports by a large margin. If this imbalance continues, American automakers may find that investment in local production facilities will not necessarily produce large market share.[21]

ORGANIZING TO DO BUSINESS IN CHINA

When the decision is made to go ahead with a major commitment to the China market, a variety of entry strategies have proved useful to U.S. and other foreign-based firms. Often, the newcomer begins by establishing a subsidiary or holding company in Hong Kong to take advantage of the colony's more flexible investment and tax regulations. In turn, the shell company coordinates investment projects in China.

Some of the most successful American ventures on the mainland—Toys 'R' Us, Bausch & Lomb, and Campbell Soup—have taken this route. More than 200 other American companies have established regional headquarters in Hong Kong and are thus in a relatively good position to develop business relationships with enterprises in China. About 70 percent of all U.S. firms with headquarters in the Far East have chosen a Hong Kong location. Prominent examples are Bank of America, Dun & Bradstreet, Exxon, Hyatt, May Department Stores, Motorola, PepsiCo, Polaroid, Time-Warner, Walt Disney, and Xerox. The American Chamber of Commerce in Hong Kong is now the largest U.S. chamber outside the United States.

Altogether, about 900 American firms have established some type of presence in Hong Kong, be it a sales office or a branch of a Tokyo-based regional headquarters. It is intriguing that, as a result of this increased U.S. presence and the exodus that followed the 1984 joint declaration of the United Kingdom and the PRC, fewer Britons now live in Hong Kong (19,000) than Americans (23,000).

U.S. companies doing business in China through Hong Kong have shown a particularly strong preference for joint ventures. This type of cooperative business relationship has accounted for the great majority of U.S. investment in China since 1979. Usually, the U.S. investor's share of the enterprise is based on its contribution of technology, equipment, industrial property rights, and foreign currency. The Chinese partner contributes land, factory buildings, raw materials, currency to pay the domestic costs of the business, and the intangible but often critical ability to deal with national, provincial, and local authorities.

An increasingly popular strategy for American firms is to establish a wholly foreign-owned enterprise (WFOE). As discussed in Chapter 3, WFOEs are generally discouraged by the Chinese government and do not enjoy the same privileges as joint ventures. Nevertheless, WFOEs can be the organization of choice for U.S. firms concerned about advanced technology transfer or unwilling to compromise their control over business decisions. Motorola, whose Chinese equipment sales exceeded $2 billion in 1994, has established a massive WFOE in Tianjin. The large-scale, high-tech manufacturing operation produces pagers, semiconductors, cellular phones, and microprocessors. Ultimately, the company hopes to manufacture an even wider range of products at its Tianjin facilities.[22]

3M China Limited was the first wholly foreign-owned enterprise to operate outside the four Chinese Special Economic Zones. Since its initial registration in 1984, 3M has introduced more than 2,000 products to the Chinese market and has expanded in scope to cover 20 of the 29 Chinese provinces. Nevertheless, its total Chinese operation remains modest compared to 3M activities elsewhere. 3M's 1993 sales volume in what it calls the "China Region" was $200 million, compared to a total corporate volume of $14 billion.[23]

In a limited number of cases, large and well-known American corporations are authorized to establish "umbrella enterprises." Such China-based subsidiaries are designed to integrate a whole range of operations—manufacturing, investments in new projects, purchases of raw materials and components, and the sale of the items produced. However, an umbrella enterprise may neither import finished products nor sell them in China. DuPont and IBM have set up such wholly owned umbrella enterprises in China. Coca-Cola maintains one as an equity joint venture with the China International Trust and Investment Corporation, a major government-owned finance and entrepreneurial unit.

SPECIAL PROBLEMS FOR AMERICANS

Judging by the experiences of Americans and other foreigners who do business in China on a continuing basis, it is clear that hard knocks are to be expected, especially at the outset. Even one of the most experienced Hong Kong entrepreneurs got burned after opening a restaurant for tourists near Tiananmen Square—just a week before the shooting started in 1989. No amount of *guanxi* or due diligence is likely to have prevented that fiasco.

But Americans doing business in China encounter a particularly daunting host of obstacles. Some of the cultural barriers described in the previous chapter face all foreigners. Other problems are peculiar to Americans. For example, U.S. citizens who pay bribes to Chinese officials find that such practices are more than just costly and distasteful. They are illegal under the U.S. Foreign Corrupt Practices Act and subject perpetrators to a fine of up to $100,000 plus five years in jail (the penalty for a company can be as much as $2 million). Perennially, American companies doing business overseas gripe about how the Foreign Corrupt Practices Act prevents them from being competitive with companies from other nations, which can be more relaxed about such ethical matters.

On the positive side, however, savvy American companies use the Act to turn down overtures for bribes. In the words of one U.S. business executive, "Once you get the reputation of never paying, they will stop asking."[24] That course of action is easier for the larger and higher-tech firms that have more leverage with the PRC authorities. Small, low-tech companies do not have that advantage.

The U.S. government has tried repeatedly to get the Chinese to reduce the obstacles facing American business. In 1992, the governments of the two countries entered into two Memoranda of Understanding. Under the first, dealing with market access, the Chinese authorities promised to eliminate import barriers by 1997 and to publish the laws and regulations governing international trade. The second agreement, covering intellectual property rights, is designed to provide stronger protections for patents, copyrights, trademarks, and trade secrets. The lack of effective protection of intellectual property rights is a basic barrier to market access for important sectors of the economy, especially U.S. companies in the recording, motion picture, and computer software industries.[25]

Some progress has been reported in carrying out the commitments embodied in the two agreements. In October 1993, China's Ministry of Foreign Trade and Economic Cooperation established a daily publication (akin to the U.S. Federal Register) to serve as a central repository for trade-related laws, regulations, and announcements. Within the first 15 months, the ministry published 93 previously confidential trade documents and rescinded 391 others. The government also released lists of products subject to import licenses, quotas, and import controls plus two volumes of additional trade and investment regulations. By 1994, the number of nontariff barriers had been cut from 3,000 to about 400.

The flurry of activity has a good news/bad news aspect. On the positive side, it is helpful to Americans and other Westerners doing business in China to see what the rules are—and to see a reduction in their number. On the negative side, the vastness of the remaining restrictions is discouraging. Overall Chinese tariff rates are still prohibitively high. Substantial barriers to market access and widespread infringement of intellectual property rights persist throughout China. Laws to prosecute those accused of pirating American product designs are weak. Moreover, enforcement is sporadic and occurs mainly in response to U.S. governmental pressure. Buck-passing is commonplace. The State Administration for Industry and Commerce says it lacks sufficient manpower for adequate enforcement, and local police contend that they are not responsible for enforcing antipiracy laws.

In response to numerous U.S. complaints—from both government agencies and private companies—China has begun to require compact disc factories to stamp a factory of origin mark on each disc. That simplifies legal action against illicit CDs or CD-ROM software. Under the new Chinese rules, any disc without such an identifying mark is illegal. As with past efforts, Beijing continues to have great difficulty enforcing these regulations. Many of the factories making counterfeit discs are owned by local governments, which shield them from the central government's crackdown. When national authorities arrested managers of a pirate CD factory in Guangdong, local officials released them before they could be brought to trial.[26]

In February 1995—after the United States threatened to retaliate for repeated and blatant piracy of U.S. software—Chinese officials began a modest effort to curb this widespread practice. Investigators seized several boxes of discs and CD-ROMs in Shenzhen but left after two hours without making any arrests. Of greater significance was the shutdown of seven compact disc factories, including Shenzhen's Shenfei Laser and Optical System Company, one of the leading counterfeiters. By June, however, six of the factories had reopened while construction of an additional factory was under way.

Beijing has promised to investigate other factories suspected of pirating activities and to destroy any equipment used to make counterfeits. Of course, such crackdowns may be a response to

Chinese interests rather than U.S. pressures: cheap, skilled labor has fostered China's *own* software industry, which must be protected from domestic pirates. Likewise, China's heavily protected cigarette industry has found itself battling domestic producers of counterfeit brands.[27]

Moreover, China threatens to retaliate if the United States responds to the infringement problem by imposing punitive tariffs on products that China exports to this country. Beijing talks about suspending talks with American automakers that wish to produce cars and components in China. Such action would give the European companies already in China—Volkswagen, Citroen, and Peugeot—a great opportunity to increase their penetration of that large and growing market.

OPPORTUNITIES FOR AMERICAN BUSINESS

Despite all the difficulties that arise, American companies continue to enter the Chinese market and to increase their investment there when they already have a presence. In mid-1994, Caterpillar unveiled a joint venture to build hydraulic excavators, Apple Computer announced plans to begin production of components, and Ford Motor Company signed agreements for two joint ventures to produce auto parts. Ford is teaming up with Shanghai Automotive Industry Corporation to make seats and instrument panels and with Shanghai Yaohua Glass Works to produce glass products. The American firm owns 51 percent of both operations.[28]

It is an axiom of business finance that high risk accompanies high expected returns (the Chinese might put the matter more delicately as the *yang* and *yin* of challenge and opportunity). The growth of Greater China, especially on the mainland, continues to attract interest on the part of American investors willing to take such risks. At a time of modest growth prospects in North America and Western Europe, the rapid industrialization of China is creating important opportunities for U.S. companies—and no shortage of dangers.

Many U.S. firms find themselves caught in a difficult dilemma.

If they respond aggressively to the attractive long-term potential of the Chinese market by entering the mainland quickly—without getting their feet wet first—they will head off potential competitors. But in doing so they may lose their shirts. On the other hand, in the presence of great political and economic uncertainty, they could proceed more slowly and cautiously, expanding their business relationships with the mainland only a step at a time— or delaying entry outright until China's "market socialism" is more market than socialism. In the latter case, other businesses may jump the gun on the more timid U.S. companies and forge ahead.

Not surprisingly, most U.S. firms take a halfway approach: they make contacts, establish offices, and set up limited production capabilities in China but remain reluctant to sink large amounts of capital into fixed investment. As a result, most investment in China to date has been made by less cautious overseas Chinese companies.

A typical American experience is that of the large petroleum corporations. They possess the special ability, lacking in China, to explore, produce, and market oil and its derivatives in large quantities. However, the State Planning Commission has declared petrochemicals to be one of China's "pillar industries," along with automobiles, telecommunications, and transportation. Because of its strategic importance to Beijing, the petrochemical industry is heavily insulated from foreign ownership or competition. The China National Petroleum Corporation (CNPC), formerly part of the now defunct Ministry of Petroleum, accounted for 99 percent of crude oil output in 1990, 98 percent in 1991, and 97 percent in 1992. This leisurely decline shows little sign of accelerating: even long-range forecasts predict that CNPC will continue to produce over 90 percent of China's crude output.[29]

However, CNPC lacks the capital, technology, and expertise needed to meet the coastal provinces' insatiable energy needs. China's domestic crude oil output is virtually stagnant, growing at only 1.2 percent annually, far below demand growth rates that are ten times higher. In recent years, China—the world's fifth largest oil producer—has become a net importer of oil. All this has forced the relaxation of some of the restraints on foreign investment in the energy sector.

Despite this new openness, substantial restrictions still deter U.S. firms from tapping into China's vast oil reserves. Import bans, price controls, and other governmental efforts to retain control over energy are continually in flux, preventing the openness necessary for firms to make effective, long-term decisions. One particularly disturbing restriction facing foreign firms is that CNPC holds a monopoly on purchasing rights to all oil extracted on the mainland and does so at a price to be determined by the Chinese after the fact. To put it mildly, that is a substantial deterrent to any petroleum company thinking about making a large investment.

The Tarim Basin, located in the politically volatile western province of Xinjiang, holds such tremendous potential that many firms are interested despite the government's substantial restrictions. This vast area—approximately the size of Texas—may contain upward of 100 billion barrels of oil. Some call the region "Saudi Arabia in China." State-owned firms have had little success in exploring Tarim because of harsh surface conditions and the extreme depth of drillable oil. Even if oil could be extracted, it could not be transported out of the region in large quantities, as existing pipelines, railways, and roads are not up to the task. A pipeline across China to the coastal regions could cost up to $20 billion and would require technical resources that China lacks.

Despite their own very limited ability to extract Tarim oil, Chinese officials have offered only the lowest-quality tracts to foreign investors. Of five initial blocks opened to foreigners, two had such poor potential that they attracted no bidders. Furthermore, Tarim's remote location makes exploration and transportation costly, a concern reinforced by the presence of oil price controls. The companies contemplating bids do not even know whether China will pay world market prices for oil produced by foreign companies onshore. If not, oil production and transportation will be too costly. As a result of these problems, Tarim oil accounted for barely 1 percent of China's total output in 1994. Nevertheless, some Western firms are so eager to get their foot in the door that they are purchasing unprofitable blocks in the hope that they will be offered more lucrative sites later.

Overall, American oil companies continue to invest in China—because of the attractive combination of large reserves and long-term market growth—to the tune of more than $1 billion since 1978. So far, these companies have only small finds to show for their labors and most of them have not been profitable. The best producers are two fields operated by a consortium consisting of Chevron, Texaco, and Agip. The fields are near the mouth of the Pearl River in the South China Sea and are being developed at an investment commitment of $280 million. The oil is needed to help meet the burgeoning energy requirements of nearby Guang-dong province.

Meanwhile, the Chinese authorities give preferential treatment to their own government-owned corporations. The hazards associated with "upstream" activities such as exploration have forced most foreign firms to concentrate on refining, retailing, and other "downstream" operations that require less fixed investment. Beijing has allowed foreign investment in downstream activities only since 1991, but already several major foreign companies have moved into this market. Shell Oil began building a $5 billion refinery in Guangdong province in 1992, which is expected to be operational sometime in 1995.

JOINING EAST AND WEST

If there is one overarching lesson to be learned by American business experiences in Southeast Asia, it is that a strong domestic position does not automatically ensure success in the Chinese market. Given the many barriers that confront Western business and the advantages offered to the bamboo network, foreign firms that hope to carve out a market niche must bring something special to the bargaining table. Broadly speaking, two types of companies have succeeded in doing this. In the case of both of them, the strengths of American companies compensate for the relative weaknesses of the bamboo network and of mainland China's industry.

The first successful category is the high-technology firm that offers products, manufacturing processes, or research capabilities not available on the mainland. The Chinese government is anxious to obtain new technologies in order to compete with other regional powerhouses—namely Japan and South Korea—in the next century. Furthermore, if Beijing is going to sustain China's rapid development, it must allow imports of telecommunications, pollution control, energy generation, and a number of other technologies. Given these needs, it is little surprise that firms such as Boeing, McDonnell-Douglas, Motorola, and General Electric have led the way for other U.S. corporations.

The second category of successful foreign firms operating in China is the low-tech but marketing-intensive company that has worldwide brand association. Despite tough import restrictions, rising incomes and a growing consumer consciousness have fueled demand for traditional Western goods: soft drinks, cigarettes, fast food, and other consumer products. The future growth industry, provided Beijing relaxes its censorship laws, may be American culture: movies, magazines, and MTV.

Regardless of whether they are high- or low-tech, most American companies successfully doing business in China have one thing in common, especially when they are getting started: an ethnic Chinese joint venture partner. The list of U.S. corporations that have teamed up with a bamboo network business group is long and distinguished: Chrysler, Coca-Cola, Kentucky Fried Chicken, Lockheed, Motorola, Procter & Gamble, Wal-Mart, and many others. These joint ventures are not necessarily a one-way street; rather, they may bring together two complementary organizations. The overseas Chinese have considerable organizational resources and the connections on the mainland that are necessary to get things done. However, they lack the technology and marketing ability necessary to sustain a large manufacturing enterprise.

Because of its extensive operations on the mainland, many Western companies seeking to do business in China view the CP

Group as an ideal partner. Heineken looked to CP when it needed a partner to produce and distribute its beer on the mainland. In 1995, U.S. retail giant Wal-Mart linked up with Ek Chor Distribution System (a subsidiary of CP) to develop and operate warehouse clubs in Hong Kong, Shenzhen, and Shanghai. CP has also helped Kentucky Fried Chicken to establish a presence in Shanghai. Thirayut Phitya-Isarakul, senior executive vice president of CP, explains this activity in a very straightforward way: "After 14 years in China, we have all the connections, from the top of the government down to the county level."[30]

CP's joint venture with NYNEX—Telecom Asia—illustrates the potential of linking Western firms with successful overseas Chinese groups. NYNEX supplies the high technology and institutional expertise needed to install 2 million new phone lines in Thailand. CP possesses good relationships with Thailand's high-level government and business officials, as well as the regional name recognition that attracts top engineering and business graduates from local universities. In 1995, Telecom Asia's stock market capitalization reached $9 billion. The venture also provides a regional footing from which to jump into other local markets, such as the Philippines, Vietnam, Indonesia, and possibly China.

President Enterprises Corp. (PEC) is another popular partner for many U.S. firms trying to crack the China market. Based in Taiwan, PEC produces and markets basic foodstuffs, such as instant noodles. Business is good: in 1994, the company earned after-tax profits of nearly $7 billion on reported sales of almost $25 billion. The firm's main competitor is Thailand's CP Group. And, like CP, PEC is teaming up with Western firms. Recent joint venture partners include PepsiCo and 7-Eleven.

Whirlpool's foray into the mainland—in the form of four joint ventures to produce household appliances—has been led by Wah-hui Chu, an experienced, Western-trained native of Guangdong. Mr. Chu heads Whirlpool Greater China, Inc., serving as a middleman between the firm's Western headquarters and its joint venture partners on the mainland. It is too early to gauge Whirlpool's success in the region, but the company apparently wants to establish a long-term presence. In 1994, it followed the advice of a *feng shui* consultant who suggested alterations to a training facility near company headquarters in order to better accommodate Chinese visitors.[31]

Li Ka-Shing has helped some of the largest, most capable Western firms to penetrate the Greater Chinese market. Procter & Gamble was unable to establish a manufacturing plan on the mainland until it began working with Li. Lockheed teamed up with Li to start an aircraft maintenance business in Guangzhou, as did Motorola in establishing its cellular phone business in Hong Kong. MTV used his expertise to start up its satellite television service in Asia.[32]

Although it is difficult to do so, some Westerners manage to directly tap into the bamboo network. For these few, the payoffs can be very high. Consider the case of Bruce McMahan, who heads the U.S.-based firm of McMahan Securities. For years, McMahan has been heavily involved in a foundation that donates computers to disabled children in the United States and abroad. One of the recipients of McMahan's generosity has been the China Disabled Persons Federation, headed by Deng Pufang— the eldest son of Deng Xiaoping. McMahan and Deng have developed close, personal ties through their joint charitable work.

Years after their first meeting, these ties provided the necessary foundation for a private business venture. In 1992, the China Huaneng Group, a large state-owned industrial conglomerate, was trying to raise funds for its Shandong Huaneng Power Development Company. Underwriter competition for the project was fierce, with many of the largest Western financial firms jockeying to establish their presence on the mainland. Nevertheless, McMahan's relatively small firm managed to claim a spot on the underwriting team, in part because of his high-level connections. It turns out that Deng called Zhu Rongji, China's Deputy Prime Minister and former central bank governor, to recommend McMahan.[33]

Despite the assistance it provides to U.S. firms wishing to get started on the mainland, the bamboo network also constitutes a major problem for Western businesses. In some market areas, overseas Chinese firms represent the future rivals of American manufacturers. Using a combination of advanced Western technology and low-wage labor, conglomerates such as CP may well become the Sony or Toyota of the next 50 years.

Indeed, the successful high-tech firms in Taiwan and Hong Kong and on the mainland are run by overseas Chinese with advanced engineering degrees from top-tier Western schools. Even more valuable than the technical skills they gained at these universities is the business savvy they acquired by working for American firms such as Microsoft, Sun, or Bell Laboratories. Their education, along with their Chinese background, enables these businesspeople to become "knowledge arbitrageurs," tapping into the pool of highly educated, cheap labor on the mainland to start up their own high-technology ventures.

An example is Horace Tsiang, who was born on the mainland, acquired U.S. citizenship, and then worked at Wang Laboratories for 23 years before that company was edged out of the personal computer marketplace. Today, Tsiang is CEO of Taiwan's First International, a PC firm valued at $600 million. Working alongside him are many of his former Wang Labs employees.

Allan C. Y. Wong was educated in the United States before becoming an electrical engineer at NCR Corporation. Today, he runs VTech Holdings Ltd., a Hong Kong-based firm that supplies cellular phones and educational toys such as children's computers. In 1994, VTech was valued at over $500 million. Wong's goal is to quadruple the company's size by expanding his manufacturing operations on the mainland.[34]

Western firms doing business in Southeast Asia must come to terms with the fact that the overseas Chinese are a force to be reckoned with. Doing business in that region very often means dealing with the traditional Chinese middlemen, whose grip has grown increasingly strong. Those middlemen include local distributors, after-sales service agencies, transportation companies, intermediate processors, insurance agents, accounting firms, advertising agencies, and warehousing companies.[35]

Nevertheless, ethnic Chinese firms themselves face long-term limitations. As noted earlier, their most noticeable weakness is a reluctance to enter the world of brand-name goods and mass marketing. Inevitably, family businesses face size limitations that restrict the range of activities that can be managed inside their boundaries. As a result, these firms often need the international marketing capabilities that a Western company can offer. Alliances between Western and overseas Chinese firms can prove beneficial to both parties, a marriage of high technology and regional business savvy.

Reluctant to destroy their bridge to international markets, overseas Chinese firms are not likely in the short run to expand their activities to include the specialized functions of their Western partners. Because of this, partnerships can be long lasting if both players appreciate the differences in each other's operating methods. Attempts to transform an informal Chinese enterprise into a more bureaucratic, Western-style corporation are not likely to succeed. Although some of the leading overseas Chinese tycoons, such as Li Ka-shing and Mochtar Riady, have begun to hire Westerners for top-level corporate slots, the family business remains the standard organizational form in the bamboo network.

A LOOK TO THE FUTURE

U.S. companies have invested in more than 2,000 projects in China, with a combined contract value of over $6 billion. In an extensive federal government survey of American firms interested in doing business in China, that country's great market potential was identified as the primary reason for wanting to do business there. The second most important factor was the increasing pace of economic reform and liberalization. (Chapter 8 analyzes the likelihood of the reforms continuing.)

Americans are investing in China at a rapid pace. By the end of 1994, more than 80 of the top 500 U.S. corporations had established some form of joint venture in China. One development area near Beijing has attracted General Motors, AT&T, and General Electric, as well as Germany's Bayer, Sweden's ABB Corporation, and Japan's National Electric. Ford has signed a $20 million joint venture with the Shanghai Yaohua Glass Works to produce automobile windshields for export. Amoco is in the process of investing $1.2 billion to explore petroleum reserves in Hainan province and to lay a connecting pipeline to Hong Kong.[36]

In January 1995, four U.S. institutional investors formed a joint company to make $100 million in direct investments. The partners—Bridgewater Associates, the Hughes Investment Company, the Rockefeller Foundation, and U.S. West, Inc.—set up a representative office in Beijing to oversee the investments. Rather than financing new ventures, this fund will specialize in buying into China's government-owned enterprises. Beijing is still debating the amount of foreign ownership that will be allowed.[37]

The difficulties of doing business in China are also becoming clearer. In January 1995, Chrysler announced that there was less than a 50 percent chance that it would reach an agreement with the Chinese government to build minivans in that country. Apparently, the Beijing authorities were insisting on conditions not acceptable to Chrysler. The company had hoped to invest $500 million in a joint venture to assemble 60,000 vehicles a year at a factory in Guangdong province, but had learned that a Chinese factory located near its own production facility was turning out knockoffs of its locally produced Jeep.[38]

The company's prediction turned out to be accurate. In July 1995, the Chinese government announced that its $1.2 billion minivan joint venture contract would be awarded to Germany's Daimler-Benz. Although the German manufacturer may well have won the contract for economic reasons, the timing of the announcement (shortly after harsh criticism from Beijing regarding Taiwanese President Lee's U.S. visit) led many to believe that the decision was politically motivated. As evidence, automobile analysts pointed out that Daimler-Benz had never produced a passenger minivan, whereas Chrysler had extensive, worldwide expertise in minivan production. For its part, Chrysler downplayed the incident, stating that it had lost the contract because of its demand to retain control over Chrysler technology; its German competitor was more complacent on that score.[39]

Because of these problems and uncertainties, many American businesses are examining the very substantial opportunities that are becoming available elsewhere in Southeast Asia. Often, those opportunities involve far less hassle than is the case in China, although they also have substantially less long-term market potential. Nevertheless, the economies of Malaysia, Indonesia, Singapore, Thailand, and Vietnam are registering healthy economic growth rates in the neighborhood of 8 percent a year—while keeping inflation in single digits.

As in China, the major investors in these countries are overseas Chinese, plus many Japanese and Korean companies. However, U.S. companies also have an important and expanding presence in this region. Exxon is developing a major national gas field in Indonesia, General Motors has built automobile plants in Indonesia and Thailand, and IBM is opening a large disk-drive factory in Singapore.

Each of the Southeast Asian nations has its own set of pluses and minuses that need to be evaluated on a country-by-country basis. Typically, the advantages include government encouragement of foreign investment, a productive workforce, and relatively low costs of production. The disadvantages include a history of violent reaction against foreign (but mainly Chinese) businesses and, on occasion, the violent overthrow of the government in office. In recent years, the situation in the region has been much more benign.

The extent to which U.S. and other Western investors will emphasize China in their future plans will depend upon the attractiveness of that impressively large and rapidly growing market—in both absolute terms and relative to alternatives in the region of which it is such a large part. To a substantial extent, there is competition among the various Southeast Asian nations for the foreign funds so necessary to their continued economic development.

From the viewpoint of Americans and other foreign investors, China and Southeast Asian markets generally represent important opportunities for diversifying their portfolios. Historically, Western business has focused elsewhere, especially in Europe and North America. As we saw in Chapter 2, overseas Chinese businesses are expanding their investments beyond both the

country in which they are based and their ancestral homeland—
to include the entire Southeast Asia region, as well as Australia
and North America. In both cases, business leaders—Western
and ethnic Chinese—are responding to the increasing globalization of markets made possible by technological advances in transportation and communications.

Clearly, companies around the world respond to government
actions that make a country's economy more—or less—inviting
to foreign investors. China's future success in attracting capital
from American and other foreign investors will depend upon the
extent to which it takes strong action in several key areas well
within its control—strengthening its legal system, enforcing contracts and establishing property rights, and protecting residents
against arbitrary governmental actions. So long as uncertainty
characterizes this challenging business environment, the companies of the bamboo network will continue to benefit from their
special relationship with and understanding of China. American
business needs to pay more attention to the ways in which it can
take advantage of that special relationship and understanding.

PART IV

THE FUTURE

CHAPTER 7

International Implications
of a Greater China

Business is the ultimate force for democratic change in China.
—Dissident Li Lu

Throughout the twentieth century, mainland China has remained outside the circle of traditional world superpowers, but that isolation is ending as the PRC takes a more active role in the international community. The established superpowers, as well as other nations, will increasingly feel the effects of that more active role. However, a great deal of uncertainty attaches to almost every aspect of China's relationship with the rest of the world.

During the Cold War, China succeeded in commanding international power and respect as a member of the nuclear "club." Nevertheless, it was still perceived in most other matters as a backward Third World nation, one of the poorest in the world. The economic failure of communism contrasted sharply with the success of nearby Hong Kong and Taiwan. Politically, China shut itself off from the world during this era. Closing off its borders to trade and investment turned out to be a much more effective barrier to Western "invaders" than the Great Wall, erected over 2,000 years earlier, had been.

185

Militarily, China has lacked the ability to project its power over water, and its technologically outclassed forces were unable to fight a modern ground war. Even at the height of the Cold War, China never represented a serious military threat to any Western power. Indeed, some American strategists spoke flippantly of "playing the China card," implying that the mainland was merely a pawn in the struggle between the United States and the Soviet Union.

All of these factors have changed dramatically in recent years. As we have already seen, economic progress since the death of Mao Tse-tung is unprecedented. Sustained double-digit growth rates have quadrupled aggregate economic output. In an almost symbiotic relationship, Hong Kong and Taiwan have also experienced breathtaking growth during this period. With the help of the mainland's cheap labor, these smaller economies have been able to penetrate many product markets once dominated by the United States, Europe, and Japan.

Such international competition has not been limited to the economic arena. With its newfound wealth, China is also emerging as a military superpower. Economic growth has allowed the People's Liberation Army (PLA) to procure more sophisticated military hardware and to increase its power radius to include Vietnam, India, Korea, southern Russia, and Japan. Furthermore, by opening its borders to trade, China is rapidly becoming a major voice in world politics through its membership in United Nations organizations.

This chapter explores some of the international consequences of Greater China's economic transformation that have already come about, as well as the long-term implications associated with the rise of this new Asian superpower.

GROWING MILITARY POWER

Effective military establishments—those that can project force and fight wars, rather than simply suppress internal dissent—are expensive. This simple fact has severely constrained membership in the club of major military powers since the end of World War

II. With its newfound wealth, however, China is increasingly capable of funding a modern, large-scale military establishment.

The Gulf War shocked many of the world's military leaders—including China's—into recognizing that success on the modern battlefield requires technologically advanced combat and support units. Large stockpiles of outdated equipment are of little use in a conflict against a more advanced, mobile opponent. Realizing this, the PLA is striving to reshape its armed forces, focusing on firepower, mobility, and the ability to project its military strength in a variety of operational environments.

Many national security and political analysts have voiced concern over these recent efforts to upgrade China's military capability. Underlying much of this concern is fundamental uncertainty concerning the size of the PLA's budget. There is no doubt that it has increased substantially in recent years. On the basis of official data, the PLA's budget rose over 50 percent (in real terms) between 1988 and 1993, to roughly $7.5 billion (as measured by international exchange rates).[1]

However, such official budget numbers are routinely dismissed by national defense experts as too low. In addition to the standard problems of currency conversion (as described in Chapter 4), Chinese defense budgets exclude expenditures for many items that are crucial in determining military effectiveness. Weapons research and development is included in the civilian category of scientific and technological activities. For example, the Ministry of Light Industry is responsible for the development and manufacture of conventional weapon systems. Likewise, the Ministry of Energy Resources is partially responsible for the enhancement of nuclear capabilities (as in the case of the U.S. Department of Energy, some of the results are applied to military use). Military budgets also omit expenses for military academies, civilian employees of the Ministry of Defense, and procurement of weapon systems from other countries (such as the Sukhoi-27 interceptor aircraft purchased from Russia).

Efforts to translate the published budget figures into estimates of actual military spending are little more than educated guesses. An upper-bound rule of thumb is to multiply the official budget fivefold, which would increase the 1993 figure to roughly $35 billion. However, this crude approximation does not address the critical issue of purchasing power parity. Labor costs, for example, are a large component of most Western military budgets. In China, extremely low labor costs bias any attempt to make cross-country comparisons of defense expenditures.[2]

Even when adjusted for such cost differentials, military expenditures do not necessarily indicate the technological quality of a nation's armed forces. Thus, instead of focusing merely on the raw numbers contained in defense budgets, we must examine tangible changes in Chinese military equipment and organization in order to assess the PLA's ability to fight and win a modern conflict.

It is clear that the PLA has been engaged in a military spending spree over the last decade, acquiring a wide variety of high-technology equipment from other nations. In particular, the mainland has done substantial business with the cash-strapped countries of the former USSR. Purchases of SU-27 attack aircraft, MIG-31 fighters, T-72 tanks, and Mi-17 helicopters are the most visible examples of this trading relationship. However, these high-profile weapons are probably less critical than other procurements of advanced technology—such as air defense, electronic warfare, transport aircraft, and airborne early warning systems—that signal a broad-based effort on the part of the PLA to improve its fighting capability. In recent years, an informal military exchange program has developed between China and Russia, with Russian scientists visiting China to provide technical assistance and Chinese officers visiting Russia to receive training.[3]

In light of these developments, other Southeast Asian nations have boosted their military capabilities in recent years. Taiwan has ordered six frigates from France and is building eight more under license from the United States. Thailand has acquired three frigates from China and Indonesia has purchased 39 naval vessels formerly owned by East Germany. Singapore is building five corvettes under license from Germany, while Malaysia has ordered two missile frigates from Great Britain.

The age-old regional rivalries that exist in the area contribute to this buildup in weaponry. The size of the Vietnamese Army (700,000 troops) is cited by Thailand as a reason for its military expansion. The Thais are building new air and naval facilities on their southeastern coast, giving them a greater military presence in the South China Sea. The steady improvement in the military capabilities of Malaysia and Indonesia is a source of concern in Singapore.

Michael Klare, director of the Hampshire College Program in Peace and World Security, notes that China and the other East Asian nations are not content simply to purchase their arms on the world market. Instead, they seek the technology to manufacture arms of their own. This is unlike the tendency of the other developing countries (in Africa, Latin America, and the Middle East), which prefer to import finished weapon systems from more developed suppliers.[4]

China in particular has become increasingly capable of producing its own high-tech military equipment. It has always enjoyed a skilled stock of scientists, although their training has often been more theoretical than applied. Over the last decade, China has been producing an array of standard military items, mainly based on Soviet designs going back to the 1950s and 1960s. Today, joint ventures with foreign investors expose Chinese engineers to more advanced manufacturing technologies. Eased emigration laws also allow Chinese students to study at leading Western engineering schools. Closer links with Taiwan could provide the technological know-how to produce sophisticated computer and electronic components. Meanwhile, Taiwan is developing its Indigenous Defensive Fighter and a variation of the Patriot missile.

Both China and Taiwan are expanding their military arsenals at a rapid rate. Under present circumstances, Taiwan is reluctant to help the mainland produce weaponry that might one day be used against itself. Increasingly friendly ties with Beijing in the future and burgeoning informal trade could counteract this mistrust.

U.S. aerospace and electronics companies already sell China a variety of end products and advanced technologies that have potential military applications. Chinese procurement teams have been buying up used aerospace machinery and reportedly shipping entire military production lines to China. Much of the equipment has dual uses. For example, the gas turbine engines sold by Garrett Engine Company power jet trainers but might also be used to make an improved Chinese cruise missile. Even more disturbing is the fact that some of these parts may be re-exported to nations such as Iran to earn foreign exchange and expand China's access to Middle Eastern oil.[5]

The enhancement of China's military technology can be interpreted as aggressive and threatening to neighboring countries—and it may well be. Nevertheless, it can also be argued that, in the dangerous world in which we live, it makes good sense for a nation that has achieved a tremendous increase in wealth to invest in more and better military equipment. The more important issue to consider is whether the *nature* of the PRC's military strategy has changed to a more offensive stance. That is, do China's new military capabilities signal a desire to develop the potential for offensive operations and to shift the strategic balance in Asia? Some inferences can be made from shifts in the composition of its military budget.

Historically, the Chinese military has been landlocked, relying upon vast numbers of infantry and low-tech artillery for the bulk of its power. The PLA has never been able to develop a modern navy. Its warships have little or no air defense, its radars have extremely limited range, and its submarines are noisy and fitted with unreliable torpedoes.

Recently, however, the PRC has aroused the suspicion of its neighbors with significant acquisitions of more advanced naval technology. Many of these new purchases—such as amphibious assault ships, missile frigates, and destroyers—are clearly intended for projection of naval power. China is also negotiating the purchase of 22 Kilo-class submarines from Russia. And, most ominously to some, China has expressed a desire to acquire the quintessential symbol of modern military power: an aircraft carrier. Clearly, an attempt to transform the Chinese navy from a "brown-water" to a "blue-water" navy is well under way.[6]

Another potentially disturbing development is China's continued modernization of its nuclear forces. China already possesses land-based intercontinental and intermediate-range ballistic missiles, as well as a ballistic missile submarine with a striking range of over 1,000 miles. However, the quality of these existing systems (particularly the submarine, which reportedly spends most of its time in dock) is very low. Concerned about the reliability and survivability of its admittedly primitive delivery systems, the PLA is aggressively moving forward to develop a credible, twenty-first century nuclear deterrent. Some believe that Russia and Ukraine may be assisting in these modernization efforts by exporting technology for use in mobile missile systems (Beijing began testing a mobile ICBM in mid-1995). As further evidence of its intentions, China continues to test large-yield nuclear weapons.

In all, China is believed to possess roughly 400 nuclear warheads. Ranked by explosive power, its nuclear arsenal is the world's third largest, behind only the United States and Russia. In addition to its ballistic missiles, the PLA has a force of about 200 bombers that supposedly are capable of delivering nuclear payloads. No other nation in the area even begins to possess such a strategic capability.

Despite obvious concerns, the PLA's arms buildup may have purposes beyond offensive military action. Advanced defense technology could serve as a source of national prestige. More concretely, a powerful military provides an equally strong deterrent. China continues to perceive Russia and the United States as potential strategic enemies. Thus, it is difficult to argue that China should not build up its military readiness to a level commensurate with other nations that could project substantial military power in the region. Russia's nuclear arsenal dwarfs that of the PLA, Japan maintains an advanced air force and navy, and India currently possesses two aircraft carriers (and seeks to acquire more). China's desire for a strong military is even more understandable, and perhaps even appropriate, given its long history of exploitation and defeat by foreign aggressors. Lastly, it should be remembered that, before China can become an effec-

tive world power, it likely will take decades for the PLA to rework its backward logistics, training, and command and control
systems.

Indeed, efforts to upgrade the PLA's fighting ability may be
counteracted by its forays into the private sector. PLA factories
produce motorcycles, washing machines, refrigerators, clothing,
and many other items for sale in civilian markets. Corrupt military officials earn extra money by selling weaponry, raiding local
shipping, and selling military license plates that allow the bearer
to avoid inspections and tolls. In 1994, the particularly enterpris-
ing PLA command in Guangdong announced the establishment
of a "military tourism zone" where visitors can fire weapons,
parachute from military aircraft, and even take part in PLA ma-
neuvers.

Despite these distractions, the continued modernization of the
PLA, particularly of its capability to project force within the region, is potentially destabilizing. The rapid decline in the readiness of the Russian armed forces, plus recent dramatic cutbacks
in American military spending, have created a strategic vacuum
in Southeast Asia, one that China seems to be moving to fill.

As evidence of this, China has begun to export its domestically
produced weaponry throughout the region. Chinese defense specialists are suspected of collaborating with North Korea to build
long-range missiles. Weapons exports to Myanmar have included
tanks, armored personnel carriers, and multiple rocket-launcher
systems. Despite Chinese pledges not to arm the Khmer Rouge,
several large caches of Chinese weapons have been discovered in
Thailand near the Cambodian border. Not all of these transactions represent official Chinese policy: corrupt PLA officers are
suspected in these cross-border trades.[7]

Some Western military experts interpret the PLA's modernization as a concerted effort to position China as the predominant
military force in Asia early in the twenty-first century.[8] This potential shift in geopolitical power has created a climate of uncertainty if not tension all through East Asia. These fears are compounded by the territorial disputes among China and its
neighbors, the most dramatic of which concerns the sovereignty

of Taiwan. A PLA invasion of Taiwan would face stubborn resistance from modern, entrenched forces. Furthermore, despite Taiwan's unofficial status in the international community, the United States is not likely to ignore such open aggression. The American response to an invasion could range from economic sanctions to direct military intervention. At present, there seems to be little potential for overt hostilities between the mainland and Taiwan, outside of an unintentional blunder into armed conflict.

Other disputes are more likely and thus more troubling. One potential military flashpoint is the South China Sea, parts of which are claimed by China, Vietnam, Malaysia, Brunei, Taiwan, and the Philippines. This region has tremendous strategic significance. All ocean shipping among those six countries, as well as the transport of oil from the Persian Gulf to Japan, takes place across the South China Sea (see map). Furthermore, the area contains the disputed Spratly Islands (or Nansha Islands, as they are called by the Chinese), a chain of roughly 60 islands around which are located vast oil and gas reserves. The value of the petrochemical deposits surrounding the Spratlys has been estimated at over $1 trillion. Estimates of recoverable oil range widely, from 11 billion to almost 160 billion barrels. Not too surprisingly, China considers control of the South China Sea to be essential to its future.

A serious territorial dispute in the South China Sea could provide the spark to ignite a regional conflagration. As early as 1951, Zhou Enlai, then foreign minister of the PRC, insisted upon the "inviolable sovereignty of the People's Island and the Paracel archipelago."[9] Beijing has declared that it will not use force to settle the Spratly dispute, yet in the past it has not hesitated to flex its muscles. In 1988, China invaded seven islands controlled by Vietnam, killing roughly 70 Vietnamese soldiers in the process. The following year, elements of the Chinese navy engaged Vietnamese merchant vessels, forestalling any reinforcement of Hanoi's claim to the islands.

Since 1991, when the U.S. Navy withdrew from the Philippines, tensions in the region have become more pronounced.

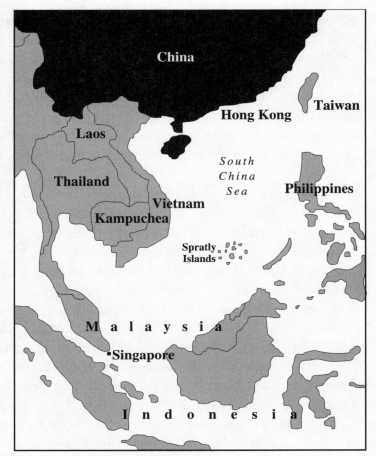

South China Sea: A Strategic Area

Most of the six nations that have claims on some portion of the Spratlys have placed military forces on the islands they currently hold. In January 1992, the PRC sent 132 officials to make a circuit of the Spratly archipelago. These representatives from the army, the navy, and the Communist Party posted claim plaques on the major islets, atolls, and sand banks of the Spratly chain. Later that year, China made the particularly aggressive move of allowing a Colorado-based firm, backed up by PLA forces, to explore for oil in Vietnamese-controlled territory.

The Spratlys are only one potential target within the South China Sea. In 1992, the National People's Congress issued the

"Law on the Territorial Waters and their Contiguous Areas," laying claim to 80 percent of the South China Sea. Included in this area is the Natuna gas field, currently controlled by Indonesia.

China's military modernization efforts seem directed toward potential conflict in the South China Sea. The PLA has constructed a military airstrip capable of landing fighter bombers and transport aircraft on one of the Paracel Islands, which it took from Vietnam in 1974, potentially providing support for an invasion of the Spratlys. Furthermore, the PLA is developing the ability to deploy troops rapidly throughout the region. It has organized several marine units for amphibious assault, as well as airborne forces that could be dropped from its Russian-made transport aircraft. From time to time, each of the countries bordering the South China Sea has sent naval vessels into the area to assert its claim. Indonesia has increased its air patrols around the Natuna Islands.[10]

Japan also has reason to be concerned over the PLA's modernization. Despite its declared pacifism, Japan has developed a formidable military capability by using its economic wealth to procure advanced fighter aircraft and state-of-the-art naval technology. But China is rapidly overtaking Japan in terms of both aggregate economic size and military strength. Both of these trends point toward an impending fierce competition between China and Japan for Asian leadership.

Clearly, the military balance of power within Southeast Asia is shifting. The military buildup of China, and also of its neighbors, points to a change in war-fighting strategies, technologies, and attitudes. Surely this buildup signals that—despite the concentration on economic progress—military strength continues to be an essential element of foreign policy in the region.

THE POLITICS OF TRADE

The impact of China's emergence as an economic and military superpower will not be confined to Southeast Asia. Both the benefits and the costs of economic development spill across national boundaries. In the case of China, its massive size threatens to alter fundamentally the world balance of economic, political, and military power. Fitting Greater China into the club of large developed nations will not be easy. Mutual accommodations will have to be reached. Sooner or later, Western nations will have to accept the realities of a new world economy with three distinct trading regions: North America, Europe, and East Asia.

On the surface, Japan appears to be in the best position to seize the opportunities provided by a rapidly growing East Asia. In 1994, Japanese exports to East Asia topped $130 billion, over 20 percent more than Japan's exports to the United States. Half of Japanese overseas employees are located in East Asia, as are 40 percent of Japan's overseas manufacturing investments. Studies by Japan's Ministry of International Trade and Industry (MITI) report that Japan's most profitable current investments are in the East Asian region.

Nevertheless, although Japan's edge over Western nations in this region is substantial, the PRC presents a rapidly emerging threat to Japanese dominance. In the short run, China faces the challenge of managing its transition from a xenophobic, socialist nation into a mature market economy. The productive forces that have been unleashed in the coastal regions are still restrained by government policies and fundamental uncertainty about the future (several alternative scenarios are explored in the next chapter).

If the West could find an acceptable way to assist China through this transition, that would be of mutual benefit. Such a display of enlightened self-interest, could it be achieved, would minimize the instability arising from dramatic change. Both parties would be the beneficiaries of increased economic—and thus political—openness.

To date, however, the role of the United States in this process has not been clearly defined by its leaders, as evidenced by the persistent controversies surrounding human rights, trade, and diplomatic issues. Economists in general believe that free and open trade between the United States and China would be of mutual economic benefit and would likely help to improve relations between the two nations. Nevertheless, many activists consider it essential to use trade with

China as a lever to force changes in that country's internal policies and as a statement of American opposition to human rights abuses and political oppression.

Memories of the 1989 Tiananmen Square episode remain vivid to many Americans. A rare public analysis by U.S. military officers attached to the commander-in-chief of the U.S. Pacific force concluded that the Chinese leadership inexcusably overreacted in the face of what was perceived as a serious challenge to public order: "They badly mishandled an extremely volatile situation."[11] China's unwillingness to admit that it erred, much less to apologize, keeps the wound open.

However, instead of providing support for continued violations of human rights, free trade may hasten their end. We share the view of numerous analysts that closer economic ties will help China to better understand the close connection between economic freedom and personal liberty. As we have already seen, economic growth has improved the welfare of hundreds of millions of Chinese citizens. Commercial products and advertising carry messages of personal choice. American companies that hire Chinese labor inevitably transmit Western political and economic values.

Barring trade between China and the United States would not only prevent the continuation of these positive trends but would also smack of a rather hypocritical moral superiority. Can the United States credibly demand an end to prison labor when U.S. military procurement regulations require defense contractors to purchase designated items from the Federal Prison Industries, an agency of the federal government that sells products made in our jails? A related argument in favor of continuing most-favored-nation treatment of China is more practical: to ensure that American firms and workers are able to participate in the area's rising economic opportunities.

Nevertheless, one major American company—Levi's—has terminated most of its business dealings in China because of "pervasive human rights abuses." However, Levi's involvement in China was not large. The company bought shirts and trousers worth about $50 million a year from Chinese subcontractors. Although it continues to buy fabric from mainland sources, Levi's believes that the negative repercussions of purchasing finished goods from China outweigh any immediate business interests. In the long run, however, Levi's may be sacrificing a great deal—the potential loss of the Chinese consumer market. As one analyst notes, "If Levi's decides to return to China, it may find the door locked."[12]

Other companies have developed more targeted means of ensuring that their business dealings in China do not encourage human rights abuses. Nike has developed a corporate code of conduct that it asks its subcontractors to sign. Sears, Roebuck, and Co. has announced that it will not import any goods produced by prison labor.[13]

These experiences illustrate the inevitable link between politics and business. Trade quotas, government contracts, tariffs, and a host of other economic weapons allow government to exert its influence over private markets. In China, given the importance of state-owned firms to the national economy, this influence is extremely pervasive. Fallout over Taiwanese President Lee's visit to the United States in 1995 caused the mayor of Shanghai to cancel a high-profile meeting with the chairmen of Ford, GM, IBM, AT&T, Intel, Citicorp, Boeing, and several other major corporations.[14]

In its dealings with China and other developing countries, Germany has adopted a policy of "critical dialogue" meant to minimize political confrontations while maintaining strong economic ties. From a business perspective, this policy appears to work quite well. Germany has become China's largest European trade partner and has secured a number of high-profile automobile contracts (including the minivan deal discussed in Chapter 6).[15]

In recent years, Beijing–Washington relations have stumbled through a number of high-profile incidents, raising doubts about a long-term beneficial relationship between the two. China seeks definite assurances that the United States will not recognize Taiwan and will remain committed to economic trade by maintaining China's most-favored-nation status. Unfortunately, recent U.S. policy has not sent clear signals on either of these issues or on other areas of concern, such as human rights and the proliferation of military technology. Part of this indecision may be a calculated effort to restrain China's ascent as a world power. On the other hand, it may simply be diplomatic fumbling by unfocused administrations. Whatever the reason, U.S.–China relations leave a great deal of room for improvement.[16]

Frequently, U.S. businesses end up paying the price of arbitrary governmental policy. Such was the experience of Westinghouse and Hughes Electronics. American suspicions that China was aiding Pakistan with its nuclear weapons program led to a 1985 ban on sales of nuclear technology to Beijing. This sanction was tightened further in 1989, following the Tiananmen crackdown, when exports of all components for use in Chinese nuclear power plants were halted. It took Westinghouse Electric until 1995 to secure a contract for the sale of steam turbine and generating equipment, and then only with the blessing of a special waiver from the Clinton Administration.[17]

Hughes Electronics has also had to navigate its way through an ever-changing political battlefield. Hughes, a subsidiary of General Motors, is the world's largest producer of telecommunications satellites. As we have already seen, China's existing telecommunications infrastructure has been unable to meet rising consumer demand. Because of this, the Greater Chinese market is expected to require 20 to 30 new telecommunications satellites over the next decade. In 1993, Hughes was poised to sell at least ten of these satellites to the PRC. In August of that same year, however, the American government abruptly banned all satellite exports to China in response to evidence that Beijing had exported missile technology to Pakistan.

Cut off from American markets, Beijing went forward with a joint venture between China Aerospace Corporation and Deutsche Aerospace to produce satellites comparable to those offered by Hughes. (The first is expected to be launched in 1996.) In 1994, however, the U.S. government lifted its export ban after the Chinese agreed not to sell its missiles to Arab countries. Although the short-term political objective was achieved, Hughes and other U.S. satellite manufacturers are now playing catch-up in an effort to regain their competitive positions in China.[18]

Arguments that promote the economic isolation of China often miss the central point. Amidst the heated rhetoric, the serious and more practical question—What is the most effective way of helping the Chinese people achieve more freedom?—is not asked. The irony is that the major victim of a reduction in U.S. trade relations with China would not be Beijing's communist leadership. The impact of trade restrictions on state-run monopolies and on the more repressive rural provinces would be secondary at best. Rather, Hong Kong, Guangdong, and Fujian—the regions that have made the greatest strides toward economic and personal freedoms—would be hurt most.

Judging by the negative Chinese responses to highly visible cajoling and needling from U.S. officials, threatening China with economic punishment does not serve to advance the cause of freedom and democracy. Given its long history of occupation by Western powers and Japan, the government of China is understandably touchy about infringements of its sovereignty. Westerners may have forgotten those unfortunate episodes but the Chinese surely have not. Given our own shortcomings, it is unseemly for Americans to publicly lecture another nation on its morals. As a practical matter, it is not a sensible or effective way of conducting international diplomacy.

All of these concerns, however, do not constitute an adequate excuse for ignoring the subject of human rights. Rather, more sensible ways of encouraging China to improve its track record need to be identified and pursued. Some useful insights can be gained by examining the recent experience of China's neighbors. At the end of World War II, South Korea and Taiwan were also governed by totalitarian governments that severely restricted the liberties of their citizens. Not bound by Western traditions of personal liberty, both of these Asian countries instituted policies to promote private enterprise while maintaining the other aspects of a totalitarian society. Not until much later did they begin to carry out reforms to enhance political freedom.

Clearly, most Americans prefer things to work the other way around. The prevailing Western view is that political freedom is paramount and economic freedom will inevitably follow. However, we must admit that this approach has not worked very well in Russia and the other former republics of the USSR. The loosening of restrictions on personal liberties, however welcome, has not satisfied the needs of people who suffer economic deprivation. The widespread substitution of private tyranny (the Russian mafia) for formal Soviet police power is not viewed by the typical Russian as much of an improvement. Many long for the prereform days, when safety, as well as poverty, was ensured.

How different the situation has been in Taiwan and South Korea. In both cases, greater economic freedom has led to tremendous economic growth accompanied by substantial increases in wealth and income. The rise of a large array of private enterprises has substantially decentralized power in those formerly totalitarian or authoritarian societies. Moreover, the development of a strong middle class has generated pressures for political liberalization. This, in turn, has led to important movements toward more democratic political structures, including open national elections. On balance, the lot of the average citizen of Taiwan and South Korea—economically and politically—has improved markedly since the process of liberalization began.

Singapore's combination of economic prosperity and tough social control, another variation of the "Asian model," is an example that many government planners in China would like to follow. They believe that this approach will enable them to keep their power and avoid the experiences of the former Soviet Union while gaining the benefits of economic growth. Singapore has had the same ruling party for 37 years, providing a high degree of internal stability amidst rising levels of income and employment. At least during this period, market capitalism and strict internal political and social rule have been quite compatible.

To a degree, China has been following the Asian model. As we have seen, the government of the PRC has embarked on selective liberalization, mainly in the coastal Special Economic Zones, which have attracted large amounts of foreign investment and technological know-how. The resultant rapid economic growth in these areas has led to some decentralization of power from Beijing to the provinces. Certainly the personal freedoms available to the Chinese people are very limited by Western standards. However, the visible creation of income and wealth in the new zones has led to some loosening, at least informally, of the severe limits on personal liberty. In Guangdong, especially, foreigners report an improvement in the everyday lives of the citizenry.

Foreign investment has provided more than financial resources. It has also carried new cultural and technological ideas to the mainland. Throughout the coastal areas, posters of communist rhetoric have been replaced by advertisements for consumer goods. Privately owned satellite dishes receive Western programming, including uncensored international news broadcasts and some of the less savory aspects of American culture, such as "gangsta rap." Beijing has largely given up its effort to ban these satellite dishes.

Another example of the power of technology to erode the power of the state is the globalization of the Internet, the open communications system that operates via computer networks. By the end of 1995, China's top 100 universities had access to the Internet. By the year 2000, all Chinese universities are expected to be able to access the uncensored bulletin boards, databases, and news services that are available on the Internet. The Ministry of Posts and Telecommunications has already begun providing commercial Internet access to citizens not affiliated with universities.[19]

As the liberalization accompanying the formation of the Special Economic Zones extends further inland, the role of the private sector in China is continuing to expand. The result is likely to be a continued gradual movement away from totalitarianism.

"I firmly believe that business is the ultimate force for democratic change in China."[20] That is the statement not of a U.S. corporate spokesman but of Li Lu, an exiled Tiananmen Square student leader now studying at Columbia University. His words remind us of another benefit of an open relationship between China and the United States—students and professors from one country who work and study in the other constitute a human bridge between the two nations.

Treating China as a pariah would interrupt the process of liberalization now under way. It would disproportionately injure Guangdong—the province in the forefront of economic reform, with the least number of human rights violations. Here at home, removal of China's most-favored-nation status would be a victory for domestic protectionists who always advocate the restriction of imports into the United States—for whatever reason and regardless of the adverse effect on American exporting industries.

Viewed in a broader context, both China and the United States have a great deal to gain from developing a closer relationship. The United States represents the best partner to help China upgrade its technology through investment and joint venturing.[21] That vital and dynamic factor is additional to the more obvious role of the United States as China's leading export market.

However, this relationship should not be one-sided. For the United States, China is the most promising market for American business. Over a substantial period of time, its huge development and infrastructure needs will produce enormous export and investment opportunities for U.S. companies seeking geographic diversification.

From a strategic viewpoint, China is increasingly an important player on the world stage. It is a large and powerful factor in global power equations, representing a quarter of humanity and containing the fastest growing large economy in the world. It is also a major producer of armaments and a longtime member of the nuclear weapons club. It sees itself as a key spokesman for the developing world and takes this role seriously. Moreover, China is a permanent member of the Security Council of the United Nations. Its veto, had it been used, could have undermined the unified international effort in Desert Storm and prevented the application of economic sanctions against Iraq, Libya, and Serbia.

Clearly, attempting to isolate China would prove counterproductive from a great variety of viewpoints, from economic to social to political to national security.[22] A positive array of active relationships, involving both the public and the private sector, is likely to be far more productive.

ENVIRONMENTAL PROBLEMS

China's recent economic transformation has not occurred without significant pressure on the environment. Economic progress can mean ecological degradation, especially if environmental impacts are not given much weight in government and business decision-making. Erecting thousands of factories in Guangdong and Fujian within the last decade has been a boon to job creation; those factories, however, also discharge substantial amounts of surface, air, and water pollution. Likewise, automobiles and motorcycles, rather than bicycles, transport a new middle class and an expanded working class to and from these factories—generating substantial air pollution at the same time that they ease people's physical burdens. Villages are quickly growing into cities that require more energy, land, and other natural resources. All these developments have strained the ability of society to maintain economic growth without severely damaging the environment.

Nowhere is this situation more evident than in economically liberal Guangdong province, where development has been extremely uneven. The construction boom has created both modern skyscrapers and instant slums. Despite the predominance of bicycle traffic, the air is polluted and the streets are perpetually congested by a variety of motorized vehicles. In northeastern China, air pollution around the coal city of Benxi is so bad that it masks the area from the sight of reconnaissance satellites. Nearby Shenyang has the world's second highest level of suspended particulates.[23]

Environmental damage is not limited to China's urban areas, however. Short-sighted industrial, energy, and deforestation projects have caused widespread soil erosion and desertification. Some estimate that, since the Communist Revolution, China has lost a third of its crop land, a trend that shows no sign of reversal in the near future.[24]

Although there have been relatively few publicized ecological catastrophes in China, there is little doubt that its environmental quality is poor and deteriorating, and far more rapidly than in the West. Most of the southeastern coastal region suffers from acid rain. Mercury and lead poisoning among children is rising. Uncontrolled use of pesticides and fertilizers reportedly poisoned more than 100,000 Chinese during 1992 and 1993, killing more than 14,000 people. In July 1994, a chemical spill in the Huai River killed more than 13,000 tons of fish and contaminated the drinking water of thousands of people.[25]

Enforcement of antipollution laws is undermined by corruption. Offending factories are frequently owned by senior members of the Communist Party, who have the necessary *guanxi* to avoid shutdowns or fines. Furthermore, many believe that environmental quality is a luxury to be enjoyed only after China is wealthier and has developed a more advanced industrial base.

The heated debate in the United States preceding the approval of the North American Free Trade Agreement (NAFTA) highlighted the worries of many Americans over the adverse side-effects of the economic development of Second and Third World nations. At times, the high-minded concern over environmental factors seems to be motivated, or at least reinforced, by the less noble desire to eliminate low-cost foreign competition. For example, the *maquiladoras*—foreign-owned firms that receive preferential treatment in Mexican governmental policies, such as the duty-free importation of goods intended for reprocessing and export—are quite similar to China's Special Economic Zones. The largely unregulated *maquiladoras* have been successful in attracting foreign investment capital because of their low labor costs. However, they also have contributed to poor environmental conditions along the U.S.–Mexico border.[26] *Maquiladoras* found themselves assaulted in the NAFTA debate by both environmental and union activists. Likewise, China is frequently portrayed as an unfair economic contender: a low-wage country oblivious to the adverse impact of its industry on the global environment.

Realistically, some amount of environmental damage is to be expected in China. After all, environmental impact was routinely ignored during our own transition from a developing to a highly industrialized nation. Thus, it is unseemly for the United States—still one of the world's leading polluters—to pass judgment on the environmental policies of poorer developing nations. Nevertheless, China's combination of enormous population, rapidly growing economy, and expanding environmental problems has aroused the attention of environmentalists. They fear that unbridled development will have severe long-term consequences for the rest of the globe. The effects of air and water pollution are not limited by political boundaries. The Mekong River flows from China into Laos and Vietnam, the Salween River into Myanmar.

The relationship between economic development and the environment, however, is not clear or simple. Economists have identified three distinct links between economic growth and environmental quality—and they are not uniformly positive or negative.[27] First, and most obvious, expanded economic activity tends to require more natural resources and generate more pollutants. We must add a proviso often neglected by ecologists: this is true unless the production process is changed to reduce environmental degradation. Second, as a nation opens up to foreign trade, it specializes in sectors where it holds a comparative advantage. Part of this advantage can arise from the relative laxness of local environmental regulation. Because of this, nations with weak environmental laws may specialize in types of manufacturing that have particularly onerous environmental effects, because they can do so at lower cost than nations with more stringent pollution legislation.

Both of these effects imply that economic growth and environmental quality move in opposite directions. Yet high-income countries tend to have *lower* levels of air and water pollution than low-income countries.[28] This seeming anomaly can be explained by a third factor. Production techniques change as economies modernize. Richer nations can afford to utilize newer, cleaner, and more efficient (albeit more costly) technologies—and they usually do so. Spending for a clean environment rises even faster than income. That is, a wealthy citizenry can afford to place a higher value on environmental quality than a poor one. More stringent pollution standards appear to be a direct consequence of an expanding economy, and they offset some or all of the adverse environmental effects of economic growth.

All in all, how should we characterize the complex relationship

between growth and environmental quality? Princeton economists Gene Grossman and Alan Krueger have empirically estimated this relationship using data from the Global Environmental Monitoring System (which measures ambient levels of
pollutants such as sulfur dioxide, dark matter, and suspended
particles of dust and smoke in urban areas throughout the
world). When they control for other factors such as site location
and population density, Grossman and Krueger find that pollution levels do generally rise as per capita GDP increases—but
only at very low levels of national income.

When a country achieves a higher level of income, the relationship goes the other way: pollution levels begin to fall as income rises. The turning point occurs at a level of per capita income somewhere between $5,500 and $7,000, measured in
1994 dollars.[29] Mainland China's per capita income is substantially below this level. Therefore, we should expect its environmental quality to continue to deteriorate for a while as economic
development progresses—until China reaches the turning point
in the relationship between economic growth and environmental
quality.

As a practical matter, little environmental progress is likely to
be made so long as China's primary energy source continues to
be coal, the dirtiest of all fuels in terms of carbon dioxide emissions. Reliance on coal for roughly 75 percent of the energy of its
massive population has caused China to rank third in carbon
dioxide emissions (behind the United States and the former Soviet Union), despite its low per capita output. Coal consumption
has been rising despite dramatic increases in energy efficiency
over the last decade. Energy use has grown at only half the rate of
economic expansion. Nevertheless, coal consumption is fore-
casted by many analysts to rise rapidly, from 1.1 billion tons in
1993 to over 1.4 billion tons a year by the end of the century.
Such findings have led some to forecast that China will become
the world's biggest generator of carbon dioxide, possibly by the
year 2025. Meanwhile, coal-fired power plants dump roughly 15
million tons of ash into China's rivers each year.[30]

There are signs, however, that China is trying to reverse these trends. In 1995, the Guangdong government declared that it would accept no new coal-burning power plants and that existing factories would have to install pollution-control equipment. Increasingly, Beijing is looking toward nuclear power to satisfy both its energy and its environmental needs.

Nevertheless, China's future environmental progress is dependent upon increases in its per capita income. So long as China remains poor, it can be expected to continue to downplay environmental concerns. There is no assurance that rising living standards will automatically make environmental cleanup a higher priority—but the economic wherewithal to do so will be present. In some of the coastal regions, incomes have already risen to the turning point experienced by other developing nations.

CONCLUSION

The rapid political, economic, and military changes occurring in Greater China are too profound to be ignored by the rest of the world. China is rapidly becoming a major world power. Some of the overt manifestations of its newly found strength—notably muscle flexing in the South China Sea—raise concerns among the other nations of Southeast Asia. Economic and political competition from the PRC generates broader repercussions around the world. Yet important positive developments must also be acknowledged. Over the past 20 years, China has made great strides toward opening its society. Although far from complete, the magnitude of this change is immense.

There are no assurances that Beijing will continue to reform its economic and political institutions or that it will limit its international competition to economic and business matters. But without substantial Western involvement, China could revert to being a closed society isolated from the international community. Such mutual withdrawal would be to our mutual disadvantage.

A less sanguine view of these matters, however, is held by a distinguished political scientist, Samuel P. Huntington of Harvard. He sees a "clash of civilizations" taking place between the advanced industrialized nations of the West and China and other sectors of East Asia dominated by Confucian thought and culture. Huntington notes that, with the end of the Cold War, the underlying differences between China and the United States have reasserted themselves in such important areas as human rights, trade, and weapons proliferation. He sees these differences as unlikely to moderate.[31] Worse yet, in the eyes of other analysts, it is possible that China could embark on an aggressive military campaign at the expense of its smaller neighbors. In the past, such regional conflicts often have widened to include the major military superpowers of the day.

The great uncertainty about the future direction of China has resulted in diametrically opposed forecasts by individual scholars. Professor Jack A. Goldstone of the University of California at Davis warns us that "We can expect a terminal crisis in China within the next 10 to 15 years."[32] At the same time, Professor Yasheng Huang of the University of Michigan explains "why China will not collapse."[33] In this vein, the eighth and final chapter of this book examines several alternative scenarios that describe China's future direction, and the possible responses by the bamboo network.

CHAPTER 8

The Foggy Crystal Ball:
Three Scenarios

For China's economy, the future is bright, the burden is heavy,
and the road is long.
—Liu Tonglin[1]

It is easy to speculate that China will follow the same path of rapid economic development as other Asian "dragons" such as Japan and South Korea. Given China's immense population, such a forecast implies staggering changes in the world's economy. Indeed, a small cottage industry has sprung up that engages in this particular form of intellectual entertainment.

However, it is not sensible to do a straight-line extrapolation of China's recent economic success for any long period of time. The future of the mainland—and, with it, all of Greater China—is tenuous and uncertain. Its distance from the West is far greater than a glance at the globe suggests. Fundamental differences in cultural orientation and political institutions complicate comparisons of China with more advanced economies. The gap in living standards between China and the developed nations of Europe, North America, and Asia has narrowed dramatically since 1978. A much greater and more difficult journey, however, remains to be traveled if even rough equality is to be achieved.

211

An unabashedly optimistic forecast is just not realistic given the array of political, social, and economic barriers to China's continuing development. After almost two decades of rapid change and growth, any serious observer must question China's underlying stability as well as its ability to continue moving forward with economic reforms. A Chinese saying comes to mind: "Leaders often lift up a rock only to drop it on their own feet—or on the feet of their fellow citizens."[2] Recent history, notably Mao's disastrous Cultural Revolution, vividly demonstrates China's unfortunate tendency to generate self-inflicted wounds.

TRANSITION OF POWER

The most obvious source of political and economic uncertainty in China is the question of how governmental power will be transferred after the death of Deng Xiaoping. Serving as "paramount leader," Deng lacks an official governmental post. He has little involvement in day-to-day administrative decisionmaking and is rarely seen in public (in part because of his rapidly deteriorating health). It is increasingly apparent that top Chinese Communist Party (CCP) officials are jockeying for position in a post-Deng China. Nevertheless, Deng—far more than any other individual—continues to exert considerable influence over political and economic decisions. He has done this largely by staying above the daily battles. Instead, he mediates disputes among the various factions of the CCP.

Deng is an enigmatic figure to most Westerners, who are accustomed to rigid political hierarchies and clearly defined authority. Just as the lack of efficient economic institutions in China necessitates informal, highly personalized trade, the absence of effective political law creates an environment in which individuals, even those outside of the formal political structure, can wield substantial power. When the role and authority of the public sector are ambiguous, as in today's China, government officials succeed or fail on the basis of their ability to lead, inspire, and manage coalitions of disparate or even competing interests. A master of such power brokering, Deng commands substantial authority over the CCP, the military, and, most importantly, the Chinese people.

The three main sources of Deng's authority are unlikely to be duplicated by any successor in the near future. First, he is one of the last surviving leaders of the Long March (the legendary retreat by tens of thousands of CCP members from 1934 to 1935 that saved the nucleus of the party from the forces of Chiang Kai-Shek). These senior leaders still hold claim to part of Mao's charisma and power, but they are aging rapidly. Following the deaths of Wang Zhen, Li Xiannian, and Chen Yun, the "Eight Immortals" led by Deng Xiaoping now number only five. The average age of those remaining is approximately 90. A clear successor to Deng is unlikely to emerge from this group.[3]

Second, Deng is the man singularly responsible for China's economic transformation. Through agricultural reform, he returned land to the peasants and directly improved the lives of hundreds of millions of people. His open door policy has attracted the foreign investment and management skills necessary for economic growth. Because of his leadership, the fledgling Special Economic Zones were able to set off the economic boom that has spread throughout the coastal regions. All together, Deng's economic policies have more than *quadrupled* China's output since 1978, a fact that has had an enormous positive impact on the Chinese citizenry.

Third, Deng has evolved from a mere political figure to China's symbolic emperor. His authority is accepted by many Chinese, perhaps because of both his quasicapitalistic economic successes and his communist pedigree. This ironic combination reflects the breadth of his power base. Deng has achieved a cult-like status among many Chinese. His persona may be the only force preventing political or spiritual *luan* (chaos) throughout much of China.[4]

Yet, despite his authority, splits within the CCP have produced factions highly critical of Deng and his socioeconomic policies. The quiet contempt of Deng on the part of hard-line conservatives is mirrored in Mao's characterization of him as "an arch unrepentant capitalist roader and harbinger of the right deviationist wind."[5] Deng's reputation may wane when his successor receives the inevitable public relations buildup after assuming power. It is even possible that Deng may be purged from the CCP (for the third time) after his death.[6]

The fundamental question remains: who will assume leadership of China after Deng? The lack of a formal political post of paramount leader means that there is no clear successor. Most believe that a protracted power struggle among China's senior leaders is inevitable. Deng himself has selected the CCP's General Secretary Jiang Zemin as his "preferred heir." Jiang is also state president and chairman of the Central Military Commission. Presently, he serves with Prime Minister Li Peng and Deputy Prime Minister (and economic czar) Zhu Rongji as part of a top-level triumvirate that governs China from Beijing. Li is the hardliner of the group while Zhu is Deng's protégé for continuing the economic reforms, although he has recently yielded the position of central bank chief. That certainly makes for an interesting trio, if not a particularly stable one.[7]

As Deng's chosen successor, Jiang would be expected to continue an aggressive market reform agenda. However, many view him as lacking a stable economic ideology. Nor does Jiang command the broad loyalty necessary to serve as the CCP's supreme power broker, managing coalitions to achieve difficult changes. Perhaps recognizing this, he has promoted several supporters from Shanghai, where he was mayor and party chief, to key political positions. He has also courted the military by appointing several new full generals. Over the last several years, Jiang has regularly visited People's Liberation Army (PLA) units to inspect the troops and meet the officer corps. Nevertheless, neither he nor any other members of the triumvirate has ever served in China's armed forces, a fact that limits their influence over the PLA.

A widespread lack of confidence in Jiang's ability to maintain power has led to enormous speculation regarding who will ultimately succeed Deng. Aside from the other members of the triumvirate, one potential candidate is Qiao Shi, chairman of the National People's Congress, member of the Politburo's standing committee, and former chief of China's internal security system.

Currently number three in the CCP hierarchy, following Jiang Zemin and Li Peng, Qiao abstained from the decision to impose martial law in 1989. He thus enjoys popular support among those who opposed the harsh response at Tiananmen Square. Although little is known of his stance on economic issues, Qiao has shown a strong interest in bolstering the power of the legislature. Once a rubber-stamp assembly, the congress is increasingly functioning as a true national legislature, with free debate of national policies. Qiao is not tainted by rumors of corruption that plague other potential successors and is viewed by many as a political liberal. However, his career in China's intelligence services worries many of his would-be supporters.[8]

Another candidate is Yang Shangkun, former president of the CCP. Unlike the other potential successors to Deng, Yang has close ties with the PLA. Because he is a veteran of the Long March, he maintains the image of a leading revolutionary hero. Yang is reported to be close to former CCP leader Zhao Ziyang, who was ousted (and replaced by Jiang) following the Tiananmen crackdown. Moreover, a group of influential political figures is reported to have embarked on a quiet effort to rehabilitate Zhao.

This short list of candidates is not all-inclusive. Many other figures stand poised to fill any power vacuum. All we can expect with any degree of confidence is that dramatic political maneuvering will follow Deng's death as CCP conservatives, moderates, and liberals battle to take over China's leadership. Any shakeup will have profound economic consequences, as companies and their leaders—both those in the bamboo network and those from the West—discover that their long-nurtured *guanxi* no longer have the authority to make things happen.

SOCIAL AND POLITICAL INSTABILITY

The power struggles going on within the senior echelons of the CCP are mirrored in the social and cultural clashes that permeate Chinese society. An odd climate of quasicapitalism has emerged from the combination of Deng's market reforms and the continuing socialist rhetoric of CCP hard-liners. For example, a Japanese-financed enterprise in China distributes "Lei Feng cards" to outstanding workers. The holders of these cards, which bear the name of a Chinese soldier selected by Mao as a communist role model, are rewarded with various bonuses. Such economic incentives, of course, run counter to the communist principles of sacrifice and egalitarianism. Nevertheless, the central government continues to promote "learn from Lei Feng" educational campaigns in an effort to stem the widespread adoption of "negative" capitalist values.[9] None of Deng's potential successors has articulated a solution to the social contradictions of today's China. The ultimate equilibrium of "market socialism" therefore remains in doubt.

Meanwhile, China's communist government faces steadily increasing pressure from its citizens, provincial governments, and surrounding border nations to ease—or even relinquish—its strong political control. Without a unified, central authority, the CCP will find it difficult to restrain the forces that threaten its ability to rule effectively. The challenge facing the CCP in the years ahead will be to maintain power while accommodating the separatist pressures that threaten to tear China apart.

The chaos following the dissolution of the Soviet Union bears witness to the political volatility that can accompany widespread and rapid changes in government policy and societal norms. In China, as we have already seen, heterogeneous economic policies across provinces have produced vast economic inequalities. By 1991, booming Shanghai had achieved a per capita gross domestic product *seven times* greater than that of inland Guizhou province.[10] A comparable level of inequality in the United States would mean that the average annual income of a resident of New York City was over $140,000.

Great differentials in wealth and income have effectively split the coastal regions from the traditionally rural inland provinces. The unequal pace of reforms across China's provinces has created great barriers to internal trade. Indeed, local entrepreneurs often find it easier to develop overseas customers than to market and distribute their products in another province.

Widespread unemployment is also accompanying the rapid

changes taking place in China's economy. According to government projections, the number of unemployed will reach nearly 270 million by the year 2000—out of what will then be a total population of 1.3 billion.[11] Because the actual labor force is only a fraction of the population, these numbers imply a painfully high unemployment rate. Even if the economy is able to absorb this excess labor, continued economic reforms will create distinct classes of winners and losers. As the absolute number of losers grows, and as their plight becomes more desperate, the central government will find it increasingly difficult to maintain internal political control.

The policies of the CCP are already being challenged by political dissidents, although thus far only to a limited degree. The prodemocracy movement has not been silenced despite the events following Tiananmen. A small but organized underground opposition movement—the Cooperative Committee of the China Democratic Salvation Front—was established in 1990. Larger numbers of prodemocracy dissident organizations exist outside of mainland China, headed by Tiananmen refugees.[12] If given the opportunity, these organizations will seek to generate a political crisis by tapping into the fear and anger of disenfranchised workers. This might force the CCP to institute political reforms—or to crack down again.

If threatened, the CCP may find that it has few regional allies. Indeed, many provinces appear eager to distance themselves as far as possible from the authorities in Beijing. Tibet provides the most obvious example. Only a third of the land area of Tibet that existed before the Chinese invasion in 1950 remains as the Tibet Autonomous Region. The rest has been fractured and incorporated into other provinces. Today, a garrison of about 40,000 PLA soldiers and paramilitary police presides over Tibet's 2.2 million people. The central government strictly controls access to the region by foreigners, especially journalists who might report human rights violations.[13]

The popularity and international recognition of the Dalai Lama (whose government in exile is headquartered in northern India) continue to be a source of tension between Tibetan Buddhists and Chinese communist authorities. Although an armed conflict over Tibetan independence would be distinctly one-sided, political tensions in other regions of China could incite younger Tibetans who are increasingly straying from the nonviolent approach of the Dalai Lama, a Nobel peace laureate.

Tibet is not the only region in China that seeks national autonomy. A small but growing independence movement is also present in Xinjiang province, located north of Tibet in the westernmost region of China. Bordered to the north and west by five Moslem nations (Kazakhstan, Kyrgyzstan, Tadzhikistan, Afghanistan, and Pakistan), Xinjiang represents one-sixth of China's land mass and is populated primarily by Turkic-speaking Muslims. Ethnic Chinese account for only a third of Xinjiang's 16 million people. Many of the "minority" Muslims who make up over 60 percent of the population view the Han Chinese as intruders who occupy the most powerful economic positions and rob the province of its abundant natural resources.

The strategic Tarim oil basin, in particular, is symbolic of how Xinjiang's naturally endowed wealth is being exploited by the Chinese central authorities to fuel the progress of the booming coastal regions. In 1993, over 10 million tons of crude were produced in Xinjiang, but all profits went to the central government. Chinese oil companies employ roughly 20,000 workers in the Tarim Basin, but almost all are Han Chinese rather than Muslim natives.[14] Xinjiang's citizens are also resentful of Beijing's large military presence and the continued testing of nuclear weapons in the region.

Spurred by the recent independence of the former Soviet Muslim republics, Xinjiang separatists in the last several years have been responsible for a series of terrorist bombings. Xinjiang expatriates are helping to finance the movement to establish an independent "Eastern Turkestan" (Turkestan is the historical name of the Central Asian region, whose population is primarily Turkic).

China's western regions are not alone in their desire for independence. The prosperous coastal provinces, eager to keep the wealth they have generated, also seek to distance themselves from both Beijing and the inland regions. The coastal zone is increasingly unable to cope with an incoming tide of millions of unemployed and unskilled workers. Problems with immigrants have created a strong isolationist sentiment in many coastal provinces.

Guangdong in particular has repeatedly, albeit indirectly, voiced its desire for autonomy through several dramatic confrontations with the central authorities. In 1992, Guangdong refused to pay the national government's artificially high price for oil. When Beijing threatened an energy embargo, the province chartered a Kuwaiti oil tanker to transport purchases from abroad. From 1989 to 1991, following Tiananmen, the conservative Li Peng failed in his efforts to recentralize government expenditures after several coastal provinces—including Guangdong—refused to turn over more of their tax revenues to Beijing (central government revenue as a proportion of China's GDP has fallen sharply, from 22 percent in 1984 to only 12 percent in 1994).[15]

Another example of provincial disregard for the central government occurred in 1990. Guangdong, which primarily grows cash crops rather than staples, wanted to import rice from neighboring Hunan province. Hunan officials and the central authorities demanded that Guangdong pay a premium over the low, government-subsidized price. Predictably, Guangdong firms proceeded to establish a black market with Hunan producers, paying more than the subsidized price but less than that demanded by Hunan authorities. To stop unauthorized shipments of rice, the Hunan government ultimately had to mobilize border control troops.[16]

That an individual province can display such autonomy, or that neighboring provinces can face off with military forces, is indicative of the many divisions between the CCP and local officials. When Deng met with resistance from conservatives over economic reforms, he found the support he needed from regional authorities.[17] The resultant widespread decentralization of political power has accentuated the nation's historical and cultural faultlines.

The dissolution of Beijing's ruling power could have serious repercussions. The reader does not have to go far back into Chinese history for a precedent. Early in the twentieth century, political fragmentation within China led to the rise of regional war-lords, who sparked bitter interprovincial civil wars. Today, if several individual provinces and municipalities revolted simultaneously against the central authorities, the PLA, with its own internal schisms, might be unable to respond effectively. Regional paramilitary units might also provide determined resistance to an overextended, unpopular PLA.

To some outside observers, these dangers are no worse than the threat of a unified Greater China. Many countries in the region—Russia, Japan, and Korea, for example—may prefer a China divided into competing economic and political regions to a more powerful nationalist state. Indeed, China has some sort of territorial dispute with virtually every one of its neighbors. Russia in particular would have much to fear from an economically powerful and militarily aggressive China, because much of its far eastern territory was originally China's. This sparsely populated region is an enticing target, given the abundance of natural resources (particularly energy) that China requires for its rapid economic development.[18]

ECONOMIC UNCERTAINTY

We should not forget that the primary causes of the Tiananmen Square demonstrations in June 1989 were as much economic as political. China's long-term political stability depends upon the ability of those in power to maintain economic growth, restrain inflation, and keep unemployment low. Unfortunately, many believe that it will be difficult for Beijing to achieve these goals. With the easier reforms already implemented, China must now deal with more fundamental economic problems that will test its commitment to long-term marketization.

Beijing's reluctance to deal with the problem of the inefficient but large nationalized enterprises does not augur well. The huge subsidies required to keep these firms afloat require a constant, rapid expansion in the flow of money and credit, exacerbating an already serious inflation problem.

Despite the numerous shortcomings of state-run enterprises,

the government has not cut off their subsidies. The unemployment that would result from such economic "shock therapy" could create severe social and political consequences difficult to estimate in advance—ranging from short-term instability to outright chaos. In 1992, the government of Chongqing (a major industrial city in the inland province of Sichuan) experimented with bankruptcy reforms by shutting down a money-losing knitting mill and laying off its 2,000 workers. After overseas Chinese investors reorganized the plant, 1,200 workers were hired back. The remaining 800 workers protested their unemployment. The governor of the province then informed Chongqing's leaders that the city was dirty and they had better hire exactly 800 street sweepers to improve matters.[19]

Another important consideration is that many of the money-losing government-owned firms are controlled by influential CCP members. These individuals oppose further economic reforms on more than ideological grounds. Eliminating or downsizing these economic dinosaurs would directly impact the pocketbooks of CCP leaders.

Nevertheless, it is becoming increasingly difficult to keep the nationalized sector afloat. In addition to contributing to China's severe double-digit inflation, these enterprises want to restrict the operations of foreign joint ventures. Keeping out new competition would lower China's overall living standard, and it would also reduce the pressure to reform poorly performing government enterprises.

Even hard-line senior officials such as Li Peng have publicly recognized the problems of government-owned firms and have vowed to take corrective action. In 1993, the CCP announced an ambitious plan. By the year 2000, it would either sell off thousands of money-losing industries or allow them to go bankrupt. The verbiage is impressive, but actual progress in carrying out these large-scale reforms has been very slow. In 1994, there were 1,000 *more* state-owned factories than in the previous year. Furthermore, only 1,500 firms have applied for bankruptcy since Beijing passed its first bankruptcy law in 1988.[20]

All this leaves investors unsure about whether to believe the

CCP's rhetoric. If the nationalized sector is not dismantled, continued rapid economic growth will be difficult to achieve and reform will likely stall. However, if the central government fails to appease the millions of workers employed by these deficit-creating enterprises and the CCP members who run them, the result could be a serious backlash imperiling the reforms that have been accomplished. China's future economic success hinges on its ability to forge ahead with marketization and attract badly needed foreign investment, while simultaneously compensating redundant or inefficient workers in state enterprises. That is a very tall order.

Indeed, there is mounting pressure on top officials to slow down reforms for the sake of social stability. Mexico's financial crisis of 1995 prompted Chinese officials to reduce the foreign debt by restricting new foreign investment in certain industries. And instead of shutting down state-owned enterprises, Beijing says that it is focusing on the introduction of better management and technology to the money losers. By delaying the inevitable, the central authorities are trading away future efficiency for current stability.

In light of these tremendous social, political, and economic uncertainties, it makes sense to examine several alternative scenarios rather than insisting on the probability of a single forecast.

SCENARIO #1: SUCCESSFUL TRANSITION TO A MARKET ECONOMY

The best future for China—and for those foreigners who invest in it—would be the completion of a successful transition to a market-based, privately run economy. This relatively trouble-free scenario paints China as the next Japan, an economy that in a matter of decades vaulted from Third World status to that of a global leader.

In this scenario, market reforms continue at their recent rapid pace. After Deng's death, CCP economic reformers maintain central government control. Hong Kong is successfully incorporated into the mainland and serves as both model and incentive for future marketization. Macao also achieves its transition with a minimum of turmoil, further facilitating free and open trade within Greater China. As fears of expropriation subside, much of the investment that fled these former colonies during the mid-1990s returns to reinvigorate the already booming local economies.

Taiwan also benefits from the increasingly liberal economic environment on the mainland. Even in the absence of outright political unification, closer economic and cultural ties spell an end to the confrontational climate between Taipei and Beijing. Taiwan finds that its enhanced economic relationship with the mainland has convinced the CCP that it would be unwise to use military force to reunite the two. Strong economic and social ties become acceptable substitutes for formal national unity.

As economic reforms move inland, the role of the bamboo network in China's economic development diminishes. As we have seen, most overseas Chinese are originally from the coastal provinces of Guangdong and Fujian. They speak the same language and share the same cultural background as their joint venture partners located in those provinces. As interior regions attract foreign investment, however, these advantages diminish. Tight, family-run organizations find it increasingly difficult to cope with a national Chinese market.

While still maintaining a strong presence, the bamboo network ceases to be the principal driving force behind commerce and entrepreneurship. As concerns over political stability ease, large Western, Japanese, and Korean multinational firms—often with a higher level of technological sophistication—develop a strong manufacturing presence on the mainland. Responding to this, the management structures and ownership of ethnic Chinese firms modernize in order to compete on a worldwide playing field. Efficient capital markets eliminate many of the advantages of privately financed family businesses. Publicly held firms that can raise capital through modern investment channels emerge as more efficient alternatives to the family dynasties that utilize enormous private financial reservoirs. Stock and bond offerings become more commonplace as the government continues to lift restrictions on stock exchanges and financial markets. Investors in China show a strong interest in maintaining the momentum of both political and economic reform.

Greater wealth and prosperity—as was the case in Taiwan and South Korea—lead to political reform. Tentative steps toward democracy help ease internal pressures and boost China's world standing, particularly with the United States, which rewards China with permanent most-favored-nation status. Early in the twenty-first century, China gains membership in major international trade and financial organizations and in economic alliances. In the longer run, sustained economic development produces dramatic gains in the standard of living. Per capita income rises to levels equal to those of other Asian dragons such as South Korea.

This optimistic scenario is not realized automatically or easily. In order to fully evolve into a market economy, China continues to decontrol prices and markets aggressively. Government tinkering with market mechanisms to achieve political or social goals is abandoned. The military cooperates with the new leadership because it sees direct advantages in doing so. The PLA's numerous business enterprises, including joint ventures with foreign investors, benefit greatly from the general economic expansion. The revenues from these civilian businesses provide the PLA with substantial budgetary independence from the civilian government authorities. This independence, coupled with continued modernization, helps to transform the PLA into a more professional, politically neutral organization.

High inflation initially threatens to undermine China's economic prospects. Investors worry that the transition from explosive growth to a mature rate of economic development will burst the bubble of optimistic expectations that drives so much of the entrepreneurial energy in China. Nevertheless, the government manages to control inflation sensibly, simultaneously achieving a modest short-term slowdown in economic growth and a limited rise in unemployment. It does so by adopting Western-style monetary and fiscal policies and by phasing out subsidies to government enterprises.

State-owned firms that cannot stop the flow of red ink on their own are forced to go bankrupt. This tough action frees up capital and skilled labor for more profitable enterprises in both the public and the private sectors, especially in the expanding town and village enterprises. To help ease the plight of laid-off workers, Beijing establishes a safety net in the form of a limited social security and welfare system.

Free markets and sound monetary policy are not enough to ensure economic prosperity, however. China also finds it necessary to fully develop its economic infrastructure in order to complete its market transition. Within the next decades, key ingredients of a modern capitalist economy emerge: a body of commercial law, secure property rights, reliable accounting systems, a viable insurance industry, and a competent judiciary. These advances are accompanied by significant liberalization in foreign trade policy. Tariffs are reduced and quotas are phased out in accordance with international agreements.

Free and open trade between Taiwan and the mainland proves beneficial to both parties, saving them the expense of masking transactions by re-exporting through intermediaries (indeed, the incorporation of Hong Kong into China eliminates that "back door"). The increased mobility of capital and labor allows for the full exploitation of regional specializations. Free trade agreements, as well as technological advances in transport and telecommunications, undermine remaining barriers to trade. Owing also to the common language and culture of China and Taiwan, a level of commercial activity is generated surpassing that of the United States, Canada, and Mexico under the North American Free Trade Agreement.

In the long run, Hong Kong loses some of its privileged position as *entrepôt* to China. High real estate and labor costs in Hong Kong force more and more firms to locate directly on the mainland. The economic center of China shifts north and east as Guangzhou, Shanghai, and Beijing assume portions of the trade and financial activity formerly centered in Hong Kong. Following this shift, a free trade zone comprising Japan, Korea, and China—a "chopstick union" as overseas Chinese magnate Robert Kuok terms it—could link the region's three largest economies.

A unified, market-driven Greater China forces massive global shifts in the geographic distribution of investment, trade, production, and employment. The earlier rise of nations such as the United States and Japan is illustrative. Their admission to the club of developed nations had powerful military, political, and economic repercussions. Their success signaled an end to European domination of the globe, economically as well as politically and militarily. The resulting expansion of world trade, investment, and production brought about absolute gains for each of the world's industrialized economies, although some of the older economies experienced a declining *share* of the world market.

Figure 8 forecasts the economies of the United States, Japan, and China on the basis of this scenario. China (unified with Hong Kong) catches up to Japan in the year 2004 and then sprints ahead to rival the United States by the year 2019. These dramatic conclusions are based on several key assumptions:

1. China's economy grows at the rate of 8 percent a year. This is substantially lower than its recent double-digit pace,

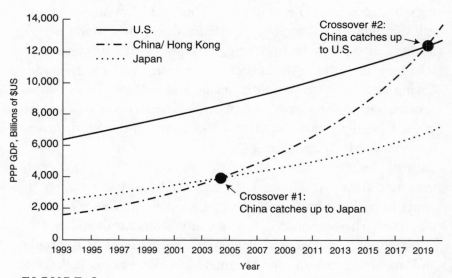

FIGURE 8
Growth Scenario Showing China Catching Up

which is probably not sustainable. The 8 percent figure is equal to the actual growth rates of other Asian dragons—Thailand, Hong Kong, Singapore, and South Korea—over the last 25 years.

2. U.S. growth is 2.6 percent a year while Japan's is 3.8 percent a year. The U.S. figure is the average of the long-range predictions of two well-known forecasters: Oxford Economic Forecasting and Laurence H. Meyer & Associates. The Japanese projection is consistent with its experience over the past 25 years.

3. We use the World Bank estimates of the Japanese and American economies (purchasing power parity—PPP—basis). Because of the considerable difficulty in estimating China's GDP, we average the World Bank's PPP estimate with the much lower, conventional GDP measure based on international exchange rates. The result is a conservative estimate of China's GDP on a purchasing power parity basis.

Although the timing of the two crossovers is roughly estimated, it is clear that China is gaining on the two economic superpowers. Undoubtedly, it is earning a position as one of the new Big Three. According to this scenario, it is only a matter of time before China moves into second place—and quite possibly into first.

The impact on the rest of the world will be profound. The presence of four superpowers—China, Western Europe, the United States, and Japan—lends itself to shifting alliances and renewed rivalries. Any balance of world power that is achieved is likely to be unstable and short-lived. In such circumstances, the most powerful competition likely will be economic and technological—although political and military rivalries will remain.

SCENARIO #2: REVERSION TO COMMUNISM

If a relatively smooth transition to capitalism in China is the dream of Western entrepreneurs, reversion to totalitarian communism is the nightmare. Parallels with the former Soviet Union abound. Widespread crime, ethnic violence, and ultranationalism are the by-products of Russia's drastic reforms, and threaten a return to communism or another form of totalitarianism. Today's China faces similar problems accompanying its rapid economic change (although so far they seem to be less virulent).

The hard fact is that China remains a communist nation. Despite the economic transformation along the coast, a relatively small number of Communist Party members—52 million, or only 4 percent of the population—continues to exercise a monopoly over political control. Thus, they retain ultimate authority over economic policies and practices, even when this power is not overtly exercised. Through its massive system of official posts and bureaucratic agencies, most of which are filled by party members, the CCP controls regulatory and legal decisionmaking. It also controls the PLA, although this relationship is more tentative: Beijing understands that the same troops that keep it in power can also, if threatened, *remove* it from power.

Some CCP members sincerely believe in the communist ideology and are bitter about the economic changes that have occurred since 1978. Many more, however, see party membership simply as a way of developing *guanxi*. CCP connections enable firms to receive preferential treatment from government regulators and inspectors who, in turn, expect rewards for their displays of favoritism. In a country where the bureaucratic allocation of labor, capital, energy, and business permits is widespread and arbitrary, CCP connections are crucial to many enterprises. Ironically, such arrangements give individual communist functionaries a vital stake in the success of private business. After all, profits can be shared only if they are generated in the first place.

In this scenario, continuing economic progress threatens to reduce the traditional power base of the CCP. Within the rural areas, the demise of communal enterprises has already reduced the influence and authority of party officials. After Deng's death, a powerful hard-line faction emerges as young CCP conservatives—many the children of senior, aging hard-liners—push to end reform. These princelings seek to retain centralized economic control and prevent the development of a middle class that could challenge CCP authority.[21] Deng's death is the pivotal event that spurs a power struggle between the hard-line coalition and economic reformers.

The role of the PLA in the ensuing conflict turns out to be crucial. Both factions struggle to retain control over the PLA, and both fear that the military's power is so great that it will resist, or even ignore, their orders. In this scenario, the PLA exhibits a high degree of loyalty to CCP hard-liners, as it did in June 1989 when its conservative allegiance was reaffirmed.

Popular support for changing China's economic policy comes, as it did in 1949, from the rural inland provinces. Since 1978, a large disaffected class has emerged in the form of vast numbers of uneducated agricultural laborers who are not needed in a more efficient agricultural sector. Many of them fill the ranks of the *mang lui*—disillusioned migrant workers who are particularly anxious for a return to communism. Even when employed, they are angered by the large and growing income differential between skilled urban workers and rural laborers. Ironically, farmers who were at the forefront of economic reform in the early 1980s now find themselves at the vanguard of a communist reversion.

With the firm support of the PLA and rural peasants, the hardliners assume power. Yang Shangkun, former president of the CCP, succeeds Deng on the basis of his close personal ties with the senior leadership of the PLA. Yang, an octogenarian, occupies the leadership for a short period of time. After his death, younger conservatives seize power. An ideologically unified group of top officials selects a new paramount leader (perhaps Li Xiaoyong, son of Li Peng). Together, the members of this conservative alliance guide China away from what they view as the corruption of Mao's vision under Deng and the pragmatist factions of the party. The unified senior leadership halts and then reverses market reform.

Within a decade, China returns to the practice as well as the theory of Marxism-Leninism. The state reassumes control of industry and allows only limited agricultural privatization in staple crops. Expansion of the Special Economic Zones ceases and many of the privileges of the existing zones are gradually withdrawn. Because these regions supply necessary foreign currency to the central government, as well as profits to CCP officials, some unofficial openness continues to be tolerated. This is especially true in Shanghai, where loyalty to the CCP was maintained throughout the period of capitalist reform.

This rapid reversal of economic policy scares many foreign investors into moving their mobile investments elsewhere. Massive capital flight ensues as overseas Chinese and other foreigners seek to remove their funds from China before widespread nationalization occurs. These efforts, in turn, force the Chinese government to severely restrict outflows of money, material, and people. Economic growth halts. The country is plunged into deep recession. Living standards plummet as enterprises cut their production and investments lose their value.

One winner in this scenario is the PLA. Strong central control over regional authorities requires a well-funded military. Senior CCP members with close ties to the PLA push for continued modernization and expansion of China's armed forces. Military power lends itself to use. Thus, in its desire to remain energy-independent, Beijing mounts a military campaign to seize disputed oil reserves in the South China Sea. In the worst-case scenario, the burgeoning independence movement in Taiwan prompts an invasion by the mainland.

The central authorities still recognize the importance of Hong Kong as *entrepôt*, financial center, and supplier of foreign capital for critical projects. This limits the squeeze they can put on that territory. Furthermore, the realities of the information age make it difficult for the communist government to fully insulate the mainland from Hong Kong and Taiwan, especially from the latter's liberal economic policies. Nevertheless, nervous investors pull out large amounts of their funds, causing a rapid deflation of property values in once-booming Hong Kong and Shenzhen. Those who remain are saddled with heavy debt.

Taiwan's already delicate political position worsens after China's drastic shift leftward, making it impossible for the island to conduct more than a limited, black market trade with the mainland. Aggressive moves by CCP hard-liners heighten fears that Beijing will seek to settle its claim over Taiwan with military force. As a hedge against such threats, Taiwan distances itself from the mainland politically and economically. Its own economy enjoys an influx of capital from investors retreating from China (which now includes Hong Kong).

As we have seen, many of the advantages of the bamboo network are based on the trust that obviates the need for formal contracts. This works well only in an environment where people have the power to keep their promises. But in a totalitarian state, layers of bureaucratic authority undermine the discretion of most people in the society. Thus, the commitments they make are less reliable. Operating costs are increased substantially by the need to negotiate a labyrinth of entanglements and a morass of official channels.[22]

After China's open door is slammed shut, the established networks of overseas Chinese investors therefore have an increased incentive to exploit the trading opportunities present in other parts of Southeast Asia. New "growth triangles" emerge to replace the trade between Hong Kong, Taiwan, and China. Due to their geographical proximity, portions of Thailand, Indonesia, Vietnam, and Malaysia become segments of these triangles. Each of these nations has experienced rapid growth over the last several decades and has established, large-scale enterprises financed by overseas Chinese. Singapore, with its large and wealthy ethnic Chinese population, replaces Hong Kong as the region's dominant center of finance, investment, and trade for overseas Chinese business interests.[23]

However, none of these new trading regions possesses the dynamism and potential of Greater China (the mainland, Hong Kong, and Taiwan). They are limited by much smaller labor forces and fewer opportunities for their entrepreneurs to utilize their financial reserves and know-how. Of greater importance, they lack the cultural homogeneity of Greater China. Differences in language, religion, and ethnic background are too great to permit the easy business relationships that were the norm on the mainland. The impressive complementary nature of the economic and natural resources of Singapore, Malaysia, and Indonesia is offset by fundamental differences in language (e.g., Malay versus Chinese), culture (Chinese versus Hindu), and religion (Moslem and animist versus Buddhist). The economic expansion and new wealth that are generated in these growth triangles exacerbate the existing tensions between overseas Chinese and the native majorities. For all of these reasons, the remarkable successes that occurred along the China coast are not repeated elsewhere in Southeast Asia.

Reversion to communist economic policies does not generate a new economic power in China or Southeast Asia comparable to the United States, Japan, or Western Europe. The status quo in the world economy is maintained. Some of the investment capital currently in the region shifts to Latin America and other developing parts of the world.

India, in particular, has the opportunity to serve as a substitute for the mainland. Relying on its unique combination of large population, an established legal system, and a substantial professional class educated in English and modern managerial methods, India tries to become a major factor in the world economy. This effort meets with some success but is limited by the country's massive entrenched bureaucracy, which inhibits entrepreneurship and innovation.

SCENARIO #3: GROWING INSTABILITY LEADING TO FRAGMENTATION

Despite the statistics that show strong aggregate growth, economic development has been far from uniform throughout China. As we have seen, tremendous disparities exist between the inland provinces and the so-called Golden Coast. Part of this difference can be explained by the coastal region's geographical and cultural proximity to overseas Chinese investors. This natural advantage is augmented by tax policies and special incentives to foreign investment that are not present in the interior and western provinces. Provincial disparities are heightened further by the wide-scale transfer of power from the central government to local and regional authorities that has occurred under Deng.

In this scenario, two distinct regions, or "empires," emerge within China as a result of social pressure generated by increasing economic inequality. The "outer empire" comes to include Tibet, Mongolia, Xinjiang, and northeastern Manchuria. Each of these areas has sharp language, cultural, religious, and ethnic differences from the more homogenous "inner empire," which includes China's southern and eastern coastline and is populated primarily by Han Chinese.[24]

Deng's demise is followed by events similar to those in Yugoslavia following the death of Tito. Political infighting within the CCP prevents the ruling handful of Deng protégés from making the transition to a strong central authority. Leadership by a committee turns out to be unstable. As a result, there is no single authority that can keep at bay the forces tearing China apart. External pressures, coupled with the centrifugal pull of China's periphery, cause the two fragile empires to fragment.

Western China in particular poses separatist challenges beyond the capability of the post-Deng government to manage. The region's strong religious, historical, and language ties to bordering Russia, Pakistan, and India provide powerful incentives for political independence. Within this region, Tibet is the first to attempt separation from Beijing. Rebellion in Tibet creates sparks in other regions, with the independence movement in Xinjiang province flaring into an armed uprising.

Encouraged by these rebellions and aware that the PLA cannot be everywhere at once, the southeastern coastal provinces declare their autonomy. Centered in Guangdong and Fujian provinces, separatists resent sharing their wealth with Beijing and the poorer provinces. As justification for their action, they point to their historical ties with areas outside the mainland. Over 80 percent of Taiwan's population are descendants of emigrants from Fujian, and most Taiwanese speak the Fukienese dialect prevailing in Fujian. Likewise, Hong Kong's citizens speak mainly Cantonese—the dialect of nearby Guangdong. These language and cultural links reinforce the economic chasm that separates the coastal provinces from the rest of China.

Guangdong is in an especially strong position to break away

from Beijing. For many years, it has been receiving only a small fraction of its capital investment from the central government. Instead, it has been financing its own development primarily by attracting investment from overseas Chinese in (or through) nearby Hong Kong.

In this scenario, the PLA is unable to put down the simultaneous rebellions throughout the country. Although Tibet's independence can be tolerated, Xinjiang's vital oil resources demand protection. Likewise, the economic wealth of the coastal regions—and the tax revenue they supply—are critical to Beijing. Nevertheless, the PLA faces stiff opposition from armed rebels and internal police units. It also encounters rebellion within its own units, some of which defect to the provinces in which they are based.

Disturbingly, some of these regional forces control nuclear weapons, elevating the situation to an international crisis. The conflicting voices emanating from Beijing do not help matters. The lack of a strong consensus prevents an effective response to the rapidly deteriorating situation. In the resulting chaos, the western provinces succeed in permanently breaking off from China, while an uneasy compromise is achieved among Beijing, Shanghai, and the coastal regions. Taiwan achieves total independence and its sovereignty is recognized by many foreign nations.

The United States, Russia, and Japan follow the developments closely. Without saying so publicly, they are relieved that China is no longer an effective rival. Concerned over the possibility of a protracted civil war such as Yugoslavia's the Big Three succeed in brokering a series of limited peace agreements.

In the longer run, the dissolution of China into region states, possibly bound together in a Commonwealth of China, could create a dynamic new trading region.[25] Unconstrained by cautious central authorities, regions could experiment with even more dramatic economic and political reforms, compete for foreign investment capital, and specialize to exploit comparative productive advantages. But that is a possibility for much later in the twenty-first century.

OTHER SCENARIOS

Most likely, none of these three dramatic scenarios will come to pass. Rather, China will experience a shifting combination of economic openness, socialist ideology, and increasing local independence, perhaps approximating the "peaceful evolution" described by Willy Wo-Lap Lam, the highly regarded Hong Kong/China watcher.[26] In that scenario, the PRC continues its step-by-step economic experimentation, gradually expanding the policies of the Special Economic Zones to some of the inland provinces while maintaining its peculiar philosophy of market socialism.

The increasingly powerful provincial authorities find it in their best interests to coexist peacefully with the CCP. As Gerald Segal writes, "Beijing will pretend to rule the provinces, and the provinces will pretend to be ruled by Beijing."[27] Likewise, the mainland's trading partners maintain their tenuous political and economic relationships within Greater China. Hong Kong is permitted to conduct business as usual under the policy of "one country, two systems." Taiwan continues its cautious approach to trade with the mainland, understanding the advantages of economic interdependence but reluctant to enter into a closer political relationship.

A historical parallel comes to mind: the key role in international commerce of the Hanseatic League during the late Middle Ages. The league tied together first the merchants and then many of the cities of northern Germany and the Baltic area. The Hanse cities did not set up a joint or unified government. Rather, business and government leaders cooperated closely on matters of mutual economic and financial interest.

Unlike the European Union or the North American Free Trade Agreement, the Hanseatic League was not a formal compact among sovereign powers. Nor did it constitute a supergovernment. Individual members continued to owe their traditional allegiance to the specific political power that controlled the part of the region in which they resided. The league was an amorphous organization, lacking legal status. It possessed neither finances of its own nor an independent army or navy.

Nevertheless, the Hanse merchants worked together in many important ways, such as providing mutual support in times of danger. They constituted an identifiable economic grouping that competed with businesses in Holland, Italy, and the nations on the Baltic Sea. The league experienced the limitations of a nongovernmental organization spread over considerable distances. Bergen in Norway was an important Hanse location, as was Novgorod in Russia. Despite this, for almost five centuries the Hanseatic League was an economic power to be reckoned with.

A somewhat similar arrangement may develop among the networks of overseas Chinese, who are not especially bothered by the lack of political union among the economically and culturally linked regions that make up Greater China. A more ambitious approach would be to seek the type of formal cooperation mandated by the North American Free Trade Agreement. Should that prove successful, the movement toward a Southeast Asian version of the European Union could be in the offing.

However, there is currently little if any talk of such a formal economic treaty among the potential participants. Political realities preclude the formation of an integrated economic bloc or common market. Instead, economic policies focus on proposals to enhance cross-border trade and investment flows through more open political relations, freer economic institutions, and better-functioning physical infrastructures.

The geographic proximity and cultural homogeneity of the key parts of Greater China do point toward some form of integration, whether formal or informal. The great and widespread gains from faster political liberalization and economic development are too important to be ignored for very long.

Nevertheless, such a situation could quickly turn sour. Just consider Mexico. At the start of 1994, Mexico seemed poised to be the next great success among the developing nations. Many nations envied its ability to control inflation, increase productivity, and achieve healthy economic growth. But within 12 months, that country suffered two major political assassinations, an armed peasant uprising, and a serious currency crisis. The peso lost over one-third of its value in the last month of 1994, and bail-out efforts by the United States and other Western powers were necessary in early 1995.

CONCLUSION

China is a world giant. The reasons for this are many: its massive population, its immense area, its rapidly developing economy, its great abundance of natural resources, and, perhaps of greatest importance, its profound influence on the language, philosophy, and culture of Japan, Korea, and Southeast Asia.

Peter Drucker believes that the explosion of economic development on the mainland will make China the world's most strategic area for the next decade. "These will be the most critical years in East Asia since the Mongol invasion. But with any luck, by the year 2005, China may also be the world's number two economic power. China is a great question mark."[28]

Drucker expects that in ten years we will see a flood of books about Chinese management. "Just as the Japanese succeeded in turning the modern corporation into a family, I think the Chinese and overseas Chinese will succeed in turning the family into a modern corporation . . . with the emergence of that new economic power, we will see the emergence of a new form of corporate governance."[29] Surely, as shown in earlier chapters, Western business managers have much to learn from the less formal, adaptive, nonbureaucratic approach of the entrepreneurs of the bamboo network.

Great uncertainty attaches to any scenario concerning the future of China and the surrounding region. Whatever the specific outcome, the bamboo network will continually seek to accommodate to and benefit from the changing political and economic environment. Driven by powerful business incentives and potential, overseas Chinese businesses have exposed themselves to significant risk through their large investments in the mainland. Thus, they have an overwhelming stake in the success of China's economic experiment. At critical junctures, they are likely to exert

their powerful influence to ensure that success. Amid all the uncertainty about future prospects, the bamboo network will turn
out to be a key factor in the economic development—and ultimately the political transformation—of China.

In the first and most optimistic scenario, the bamboo network
faces east, to China and the Asian mainland. The overseas Chinese develop closer ties with the PRC. This combination of forces
enables China to become the major superpower in Asia early in
the twenty-first century. By the year 2020 or even earlier, the
United States and China may be in a race for the number one
slot in the world economy. Given their many common interests
and the lack of any historical or geographical conflicts, the competition between the two economic superpowers could be quite
benign. Here, too, the bamboo network would provide both a
continuing demonstration of those common interests and a
mechanism for bridging the two disparate cultures.

On the other hand, should China split up or revert to communism, the bamboo network will orient itself to the West. Overseas
Chinese commercial families will develop closer ties with North
America and Western Europe. At home, they will emphasize the
substantial opportunities in Southeast Asia outside of the PRC.
Although China will still enter the global marketplace, it will remain behind the current economic superpowers.

In all of these situations, the bamboo network will survive and,
very likely, continue on its traditional path of uneven progress
amidst setbacks and opportunities. From the viewpoint of business and economics, the overseas Chinese business families will
be the major unifying force in Southeast Asia. They will simultaneously expand their role in the international economy and seek
to minimize risk and expand profits by means of geographic diversification.

The future pacing element will be the Western-educated
younger generation of overseas Chinese business leaders. They
will seek to exploit the tremendous possibilities that arise from
combining their unique cultural characteristics with modern
management and advanced technology. Their potential for busi-

ness success on a global scale is impressive. It is not a foregone conclusion that this potential will be realized. Yet the inevitable vicissitudes that the resourceful members of the bamboo network will experience in the years ahead will likely strengthen their resolve and capabilities. After all, bamboo is the Chinese symbol for durability; it is flexible and constantly developing. As the old saying goes, "Bamboo bends; it does not break."

NOTES

Chapter 1. The Strategic Role of the Bamboo Network

1. Louis Kraar, "Importance of Chinese in Asian Business," *Journal of Asian Business*, Vol. 9, No. 1, Winter 1993, pp. 91–93.
2. Steve Givens, "Best of Both Fields," *Washington University Magazine*, Spring 1995, pp. 24–26.
3. Paul Theroux, "Going To See The Dragon," *Harper's Folio*, October 1993, p. 55.
4. Nicholas D. Kristof and Sheryl Wu Dunn, *China Wakes* (New York: Random House, 1994), p. 368.
5. Ibid., p. 373; Jon Vanden Heuvel and Everette E. Dennis, *The Unfolding Lotus: East Asia's Changing Media* (New York: Freedom Forum Media Studies Center, 1993), p. 23.

Chapter 2. Understanding the Bamboo Network

This chapter draws heavily on interviews by the authors.

1. Louis Kraar, "Importance of Chinese in Asian Business," *Journal of Asian Business*, Vol. 9, No. 1, Winter 1993, p. 87.
2. Ibid.
3. Friedrich Wu and Sin Yue Duk, "(Overseas) China, Inc.," *The International Economy*, January/February 1995, pp. 33–35.
4. S. Gordon Redding, *The Spirit of Chinese Capitalism* (Berlin: Walter de Gruyter, 1990), p. vii.
5. Marcus W. Brauchli and Dan Biers, "Green Lantern: Asia's Family Empires Change Their Tactics for a Shrinking World," *Wall Street Journal*, April 19, 1995, p. 1.
6. "The Billionaires," *Forbes*, July 17, 1995, p. 117.
7. "Southeast Asia's Octopuses," *The Economist*, July 17, 1993, p. 61; Nicholas D. Kristof and Sheryl Wu Dunn, *China Wakes* (New York: Random House,

1994), p. 317; Wu and Duk, "(Overseas) China, Inc.," p. 33; Nirmal Ghosh, "Chinese Filipinos: Rich and Insecure," *Singapore Straits Times*, August 14, 1994, p. 16.

8. Henry Sender, "Inside the Overseas Chinese Network," *Institutional Investor*, September 1991, p. 40; Lynn Pan, *Sons of the Yellow Emperor: A History of the Chinese Diaspora* (Boston: Little, Brown and Company, 1990), p. 225–226.

9. "Rioters in Indonesia Demanding Higher Wages Attack Chinese," *New York Times*, April 24, 1994, p. 5.

10. "Financial Markets Turmoil in Japan Leads to 'Jewish-Conspiracy' Article," *Wall Street Journal*, July 3, 1992, p. A4.

11. James Fallows, *Looking at the Sun: The Rise of the New Asian Economic and Political System* (New York: Vintage Books, 1995), p. 292.

12. Andrew Tanzer, "The Bamboo Network," *Forbes*, July 18, 1994, p. 140.

13. "The Billionaires," p. 111; "The Business Week Global 1000," *Business Week*, July 10, 1995, p. 56.

14. "Fortune's Global 500," *Fortune*, August 7, 1995, pp. F30–40.

15. Redding, *Spirit of Chinese Capitalism*, p. 2.

16. James R. Ware, "Introduction," *The Sayings of Confucius* (New York: New American Library, 1995), p. 17.

17. Robert S. Elegant, *The Dragon's Seed* (New York: St. Martin's Press, 1959), p. 8.

18. "A Driving Force," *The Economist*, July 18, 1992, pp. 21–24.

19. Frankie Fook-Lun Leung, "Overseas Chinese Management: Myths and Realities," *East Asian Executive Reports*, February 15, 1995, p. 12; Pan, *Sons of the Yellow Emperor*, pp. 228–229.

20. Ross H. Munro, "China's Waxing Spheres of Influence," *Orbis*, Fall 1994, pp. 585–605.

21. Sender, "Inside the Overseas Chinese Network," p. 38.

22. Peter L. Berger, "Our Economic Culture," in T. William Boxx and Gary M. Quinlivan, eds., The *Cultural Context of Economics and Politics* (Lanham, Md.: University Press of America, 1994), p. 72.

23. Gary G. Hamilton and Tony Waters, "Chinese capitalism in Thailand: embedded networks and industrial structure," in Edward K.Y. Chen and Peter Drysdale, eds., *Corporate Links and Foreign Direct Investment*, (New York: Harper Collins, 1995), pp. 104–105.

24. "Asia's telecoms leader," *Euromoney sectoral guide to Asian markets*, September 1994, pp. 12–14.

25. Peter Janssen, "Grown From Small Seeds," *Asian Business*, February 1994, p. 10; Carl Goldstein, "Full Speed Ahead," *Far Eastern Economic Review*, October 21, 1993, p. 67; "A bruiser from Bangkok," *The Economist*, November 26, 1994, pp. 70–76; Michael Schuman et al., "Billionaires in the Making," *Forbes*, July 18, 1994, p. 176.

26. Quoted in Janssen, "Grown From Small Seeds," p. 11.

27. "A bruiser from Bangkok."

28. Pan, *Sons of the Yellow Emperor*, pp. 364–365; "The Overseas Chinese," *The Economist*, July 18, 1992, p. 21; Lee Han Shih, "Tycoons' Moves Point to Need for Caution on China," *Business Times*, October 22, 1994, p. 6.

29. Michael Taylor, "Have cash, will travel," *Far Eastern Economic Review*, March 5, 1992, p. 57; "The Business Week Global 1000," pp. 55–56; "CIBC Restructures Global Operations Into Single Country," *South China Morning Post*, October 27, 1994, p. 7.

30. "Creators of Wealth," *Asiaweek*, December 14, 1994, p. 60.
31. "The Perils of Connections," *The Economist*, February 25, 1995, pp. 64–66.
32. Harlan C. Clifford, "Empire of the Son," *Profiles*, December 1994, pp. 24–27; Joyce Barnathan, "The Sons Are Rising In the East," *Business Week*, December 6, 1993, pp. 64–69.
33. Hotel Properties Limited, *Annual Report 1993* (Singapore: HPL, April 25, 1994).
34. Sim Wai Chew, "Kuo-Toyota Venture Gets Nod for Viet Car Factory," *Singapore Straits Times*, February 15, 1995, p. 38.
35. "Success Secrets of Asia's Fast Movers," *Asiaweek*, December 14, 1994, p. 5a; Evelyn Yap, "Four shops in a bad market? Is she nuts?" *Singapore Straits Times*, April 10, 1994, p. 13.
36. "Success Secrets of Asia's Fast Movers", *Asiaweek*, December 14, 1994, p 5a.
37. Pete Engardio with Margaret Dawson, "A New High-Tech Dynasty?" *Business Week*, August 15, 1994, pp. 90–91; William Mellor, "The Trillionaires' Club," *Asia, Inc.*, November 1994, p. 30.
38. Hamilton and Waters, "Chinese capitalism in Thailand," pp. 102–104; Schuman et al., "Billionaires in the Making," p. 176; Pan, *Sons of the Yellow Emperor*, pp. 236–240; Loh Hui Yin, "Chartsiri Is the Name, But the Game Is No Less Tough," *Business Times*, November 7, 1994, p. 23.
39. "PACFIN," *Bangkok Post* supplement, October 17, 1994, pp. 3–5.
40. Wu and Duk, "(Overseas) China, Inc.," pp. 34–35.
41. "The Billionaires," p. 140.
42. Michael Hamlin, "Whither Asia's Business Dynasties?" *Business Times*, December 29, 1993, p. 7.
43. "The Billionaires," p. 140.
44. "Creators of Wealth," p. 60; "From Humble Beginnings," *Singapore Straits Times*, April 25, 1994, p. 11; Conrad Raj, "Robert Kuok, Liem to Form Billion-Dollar Sugar Empire," *Business Times*, April 11, 1994, p. 1; Andrew Tanzer, "First Pacific's Pearls," *Forbes*, February 13, 1995, pp. 45–50.
45. Louis Kraar, "The Overseas Chinese," *Fortune*, October 31, 1994, p. 107; "Enter the Lippo-potamus," *The Economist*, July 16, 1994, pp. 61–62.
46. Al Labita, "There'll Probably Be More Kuoks in the Philippines Soon," *Business Times*, February 18, 1994, p. 11.
47. Wu and Duk, "(Overseas) China, Inc.," p. 35; Simon Davies and Kieran Cooke, "Secret Life of the Rich and Well-Connected," *Financial Times*, September 13, 1993, p. 22.
48. Conrad Raj, "King of the malls," *Business Times*, October 1, 1994, p. 3.
49. Conrad Raj, "Going public at last," *Business Times*, October 1, 1994, p. 3.
50. "Selling Across the Pacific," *Asiaweek*, December 7, 1994, p. 44.
51. Andrew Tanzer, "We Work Harder During a Crisis," *Forbes*, August 29, 1994, pp. 44–45; *Vickers Ballas Stock Guide* (New York: Vickers Ballas), January 25, 1995.
52. Ghosh, "Chinese Filipinos: Rich and Insecure."
53. Philippe Mao, "Big Players," *Forbes*, July 18, 1994, p. 144; Wu and Duk, "(Overseas) China, Inc.," p. 34.
54. Tanzer, "Bamboo Network," p. 141; Garth Alexander, *Silent Invasion: The Chinese in Southeast Asia* (London: MacDonald, 1973), pp. 59–60.
55. Ellen Oxfeld, *Blood, Sweat, and Mahjong: Family and Enterprise in an Overseas Chinese Community* (Ithaca, N.Y.: Cornell University Press, 1993), p. 93.

56. Janet T. Landa, "Culture and Entrepreneurship in Less-Developed Countries: Ethnic Trading Networks as Economic Organizations," in Brigitte Berger, ed., *The Culture of Entrepreneurship* (San Francisco: ICS Press, 1991), pp. 53–72.

57. For analysis of transactions costs, see Douglass C. North, *Institutions, Institutional Change, and Economic Performance* (Cambridge, England: Cambridge University Press, 1990), p. 68.

58. Michael W. Bell, Hoe Ee Khor, and Kalpana Kochhar, *China at the Threshold of a Market Economy*, Occasional Paper 107 (Washington, D.C.: International Monetary Fund, September 1993), p. 23.

59. John Kao, "The Worldwide Web of Chinese Business," *Harvard Business Review*, March-April 1993, pp. 25, 39. An old Chinese saying notes, "The shrewd rabbit has three holes."

60. Amitabha Chowdhury and Barun Roy, "Fortune Shall Not Weary Them, Nor Fame Stale Their Infinite Wisdom," *Asian Finance*, October 1991, p. 35.

61. Redding, *Spirit of Chinese Capitalism*, pp. 5, 98.

62. "The Chinese Diaspora: The Fifth 'Dragon'," *Conjoncture*, November 1992, pp. 156–157; Kao, "Worldwide Web of Chinese Business," p. 25.

63. Leung, "Overseas Chinese Management," pp. 6, 12.

64. Harry Harding, *The Economics of Greater China* (Washington, D.C.: Paul H. Nitze School of Advanced International Studies, Johns Hopkins University, 1993), p. 6.

65. Hoe-Tam Ho Tai, "Market Cultures," *Social Science Research Council Items*, December 1994, p. 89; Daniel Chirot, "Outsiders and Insiders," *Social Science Research Council Items*, December 1994, p. 90.

Chapter 3. Creating a Greater China

1. "Budget: Statistics of Success," *Hong Kong Digest*, February-March 1995, p. 1; "Asia, at your service," *The Economist*, February 11, 1995, p. 53.

2. Andrew Tanzer, "Attention: Los Angeles, New York, London," *Forbes*, April 11, 1994, p. 54; Randall Jones, Robert King, and Michael Klein, *The Chinese Economic Area: Economic Integration Without a Free Trade Agreement*, Working Paper No. 124, (Paris: Organisation for Economic Co-Operation and Development, 1992), p. 7.

3. William H. Overholt, *The Rise of China* (New York: W. W. Norton, 1993), p. 189.

4. Nicholas D. Kristof and Sheryl Wu Dunn, *China Wakes* (New York: Random House, 1994), p. 372.

5. Andrew Tanzer, "The Mountains Are High, the Emperor Is Far Away," *Forbes*, August 5, 1991, p. 73; Lena H. Sun, "South China Drives Boom Region," *Washington Post*, December 2, 1992, p. A1.

6. Gerald Segal, "China's Changing Shape," *Foreign Affairs*, Vol. 73, No. 3, May/June 1994, p. 48.

7. "Hong Kong," *KPMG World*, No. 2, 1993, p. 22.

8. Kitty Y. Young, "Political Risk Under 'One Country, Two Systems': A Conjoint Analysis," *Journal of Asian Business*, Winter 1993, p. 43; "News & Developments," *Hong Kong Digest*, February-March 1995, p. 2; Edward A. Gargan, "China's Cloud Over Hong Kong: Is '97 Here?" *New York Times*, July 5, 1995, pp. A1, 6.

9. Todd Crowell, "As 1997 Nears, Hong Kong's British Firms Start to 'Sino-fy'," *Christian Science Monitor*, July 26, 1995, p. 1.

10. "The taipan and the dragon," *The Economist*, April 8, 1995, p. 62; "The Business Week Global 1000," *Business Week*, July 10, 1995, pp. 57, 59.

11. Jones, King, and Klein, *Chinese Economic Area*, p. 15; Jonathan Friedland, "A winning streak," *Far Eastern Economic Review*, September 6, 1990, p. 59.

12. Tuan Y. Cheng, *Economic Diplomacy in the Pacific Basin of the Republic of China on Taiwan* (Honolulu: Pacific Forum CSIS, July 1992), pp. 1–3.

13. Jones, King, and Klein, "*Chinese Economic Area*," p. 7.

14. "Taiwan's big prize," *The Economist*, April 15, 1995, pp. 62–63; Kristof and Dunn, *China Wakes*, p. 432.

15. "A Dangerous Warmth," *The Economist*, May 1, 1993, pp. 31–32. See also Jeremy Mark, "Taiwan Loosens Some Restrictions on China Relations," *Wall Street Journal*, August 26, 1994, p. A6.

16. Hang-Sheng Cheng, "Taiwan at the Crossroads," *Federal Reserve Bank of San Francisco Weekly Letter*, February 18, 1994, p. 2; Sheila Tefft, "Taiwan Investors Exploit Growing Ties to Mainland," *Christian Science Monitor*, February 2, 1993, p. 8; Chia Siow Yue, *Motivating Forces in Subregional Economic Zones*, paper presented at the Pacific Forum, Honolulu, Hawaii, November 30, 1993, p. 13.

17. Kristof and Dunn, *China Wakes*, p. 373.

18. "China–Taiwan Banking Link," *New York Times*, April 3, 1995, p. C2.

19. Based on a discussion with Dr. Harvey Sicherman, president of the Foreign Policy Research Institute, August 3, 1994, on his return from meetings with senior Taiwan government officials.

20. Yue, *Motivating Forces in Subregional Economic Zones*, p. 13.

21. "Taiwan," *KPMG World*, No. 2, 1993, p. 10.

22. Quoted in Edward A. Gargan, "Taiwan Pushes to Rebuild Its Place in Global Community," *New York Times*, June 26, 1994, p. 6.

23. Chen Qimao, "Sino-American Relations and Taiwan Issue," in Pacific Forum/CSIS *PacNet*, June 29, 1995, p. 1; Henry Kissinger, "Four Proposals to Get the U.S. and China Off Their Collision Course," *International Herald Tribune*, July 24, 1995, p. 9.

24. Christine Lee, "Massive Economic Landing," *China Information*, February 1994, p. 24.

25. Jon Vanden Heuvel and Everette E. Dennis, *The Unfolding Lotus: East Asia's Changing Media* (New York: Freedom Forum Media Studies Center, 1993), p. 43.

26. He Di, "China's Three-Part Transition," in Ralph A. Cossa, ed., *The New Pacific Security Environment* (Washington, D.C.: National Defense University Press, 1993), p. 105; Andrew Ma, "Hong Kong: In Search of a Chance," in Cessa, ed., *New Pacific Security Environment*, p. 211.

27. Jones, King, and Klein, *Chinese Economic Area*, p. 10.

28. Chong-Pin Lin, "China's Students Abroad," *The American Enterprise*, November/December 1994, p. 12.

29. Carl Riskin, *China's Political Economy: The Quest for Development since 1949* (Oxford: Oxford University Press, 1987), p. 296.

30. Peter Nolan, "The Chinese Puzzle," in Qimiao Fan and Peter Nolan, eds., *China's Economic Reforms: The Costs and Benefits of Incrementalism* (New York: St. Martin's Press, 1994), pp. 11–12; Philip Donald Grub and Jian Hai Lin, *Foreign Direct Investment in China* (New York: Quorum, 1991), p. 3.

31. Ross Terrill, *China In Our Time* (New York: Simon & Schuster, 1992), pp. 149–150.
32. Thomas G. Rawski, "Chinese Industrial Reform: Accomplishments, Prospects, and Implications," *American Economic Review*, Vol. 84, No. 2, July 1994, pp. 272–273.
33. Rawski, "Chinese Industrial Reform," p. 271.
34. Nolan, "Chinese Puzzle," p. 7.
35. Barry Naughton, "Chinese Institutional Innovation and Privatization from Below," *American Economic Review*, Vol. 84, No. 2, July 1994, pp. 267–268.
36. Howell Raines, "The Capitalist Road," *New York Times*, April 3, 1994, p. 10E.
37. Lena H. Sun, "|'Flexible Socialism' Fuels Chinese Growth," *Washington Post*, May 28, 1992, p. A1 et ff.
38. Fred C. Shapiro, "Letter From Hong Kong," *The New Yorker*, June 29, 1992, p. 80; *China News Digest*, August 5, 1994, pp. 4–5.
39. Rick Yan, "To Reach China's Consumers, Adapt to Guo Qing," *Harvard Business Review*, September-October 1994, p. 68.
40. "China's Open Economic Zones Are Speeding Its Transformation to a Market Economy," *IMF Survey*, April 19, 1993, pp. 114–117; Michael W. Bell, Hoe Ee Khor, and Kalpana Kochhar, *China at the Threshold of a Market Economy*, Occasional Paper 107 (Washington, D.C.: International Monetary Fund, September 1993).
41. Armin Bohnet, Zhong Hong, Zhong, and Frank Muller, "China's Open-Door Policy and its Significance for Transformation of the Economic System," *Intereconomics*, July/August 1993, p. 191.
42. Alfred K. Ho, *Joint Ventures in the People's Republic of China: Can Capitalism and Communism Coexist?* (New York: Praeger, 1990), p. 9.
43. Jin Dexiang, "The Impact of China's Economic Policies," in *China and Southeast Asia: Into the Twenty-First Century*, (Washington, D.C.: Pacific Forum/CSIS, 1993) p. 18.
44. Steven Lewis, "Marketization and Government Credibility in Shanghai: Federalist and Local Corporatist Explanations" (St. Louis, Mo.: Washington University, Department of Political Science Working Paper, 1994), p. 2.
45. "Foreign Investment in China," *International Economic Review*, July 1994, p. 13.
46. Keri Davies, "Foreign Investment in the Retail Sector of the People's Republic of China," *Columbia Journal of World Business*, Fall 1994, p. 61.
47. Brent Scowcroft, "Dangerous Shades of Gray," *The International Economy*, January/February 1995, p. 29.
48. Caibo Wang, "A Market Economy Will Generate Political Reform in China," *Berkeley Institute of Governmental Studies Public Affairs Report*, Vol. 35, No. 4, July 1994, pp. 1, 17.
49. Richard L. Grant, "China's Domestic and Foreign Policies: An Overview," in Richard Grant, ed., *China and Southeast Asia: Into the Twenty-First Century*, p. 4; Rawski, "Chinese Industrial Reform," p. 274.

Chapter 4. The Rise of China's Economy

1. U.N. Educational, Scientific, and Cultural Organization, *Statistical Yearbook* (Paris: UNESCO, 1992), pp. 5–11.
2. Nicholas D. Kristof and Sheryl Wu Dunn, *China Wakes* (New York: Random

House, 1994), p. 145. See also Nicholas D. Kristof, "The Rise of China," *Foreign Affairs*, Vol. 72, No. 5, November/December 1993, p. 62.

3. Ford S. Worthy, "A New Mass Market Emerges," *Fortune*, Special Issue: Pacific Rim 1990, p. 51.

4. See Lester R. Brown, "Question for 2030: Who Will Be Able to Feed China?" *International Herald Tribune*, September 28, 1994, p. 4.

5. See Randall Jones, Robert King, and Michael Klein, *The Chinese Economic Area: Economic Integration Without a Free Trade Agreement*, Working Paper No. 124 (Paris: Organisation for Economic Co-Operation and Development, 1992), p. 6.

6. Nicholas D. Kristof, "China's Crackdown on Births: A Stunning, and Harsh, Success," *New York Times*, April 25, 1993, p. 1.

7. See D. Gale Johnson, "Effects of Institutions and Policies on Rural Population Growth with Application to China," *Population and Development Review*, September 1994, p. 503–531.

8. World Bank, *World Development Report 1993* (New York: Oxford University Press, 1993), pp. 288–289.

9. International Monetary Fund, *International Financial Statistics Yearbook* (Washington, D.C.: IMF, 1994), various pages.

10. Ding Jingping, *China: Accelerating Economic Growth and Implications for the Asia-Pacific Region* (Honolulu: Pacific Forum CSIS, April 1993), p. 2.

11. Michael W. Bell, Hoe Ee Khor, and Kalpana Kochhar, *China at the Threshold of a Market Economy*, IMF Occasional Paper 107 (Washington, D.C.: International Monetary Fund, September 1993), p. 20.

12. International Monetary Fund, "Revised Weights for the World Economic Outlook," annex to the *World Economic Outlook*, May 1993, pp. 116–119; World Bank, *World Development Report 1993*, p. 296–297; Sheila Tefft, "Despite Rivalries, Chinese Link Their Economies," *Christian Science Monitor*, December 1, 1993, p. 12.

13. Harry Harding, "Is China A Threat to the U.S.?" *Cosmos*, 1994, p. 37.

14. Andrew Tanzer, "Attention: Los Angeles, New York, London," *Forbes*, April 11, 1994, p. 54–56

15. Liang Hong, "The New Big Three," *China Information*, December 1994, pp. 22–24; John Naisbitt, *Global Paradox: The Bigger the World Economy, the More Powerful Its Smallest Players* (New York: William Morrow, 1994), p. 186.

16. "The insatiable in pursuit of the unquantifiable," *The Economist*, March 4, 1995, pp. 71–72.

17. International Monetary Fund, *World Economic Outlook* (Washington, D.C.: IMF, October 1994), pp. 52–53; Bell, Khor, and Kochhar, "China at the Threshold of a Market Economy," p. 9; Foo Choy Peng, "Clampdown slows FDI," *South China Morning Post*, June 7, 1995, p. 4.

18. Sam Jameson, "The Asia Boom," *Los Angeles Times*, November 29, 1994, p. 1.

19. International Monetary Fund, *International Financial Statistics Yearbook*, various pages.

20. International Monetary Fund, *International Financial Statistics Yearbook*, various pages; Jingping, *China: Accelerating Economic Growth*, p. 6; Gerrit W. Gong, "China's Fourth Revolution" *The Washington Quarterly*, Vol. 17, No. 1, p. 31.

21. International Finance Corporation, *Emerging Stock Markets Factbook* (Washington, DC: IFC, 1994) pp. 18–19.

22. International Monetary Fund, *World Economic Outlook* (Washington, D.C.: IMF, May 1995), pp. 70–74; World Bank, *World Development Report 1993*, pp. 254–255.
23. James R. Booth and Lena Chua, "The Development of Stock Markets in China," *Federal Reserve Bank of San Francisco Weekly Letter*, December 9, 1994, pp. 1–3; "Slim pickings from China's financial takeaway," *The Economist*, February 11, 1995, p. 62.
24. Bo Burlingham, "China, Inc.," *Inc.*, December 1992, p. 112; Booth and Chua, "The Development of Stock Markets in China," pp. 1–2.
25. Burlingham, "China, Inc.," p. 121.
26. "Big," *The Economist*, April 30, 1994, p. 78.
27. Armin Bohnet, Zhong Hong, and Frank Muller, "China's Open-Door Policy and its Significance for Transformation of the Economic System," *Intereconomics*, July/August 1993, p. 193.
28. Mark Spiegel, "Gradualism and Chinese Financial Reforms," *Federal Reserve Bank of San Francisco Weekly Letter*, December 30, 1994, p. 3.
29. Patrick E. Tyler, "China Migrants: Economic Engine, Social Burden," *New York Times*, June 29, 1994, pp. A1 et ff; "Beijing Sets an $11,000 Fee on New Residents," *International Herald Tribune*, September 13, 1994, p. 2.
30. Nick Bradbury, "Social cost of growth leads to inflation policy retreat," *South China Morning Post*, October 6, 1994, p. 3; Uli Schmetzer, "Corrupt Officials, Foreign Businesses Spell Doom for Workers," *Chicago Tribune*, October 5, 1994, p. 8.
31. Louise Lief, "When Both Sides Blink," *U.S. News & World Report*, May 30, 1994, p. 41.
32. Joyce Barnathan and Matt Forney, "Damping Labor's Fires: Can Beijing Calm Workers and Sustain Growth?" *Business Week*, August 1, 1994, pp. 14–15.
33. "Ordinary deaths," *The Economist*, November 5, 1994, p. 32.
34. Caibo Wang, "A Market Economy Will Generate Political Reform In China," *Berkeley Institute of Governmental Studies Public Affairs Report*, Vol. 35, No. 4, July 1994, p. 1.
35. Tyler, "China Migrants," p. A1.
36. C. K. Kong and Jane Tam, "Effect of Reforms on China's Specialized Banks," *Moody's Credit Monitor, Fourth Quarter 1994*, pp. 4–5.
37. William H. Overholt, *The Rise of China* (New York: W.W. Norton, 1993), pp. 62–64.
38. Institute of Developing Economies, *Investment Risk in Post-Deng China* (Tokyo: IDE, 1995), p. 27.
39. Carl Goldstein, "Are We There Yet?" *Far Eastern Economic Review*, July 7, 1994, p. 60.
40. Andrew Tanzer, "The China bubble," *Forbes*, May 8, 1995, pp. 46–47.
41. "State Council imposes rigid controls on steel imports," *South China Morning Post*, October 5, 1994, p. B5.
42. Tanzer, "The China bubble," p. 46.
43. Andrew Tanzer, "Eating from the same pot," *Forbes*, May 22, 1995, pp. 74–75.
44. *China News Digest*, August 17, 1994, pp. 2–3.
45. National Association of Manufacturers, *The United States and China: Valuing the Relationship* (Washington, D.C.: NAM, May 1994), p. 25.
46. Sheila Tefft, "China Seeks Foreign Investment to Boost Sagging Infrastruc-

ture," *Christian Science Monitor*, October 12, 1994, p. 5; John J. Keller, "Gold Rush: Job of Wiring China Sets Off Wild Scramble By the Telecom Giants," *Wall Street Journal*, April 5, 1994, p. A1.

47. *South China Morning Post*, Business News, September 9, 1994, cited in *China News Digest*, September 10, 1994, pp. 3–4.

48. Jones, King, and Klein, "The Chinese Economic Area," p. 6; "To the letter," *The Economist*, January 23, 1993, p. 32.

49. "Powerless growth," *The Economist*, November 28, 1992, p. 32; Gerrit W. Gong and Penelope Hartland-Thunberg, *China at the Crossroads* (New York: Conference Board, July 1993), pp. 10, 32.

50. John J. Curran, "China's Investment Boom," *Fortune*, March 7, 1994, p. 124.

51. For an introduction to the Penn World Table, see Robert Summers and Alan Heston, "The Penn World Table (Mark 5): An Expanded Set of International Comparisons, 1950–1988," *Quarterly Journal of Economics*, May 1991, pp. 327–368.

52. "Big MacCurrencies," *The Economist*, April 15, 1995, p. 74; International Monetary Fund, *International Financial Statistics Yearbook*, various pages.

Chapter 5. Western Investment in China

This chapter draws on numerous conversations with Western business executives.

1. Quoted in William Flannery, "Executive Shares Tips to Ease Way Into China," *St. Louis Post-Dispatch*, May 23, 1994, p. 6BP. See also Gerrit W. Gong and Penelope Hartland-Thunberg, *China at the Crossroads* (New York: Conference Board, 1993), p. 9.

2. Margaret P. Pearson, *Joint Ventures in the People's Republic of China: The Control of Foreign Direct Investment Under Socialism* (Princeton, N.J.: Princeton University Press, 1991), pp. 81, 123–24.

3. Philip Donald Grub and Jian Hai Lin, *Foreign Direct Investment in China* (New York: Quorum, 1991), p. 72; Alfred K. Ho, *Joint Ventures in the People's Republic of China: Can Capitalism and Communism Coexist?* (New York: Praeger, 1990), pp. 15–16.

4. Land Grant, "Wiring the Middle Kingdom," *Infrastructure Finance*, Winter 1993, p. 34.

5. Pearson, *Joint Ventures in the People's Republic of China*, p. 102.

6. Julie and John Sensenbrenner, "Personnel priorities: finding and retaining good Chinese employees" *China Business Review*, November 1994, p. 40.

7. Leslie Chang, "Foreign Exporters Gripe Chinese Banks Hold Up Payments on Delivered Goods," *Wall Street Journal*, November 22, 1994, p. A14.

8. Institute of Developing Economies, *Investment Risk in Post-Deng China* (Tokyo: IDE, 1995), p. 3.

9. *South China Morning Post*, July 28, 1994, cited in *China News Digest*, July 29, 1994.

10. "Managing on the frontier," *The Economist*, June 24, 1995, p. 12.

11. Goldenberg, *Hands Across the Ocean*, (Boston: Harvard Business School Press, 1988), pp. 182–83, 129, 156.

12. "Learning From the Past," *Wall Street Journal*, December 10, 1993, p. 8.

13. "Round and Round," *Wall Street Journal*, December 10, 1993, p. R3.

14. Patrick E. Tyler, "China Holds Christian Visitors for 4 Days," *New York Times*, February 12, 1994, p. A3.

15. Pearson, *Joint Ventures in the People's Republic of China*, p. 39.

16. Lynn Pan, *Sons of the Yellow Emperor: A History of the Chinese Diaspora* (New York: Little, Brown and Company, 1990), pp. 234–35.

17. "Lucky Numbers," *The Economist*, March 26, 1994, p. 75.

18. Bernd Schmitt and Yigang Pan, "In Asia, the Supernatural Means Sales," *New York Times*, February 19, 1995, p. F11.

19. "The Old-Fashioned Way," *Far Eastern Economic Review*, November 18, 1993, p. 58.

20. Marcus Brauchli, Joseph Kahn, and Kathy Chen, "Honeymoon's Over," *Wall Street Journal*, December 2, 1994, p. A1; "China Revises Tax Policy That Hurt Foreign Firms," *Wall Street Journal*, November 22, 1994, p. A14.

21. Michael J. Dunne, "The Race Is On," *China Business Review*, March-April 1994, pp. 16–23.

22. Kathy Chen, "China Aims to Steer Foreign Investment by Giving Certain Industries Priority," *Wall Street Journal*, March 30, 1995, p. A12.

23. James D. Zirin, "Markets and the rule of law," *Forbes*, September 12, 1994, p. 114.

24. Mitchell Pacelle and Joseph Kahn, "For U.S. Developers, China Offers Opportunity, Risk," *Wall Street Journal*, October 18, 1994, p. B4

25. Paul Theroux, "Going to See the Dragon," *Harper's Folio*, October 1993, p. 39.

26. Constance R. Brown, "The Problem of Trademark 'Nicknames' in China and Some Suggested Solutions," presentation to World Trade Seminar, St. Louis, Missouri, September 8, 1994.

27. Rick Yan, "To Reach China's Consumers, Adapt to Guo Qing," *Harvard Business Review*, September-October 1994, p. 71.

28. Brown, "The Problem of Trademark 'Nicknames' in China."

29. Edward A. Gargan, "U.S. May Thwart China's Trade Goal," *New York Times*, July 24, 1994, p. 8; "Modern-Day Pirates Steal U.S. Ideas," *St. Louis Post-Dispatch*, March 10, 1994, p. 5C.

30. Amy Borrus, Pete Engardio, and Richard Brandt, "Will China Scuttle Its Pirates?" *Business Week*, August 15, 1994, pp. 16–17; Philip Shenon, "Chinese Are Accused of Pirating Disks," *New York Times*, August 18, 1994, p. C17.

31. Craig S. Smith, "In Asia, 3M Attacks Disk Counterfeiters; Its Weapon: Penlight," *Wall Street Journal*, March 10, 1995, p. B4.

32. Gong Shen, "Progress in Intellectual Property Protection," *China Information*, February 1995, p. 2.

33. Jay Javeri, "PRC IP Protection," *Am Cham* (Journal of the American Chamber of Commerce in Hong Kong), November 1994, pp. 5–7.

34. Borrus et al., "Will China Scuttle Its Pirates?", pp. 16–17; Wanda Szeto, "Raid nets one million pirate CDs," *South China Morning Post*, October 4, 1994, p. 6.

35. Ezra F. Vogel, *One Step Ahead in China: Guangdong Under Reform* (Cambridge, Mass.: Harvard University Press, 1989).

36. Gerrit W. Gong and Penelope Hartland-Thunberg, *China at the Crossroads* (New York: Conference Board, July 1993), p. 6.

37. Patrick E. Tyler, "Chinese Executive Tied to Deng Is Arrested in Corruption Case," *New York Times*, February 20, 1995, p. A2; *China News Digest*, April

28, 1995, p. 4; Steven Mufson, "China's Corruption 'Virus'," *Washington Post*, July 22, 1995, p. A16.

38. *Import and Export Tariff Schedule of the People's Republic of China*, as reported in "Freighted with difficulties," *Wall Street Journal*, December 10, 1993, p. 4.

39. Fred C. Shapiro, "Letter From Hong Kong," *The New Yorker*, June 29, 1992, p. 76.

40. *China News Digest*, August 5, 1994, p. 3; *China Business Review*, May/June 1994, p. 24; *China News Digest*, October 21–22, 1994, p. 2.

41. Alain Larocque, "Piercing Import Barriers," *China Business Review*, May/June 1994, p. 42.

42. Keri Davies, "Foreign Investment in the Retail Sector of the People's Republic of China," *Columbia Journal of World Business*, Fall 1994, p. 63.

43. Craig S. Smith, "Smugglers Hurt U.S. Companies Selling in China," *Wall Street Journal*, July 14, 1995, p. B1.

44. Louis Kraar, "Importance of Chinese in Asian Business," *Journal of Asian Business*, Vol. 9, No. 1, Winter 1993, p. 90.

45. William H. Overholt, *The Rise of China* (New York: W.W. Norton, 1993), pp. 79–80, 187.

46. Michael Selwyn, "SE Asian Chinese Head For Home," *Asian Business*, April 1993, pp. 24–28.

47. Louis Kraar, "The Overseas Chinese: Lessons From the World's Most Dynamic Capitalists," *Fortune*, October 31, 1994, p. 97.

48. Chia Siow Yue, *Motivating Forces in Subregional Economic Zones*, paper presented to the Pacific Forum/CSIS, Honolulu, Hawaii, December 1, 1993.

49. Flannery, "Executive Shares Tips to Ease Way Into China," p. 6BP.

50. Quoted in Marcus W. Brauchli, "When in Huangpu . . . ," *Wall Street Journal*, December 10, 1993, p. R3.

Chapter 6. Experiences of U.S. Businesses, Good and Bad

1. Quoted in Craig S. Smith, "Learning From the Past," *Wall Street Journal*, December 10, 1993, p. R8.

2. Craig S. Smith and Marcus W. Brauchli, "To Invest Successfully in China, Foreigners Find Patience Crucial," *Wall Street Journal*, February 23, 1995, p. 1; Peter Binzen, "A tough road in China led her to international success here," *Philadelphia Inquirer*, October 31, 1994, p. G3; Steven Schlossstein, "Kung-Fu Con Job," *The International Economy*, January/February 1993, p. 36.

3. Craig S. Smith, "U.S. Bank Cards Fight to Win China's Millions," *Wall Street Journal*, July 17, 1995, p. B1.

4. "Foreign Telecom Activity in China, 1991–1992," *Infrastructure Finance*, Winter 1993, p. 34.

5. Quoted in Rick Yan, "To Reach China's Customers, Adapt to Guo Qing," *Harvard Business Review*, September-October 1994, p. 67.

6. Nicholas D. Kristof, "Peasants of China Discover New Way to Weed Out Girls," *New York Times*, July 21, 1993, pp. A1, 6.

7. Huang Dexian, "After Boeing and McDonald's Now Comes Gallup," *China Information*, May 1994, pp. 17–18.

8. "China," *KPMG World*, 1993, No. 2, p. 38.

9. "Foreign Investment in China," *International Economic Review*, July 1994, pp.

14–15; Kathy Chen, "Chinese Army Fashions Major Role for Itself As a Business Enterprise," *Wall Street Journal*, May 24, 1994, p. 1.

10. "Coca Cola Sells 2.4 Billion Cans to Chinese," America OnLine, September 15, 1994, Reuter News Service.

11. Marj Charlier, "Injured in U.S. Beer Wars, Heileman Heads For China," *Wall Street Journal*, November 14, 1994, p. B1.

12. Mitzi Swanson, "Western pharmaceuticals in demand," *South China Morning Post*, October 6, 1994, p. 7.

13. Randall E. Stross, *Bulls In the China Shop, and Other Sino-American Business Encounters* (New York: Pantheon Books, 1990), p. 27.

14. Zhou Gengsheng, "Making Money and a Reputation," *China Information*, February 1994, p. 14.

15. *Country Marketing Plan: China* (Washington, D.C.: U.S. Department of Commerce, 1993).

16. *The United States and China: Valuing the Relationship* (Washington, D.C.: National Association of Manufacturers, May 1994), pp. 46–47.

17. Wang Xiuhong, "Cooperation With Flying Colors," *China Information*, January 1994, pp. 17–19.

18. John F. McDonnell, *Birth of an Alliance*, speech to the Harvard University Fairbank Center for East Asian Research Conference, New York City, May 11, 1992, p. 1; George Salamon, "McDonnell-Douglas: Chinese Connection," *St. Louis Business Journal*, May 2, 1983, p. 1 et ff.

19. *The United States and China*, p. 49; Ted Plafker, "China's Expansion Gives Sales a Lift," *International Herald Tribune*, September 5, 1994, p. 14.

20. Miriam Jordan, "Chinese Airlines Postpone Orders As They Focus on Safety Issues," *Wall Street Journal*, July 15, 1994, p. A5.

21. Michael J. Dunne, "Chasing Asian Tigers," *Japanese Auto Manufacturing Association (JAMA) Forum*, Vol. 13, No. 3, 1995, pp. 8–10.

22. Carol Steinberg, "The Road to China," *World Trade*, March 1994, pp. 32–33.

23. Lisa Liao, "3M Co. Expands Business in China," *China Information*, April 1994, p. 19.

24. Quoted in William Flannery, "Firms May Find Corrupt Practices," *St. Louis Post-Dispatch*, June 27, 1994, p. 6PB.

25. *U.S. Government Policy Issues Affecting U.S. Business Activities in China* (Washington, D.C.: U.S. General Accounting Office, May 1994), pp. 29–31.

26. Marcus W. Brauchli and Joseph Kahn, "China Fights Tide of Knockoffs In Face of U.S. Trade Sanctions," *Wall Street Journal*, January 6, 1995, p. A8.

27. "Sham Brands of Cigarettes Still Rampant In China," *China News Digest*, March 27–28, 1995, p. 3.

28. Amy Borrus, "China's Gates Swing Open," *Business Week*, June 13, 1994, p. 52; Joseph Kahn, "Ford to Enter China Through Parts Venture," *Wall Street Journal*, June 28, 1994, p. A14.

29. Robert Tansey, "Black Gold Rush," *China Business Review*, July-August 1994, p. 10.

30. Quoted in Peter Janssen, "Grown From Small Seeds," *Asian Business*, February 1994, p. 11.

31. Bob Hagerty, "Whirlpool Official Realizes His Dream of Leading Ventures Into China Market," *Wall Street Journal*, April 7, 1995, p. B12.

32. Louis Kraar, "Importance of Chinese in Asian Business," *Journal of Asian Business*, Vol. 9, No. 1, Winter 1993, p. 92.

33. Esther Wachs Book, "When goodwill turns to gold," *Forbes*, December 19, 1994, pp. 126, 130.

34. Pete Engardio, Peter Galuszka, Shekhar Hattangadi, and Neil Gross, "Have Skills, Will Travel—Homeward," *Business Week Special Issue on 21st Century Capitalism*, November 1994, pp. 164–165.

35. S. Gordon Redding, *The Spirit of Chinese Capitalism* (Berlin: Walter de Gruyter, 1990), pp. 228–230.

36. Richard Dai, "Ford Motor Enters Shanghai," *China Information*, February 1995, p. 19; Ren Deshan, "American Firms: Keen on Chinese Market," *China Information*, February 1995, pp. 20–21.

37. "Investment Deal in China," *New York Times*, January 23, 1995, p. C2.

38. Neal Templin, "Chrysler Says Chances for a Minivan Venture In China Are 50/50 at Best," *Wall Street Journal*, January 6, 1995, p. A8.

39. John Templeman, David Woodruff, and Pete Engardio, "How Mercedes Trumped Chrysler In China," *Business Week*, July 31, 1995, pp. 50–51.

Chapter 7. International Implications of of a Greater China

1. Nicholas D. Kristof, "The Rise of China," *Foreign Affairs*, November/December 1993, p. 65.

2. William C. Triplett II, "China's Booming Arms Buildup," *Washington Post National Weekly*, May 16–22, 1994, p. 24.

3. Lloyd R. Vasey, "China's Growing Military Power and Implications for East Asia," *Pacific Forum CSIS*, August 1993, p. 13; June Teufel Dreyer, "The People's Army: Serving Whose Interests?" *Current History*, September 1994, p. 265.

4. Michael T. Klare, "The Next Great Arms Race," *Foreign Affairs*, Summer 1993, pp. 136–152.

5. Dreyer, "The People's Army," p. 266.

6. "China's new model army," *The Economist*, June 11, 1994, p. 29.

7. Dreyer, "The People's Army," pp. 266–269.

8. Kenneth R. Timmerman, "China Shops," *The American Spectator*, March 1995, p. 32; Michael T. Klare, "The Next Great Arms Race," *Foreign Affairs*, Summer 1993.

9. Clayton Jones, "Paradise Islands or an Asian Powder Keg?" *Christian Science Monitor*, December 1, 1993, p. 14; James Gregor, "The Spratlys and the Security Environment in the South China Sea," in Ralph A. Cossa, ed., *The New Pacific Security Environment* (Washington, D.C.: National Defense University Press, 1993), pp. 217, 225.

10. Patrick E. Tyler, "China Revamps Forces With Eye to Sea Claims," *New York Times*, January 2, 1995, p. 2; "China takes to the sea," *The Economist*, April 29, 1995, p. 41.

11. Ralph A. Cossa and Michael T. Byrnes, "The New Pacific Environment," in Cossa, *New Pacific Security Environment*, p. 290.

12. William Beaver, "Levi's Is Leaving China," *Business Horizons*, March-April 1995, p. 38.

13. Steven Mufson, "The Beijing Duck," *Washington Post National Weekly*, April 17–23, 1995, p. 22.

14. Joseph Kahn, "Fraying U.S.-Sino Ties Threaten Business," *Wall Street Journal*, July 7, 1995, p. A4.
15. Alan Cowell, "Seeking China Deal, Bonn Shuns Rights Issue," *New York Times*, July 13, 1995, p. A8.
16. Kathy Chen, Bob Davis, and Robert S. Greenberger, "U.S. and China: A Trail of Misperceptions," *Wall Street Journal*, July 14, 1995, p. A9.
17. Patrick E. Tyler, "China Trip Ends with Signing of Energy Contracts," *New York Times*, February 25, 1995, p. 19.
18. "The long march back to China," *The Economist*, November 5, 1994, p. 67
19. "China Opens to Internet," *China News Digest*, April 10–11, 1995, p. 4.
20. "Chinese Dissidents Find Freedom—In Business," *Business Week*, March 21, 1994, p. 126.
21. Claude Barfield, "U.S.–China Trade and Investment in the 1990s," in James R. Lilley and Wendell L. Willkie II, eds., *Beyond MFN: Trade With China and American Interests* (Washington, D.C.: AEI Press, 1994).
22. Cossa and Byrnes, "New Pacific Environment," p. 291.
23. Colin Mackerras, Pradeep Taneja, and Graham Young, *China Since 1978: Reform, Modernization, and 'Socialism with Chinese Characteristics'* (New York: St. Martin's Press, 1994), p. 153.
24. "Growing pains," *The Economist*, March 18, 1995, survey of China, pp. 19–21.
25. Patrick E. Tyler, "A Tide of Pollution Threatens China's Prosperity," *New York Times*, September 25, 1994, p. 3.
26. Gene M. Grossman and Alan B. Krueger, "Environmental Impacts of a North American Free Trade Agreement," in Peter M. Garber, ed., *The Mexico–U.S. Free Trade Agreement* (Cambridge, Mass.: MIT Press, 1993), pp. 13–14.
27. Grossman and Krueger, "Environmental Impacts of a North American Free Trade Agreement," pp. 14–17.
28. World Bank, *World Development Report 1992* (New York: Oxford University Press, 1992), pp. 5–11.
29. World Bank, *World Development Report 1992*, p. 23.
30. Philip M. Boffey, "China and Global Warming: Its Carbon Emissions Head Toward the Top," *New York Times*, December 8, 1993, p. A14; Mackerras, Taneja, and Young, *China Since 1978*, p. 156.
31. Samuel P. Huntington, "The Clash of Civilizations," *Foreign Affairs*, Summer 1993.
32. Jack A. Goldstone, "The Coming Chinese Collapse," *Foreign Policy*, Summer 1995, p. 43.
33. Yasheng Huang, "Why China Will Not Collapse," *Foreign Policy*, Summer 1995, p. 54.

Chapter 8. The Foggy Crystal Ball: Three Scenarios

1. Liu Tonglin, "China's Economy in Fast Growth," address to the National Association of Business Economists, Washington, D.C., September 27, 1994.
2. Nicholas D. Kristof and Sheryl Wu Dunn, *China Wakes* (New York: Random House, 1994), p. 401.
3. Gerrit W. Gong and Penelope Hartland-Thunberg, *China At The Crossroads*, Global Business White Paper No. 8 (New York: Conference Board, July 1993), p. 6.

4. Harry Harding, Robert Montaperto, and Anne Thurston, "The Promise and Peril of China After Deng Xiaoping," Heritage Lectures No. 499 (Washington, D.C.: Heritage Foundation, February 3, 1994), pp. 9–10.

5. Paul Theroux, "Going to See the Dragon," *Harper's Folio*, October 1993, p. 40.

6. "Deng Turns 90, Strong New Leader Needed For Reform," *China News Digest*, August 23, 1994, p. 3.

7. See Harding, Montaperto, and Thurston, "Promise and Peril of China After Deng Xiaoping."

8. Sheila Tefft, "Top-Tier Leaders Begin Tussling for Reins of Power in Post-Deng China," *Christian Science Monitor*, August 22, 1994, p. 14; "Next?" *The Economist*, March 18, 1995; Patrick E. Tyler, "Signs of a Power Struggle Come to Light in China," *New York Times*, March 29, 1995, pp. 1 et ff.

9. "Chinese Workers Rewarded with Touch of Lei Feng," *China News Digest*, August 23, 1994, pp. 1–2.

10. William H. Overholt, *The Rise of China* (New York: W.W. Norton, 1993), p. 103.

11. "268 Million Without a Job in 2000," *China News Digest*, August 18, 1994, p. 3.

12. Ian Derbyshire, *Politics in China: From Mao to the Post-Deng Era* (Edinburgh: W & R Chambers, 1991), p. 115.

13. Lena H. Sun, "To Repair Its Image, China Fixes Tibet Monasteries," *International Herald Tribune*, September 13, 1994, p. 2.

14. Kathy Chen, "Muslims in China Hate Beijing a Little Less," *Wall Street Journal*, October 21, 1994, p. A6.

15. Gabriella Montinola, Yingyi Qian, and Barry R. Weingast, "Federalism, Chinese Style: The Political Basis for Economic Success in China," *World Politics*, October 1995; International Monetary Fund, *International Financial Statistics Yearbook* (Washington, D.C.: IMF, 1994), pp. 280–283.

16. "Cut along the dotted lines," *The Economist*, June 26, 1993, p. 29.

17. Gerald Segal, "China's Changing Shape," *Foreign Affairs*, May/June 1994, p. 45.

18. Segal, "China's Changing Shape," pp. 52–53.

19. Patrick E. Tyler, "Overhaul of China's State Industry at a Standstill," *New York Times*, December 19, 1994, p. 1.

20. Tyler, "Overhaul of China's State Industry at a Standstill."

21. Sheila Tefft, "The Rise of China's 'Princelings' Fuels a Bitter Succession Battle," *Christian Science Monitor*, November 3, 1994, p. 1.

22. S. Gordon Redding, *The Spirit of Chinese Capitalism* (Berlin: Walter de Gruyter, 1990), p. 234.

23. See Myo Thant and Min Tang, "Growth Triangles: Fad or Fact?" paper presented to the Conference on Economic Interdependence and Challenges to the Nation State, Honolulu, December 1, 1993.

24. Segal, "China's Changing Shape," pp. 43–45.

25. Kenichi Ohmae, "Putting Global Logic First," *Harvard Business Review*, January/February 1995, pp. 119–125.

26. Willy Wo-Lap Lam, *China After Deng Xiaoping: The Power Struggle in Beijing Since Tiananmen* (New York: John Wiley & Sons, 1995).

27. Segal, "China's Changing Shape," pp. 43–45.

28. Quoted in Martin A. Keohan, "Asia Now," *Business Week*, January 9, 1995, p. 126.

29. Keohan, "Asia Now," p. 125.

INDEX